REVELATION *of* TRUTH

CLINTON BEZAN

LifeRich PUBLISHING

LifeRich Publishing books may be ordered through booksellers or by contacting:

LifeRich Publishing
1663 Liberty Drive
Bloomington, IN 47403
www.liferichpublishing.com
844-686-9607

ISBN: 978-1-4897-3582-9 (sc)
ISBN: 978-1-4897-3581-2 (hc)
ISBN: 978-1-4897-3583-6 (e)

Library of Congress Control Number: 2021909266

Print information available on the last page.

LifeRich Publishing rev. date: 05/20/2021

CONTENTS

Preface

The world we live in is rapidly changing. What we thought was normal is now a distant memory as everything has been turned upside down in very short order due to a traumatic turn of events that unveiled 2020 as an unprecedented year in our history. Amid contradicting "experts" in the fields of health, climatology, and social acceptance, as well as a "biased and bought" mainstream media controlling the official narrative, society seems to have lost its sense of logic and control of any rights and freedoms it thought it had. What was once mere science fiction of Orwellian, dystopian implications has become reality and moved beyond the unimaginable and into the prophetic category of prediction of world events.

As the pieces of the prophetic puzzle fall into place, it is becoming apparent just how colossally and how completely society has been duped into accepting the deception of the powers that covertly rule the world. We have been lied to for millennia and it has become clear that the battles being fought since creation in the spiritual realms are being played out on earth right now and we are the witnesses. The cataclysmic culmination of the final battle of good versus evil is being revealed in literal fulfillment of scripture. Our generation is the generation that Paul wrote about to Timothy. "But mark this: There will be terrible times in the last days. People will be lovers of themselves, lovers of money, boastful, proud, abusive, disobedient to their parents, ungrateful, unholy, without love, unforgiving, slanderous, without self-control, brutal, not lovers of the good, treacherous, rash, conceited, lovers of pleasure rather than lovers of God – having a form of godliness but denying its power." 2 Timothy 31:5.

Western civilization is literally playing with fire as its complacency regarding world events and comfortable standard of living have resulted in a culture with little situational awareness of what is about to happen to humanity. The bubble is about to burst and personal rights and freedoms that we take for granted are being incrementally removed without any resistance whatsoever by a population that is asleep at the wheel.

In the midst of the uncertainty surrounding the origin of the COVID 19 pandemic, the BLM protests, riots and looting and the inevitable economic collapse that will soon bring down the middle class, suspicion and conspiracy theories abound and have created division, hatred, racial tension and widespread distrust of the authorities.

People are seeking truth. Apprehension and in extreme cases, panic, have many searching for God. Depression is sky rocketing. Suicide rates have risen astronomically. Domestic violence is increasing. Now more than ever, believers must stand strong and in solidarity against the anthropocentric worldview that is flourishing in secular society. The Church must wake up and tune into the signs of the times, the signs foretold by Jesus. "When these things begin to take place, stand up and lift your heads, because your redemption is drawing near." Luke 21:28.

Believers are wondering if we are in the great tribulation period written about by the prophet Daniel, or if the rapture is imminent. As some scramble for answers, others remain indifferent, saying history is repeating itself and this too shall pass. I feel it is critical to understand God's plan for the world and the forces at play in order to discern our position on the prophetic timeline and plot our response to it. Knowing the fundamentals of our faith is paramount to comprehending the wisdom of God.

Navigating through world events and history in an effort to make sense of everything is tricky business. There is a tangled web of misinformation that is much more than simply coincidental, that is often covert and is sinister to the very core of its design. The very depth of this deception is truly mind boggling and terrifying and if it weren't for the fact that is has all been prophesied in the Bible it would be hopeless to think that a positive outcome is attainable.

Ever since creation and the fall of Adam and Eve in the garden, the sinful nature of mankind has caused obstacles and barriers that prevent humanity from fully achieving the purpose of our presence in the universe.

Limited in our understanding of our Creator, we have grown to rely upon "natural explanations" for our existence and have become vulnerable to manipulation by Satan as he has craftily woven a web of lies that most accept as truth.

In my first book, *Truth Cries Out* I examined how the science of creation is observable in our world and how the theory of evolution is just a theory and not a good one at that. To embrace Darwinism and its underlying premise of naturalism you would have to believe that: 1) Nothing produces everything. 2) Non-life produces life. 3) Randomness produces fine tuning. 4) Chaos produces organization and complexity. 5) Unconsciousness produces consciousness. 6) Non-reason produces reason. Evolutionary theory raises more questions than answers and cannot explain the intelligence found in DNA, the fine tuning of the universe and the perfect balance of nature to support all life, the complexity of single celled organisms and that there has never once been a fossil of a species in transition into a new species discovered anywhere on earth. Not once!

Mankind cannot even begin to fathom the omnipotence of God. We can observe a lightning storm and contemplate the ferocity of what we perceive as uncontrollable power unleashed in a sublime demonstration of force or watch the unending persistence of waves crashing against the rocks of the shoreline with untiring, unceasing, limitless, relentless energy but the power of God is beyond our capacity to comprehend.

Despite our rebellious nature and unbelieving hearts, God's love for us compelled him to redeem us through his one and only Son who willingly laid down his life as a sacrifice for the atonement of our sins, then resurrected himself to conquer death and establish the New Covenant and the promise of eternal life for all who believe in him. Fundamental to this covenant is the promise that Jesus will return to earth and defeat the forces of evil once and for all, thereby facilitating the intimate relationship with believers that was intended from before creation.

It is an amazingly perfect plan. God has given us freedom of choice and does not force anyone into participation and partnership with him and those who choose Jesus gain a much deeper appreciation of God's love by experiencing sin and being redeemed than if they had lived sinless lives. Eternity is a long, long time and by experiencing enmity from God before entering heaven, the full impact of our salvation prepares us to desire nothing more than to remain in his presence forever.

However, Satan will not go down without a fight and each and every day he battles to usurp believers through coercion and through "the lie" that there is no supernatural realm and that mankind's only hope is through his own devices. By sowing discord in society and creating opposing worldviews, temptation into desiring the pleasures of the flesh, and through conflicts and chaos, the evil one compels humanity to despise God, his holiness and his promise of justice. The devolution of man into a species with a broken moral compass that celebrates his independence from any authority and believes he is in control of his own destiny has placed him in bondage to the great deceiver, the devil, without any awareness whatsoever of the slavery that engulfs his existence.

We have reached the point where mankind is on the brink of self-destruction, where God will move to gather those who love him and bind up Satan for eternal punishment. Satan knows his time is short, and he is about to proceed with his plans for the ultimate deception where he will mimic the ministry of Christ through his own protégé, the antichrist. This calls for discernment from the people of God so that we are not lead astray. The bible says, there will be many false teachers in the last days. When asked about the end of the age, "Jesus answered, 'Watch out that no one deceives you. For many will come in my name, claiming, 'I am the messiah,' and will deceive many.'" Mathew 24:4-5.

The fourth chapter of 1 Timothy warns, "The Spirit clearly says that in the latter times some will abandon the faith and follow deceiving spirits and things taught by demons. Such teachings come through hypocritical liars, whose consciences have been seared with a hot iron. They forbid people to marry and order them to abstain from certain foods, which God created to be received with thanksgiving by those who believe and who know the truth.

For everything God created is good, and nothing is to be rejected if it is received with thanksgiving, because it is consecrated by the word of God and prayer.

If you point these things out to the brothers and sisters, you will be a good minister of Christ Jesus, nourished on the truths of the faith and the good teaching that you have followed. Have nothing to do with godless myths and old wives' tales; rather, train yourself to be godly. For physical training is of some value, but godliness has value for all things, holding promise for both the present life and the life to come. This is a trustworthy saying that deserves full acceptance. That is why we labor and strive, because we have put our hope in the living God, who is the Savior of all people, and especially those who believe." 1 Timothy 4:1-10.

Satan is a master at deception and he has been at it a very long time. We are called to exercise discernment and stand strong in our faith. We live in a time when there is a plethora of church denominations, messages and beliefs. Being able to identify the one true gospel is paramount to keeping yourself from being deceived. Knowing the Bible and the New Covenant so that you cannot be swayed by false teachers and false doctrine will be imperative to your salvation.

The recognition that the theory of evolution has intentionally been promoted to discredit the biblical creation account and therefore all of the Bible reveals that "the lie" that Satan propagates is indeed colossal and penetrates to our fundamental worldview. Rather than seeing fossils as a historical record of life as evolutionary thinking instructs, we must interpret them as evidence of a worldwide flood and global judgement as scripture records. When we gain this appreciation for the scientific evidence we can then acknowledge that the world will be judged again as scripture foretells.

In the end times, during the great tribulation, the antichrist will take power and control and establish a one world government and new world order. "For then there will be great distress, unequaled from the beginning of the world until now – and never to be equaled again.

If those days had not been cut short, no one would survive, but for the sake of the elect those days will be shortened. At that time if anyone says to you, 'Look, here is the Messiah!' or, 'There he is!' do not believe it. For false messiahs and false prophets will appear and perform great signs and wonders to deceive, if possible, even the elect. See, I have told you ahead of time." Mathew 24:21-25.

"Therefore put on the full armor of God, so that when the day of evil comes, you may be able to stand your ground, and after you have done everything, to stand. Stand firm then, with the belt of truth buckled around your waist, with the breastplate of righteousness in place, and with your feet fitted with the readiness that comes from the gospel of peace. In addition to all this, take up the shield of faith, with which you can extinguish all the flaming arrows of the evil one. Take the helmet of salvation and the sword of the Spirit which is the word of God." Ephesians 6:13-17.

When I look back at my own life I can pinpoint the exact time when Satan took my knees out as I endeavored to draw near to God, and drove a wedge between myself and my Creator that took over twenty years to displace. Throughout our lives we are faced with temptation on a small scale as well as in enormous context and how we process that information and act on it can have tremendous implications upon the path our lives take.

INTRODUCTION

"If you know the enemy and know yourself, you need not fear the result of a hundred battles. If you know yourself but not the enemy, for every victory gained you will also suffer a defeat. If you know neither the enemy nor yourself, you will succumb in every battle." Sun Tzu, The Art of War.

History records some great battles but there is none greater than the battle for truth. Society today is rightfully skeptical of information, based on the prolific production of fake news, political word salads obfuscating agendas and disguising corruption, outright lies evidenced by the diametric interpretations of the same events by different participants of the "Me Too" movement, or the blatant manipulation of information during the catastrophic climate change debacle, the COVID narrative and the 2020 BLM and ANTIFA demonstrations, riots and fiascos.

Communist governments have a long-standing reputation for suppressing the truth and mass-producing propaganda, however today's democracies rival the most authoritarian regimes when it comes to fabricating truth. While post modernism rejected absolute truth, post truth culture dictates that personal preferences take precedence over the values of others regardless of truth. At the very core of the battle for truth is the tragedy that happened in the garden of Eden (Genesis 3:7-11).

The Greek dramatist Aeschylus is recorded as saying in 500 B.C., "In war, truth is the first casualty."[1]The last century is known as the century of war, as more than 187 million people were killed in its battles. Very little peace was experienced with conflicts raging somewhere almost constantly. In World War 1 the average weight of recruits was 138 lbs. The average weight of the packs they carried was 76 lbs. There were so many trenches dug in World War 1 that if they were laid end to end, they would have encircled the entire globe. War is a horrible thing. To quote the philosopher Bertrand Russell, "War does not determine who is right – only who is left."[2]

Over this same time period, news media transformed from a source of news reporting on world events into an institution actively involved in shaping public opinion, influencing politics and manipulating narratives with projected outcomes determined by those who control the media. Anthropogenic catastrophic climate change and the COVID 19 pandemic are at the forefront of how the media has been employed to promote predetermined pseudo-science research talking points, promoting the agenda of stakeholders.

While the move to globalization has benefited many developing nations, there is greater disparity between the wealthiest and the poorest people in the world now than before the globalists began to forward their agendas. There is also growing apprehension from industrialized nations that they stand to lose competitiveness to lower wage economies in developing nations as was evidenced by the protectionist policies of governments like the Trump administration. There is also growing concerns that a move to more globalization will eventually put power in the hands of very few elite players on the world stage.

Conspiracy theories abound and as time marches on, one has to wonder how much theory is based upon actual fact. While conspiracies make great folklore and are dismissed by most as fantasy, they give one pause when bodies begin to pile up and justice seems evasive as evidence conveniently gets swept under the proverbial rug. Despite the fourteenth century philosopher and Franciscan friar William Occam's law of parsimony, that states that the simplest explanation for an event is usually the truth, the overall trend of civilization over time is consistent with and indicative of the prophesies of the Holy Bible. Is it possible that these conspiracy theories are a lot more conspiracy than theory?

In the last days the Bible predicts that the forces of evil will gain in power and influence until they get to a point where it appears that nothing will stop them. They will then emerge from their covert posture and operate in full view of civilization, openly subjugating society to completely and totally serve cupidity. The prophecies of Daniel (629-538 BC), Jesus Christ (4 BC – 29 AD). Paul the Apostle (4 BC – 64 AD) and the disciple John, who wrote the book of Revelation in AD 95, speak of an end time when the forces of evil will culminate with the advent of the antichrist gaining control over the entire world. His totalitarian one world government and new world order will arise through initiatives disguised as "peace and safety" however, it will reveal its hidden agenda once he demands that all of humanity bow before him and worship him as God. Then the delusion will be complete and humanity will have capitulated to the "lie" that dictates the way society lives, governs the thoughts of mankind and the very beliefs in the heartbeat of humanity.

The veil of secrecy that cloaks the meetings of the Bilderberg Group, the Free Masons, the Illuminati and others has inspired conspiracy theories and alleged planning of a New World Order and one world government. Participants never speak of what is discussed at the meetings, however Denis Healy, a member of the Bilderberg steering committee for over thirty years, commented, "To say we were striving for a one world government is exaggerated, but not wholly unfair," Adding, "Those of us in Bilderberg felt we couldn't go on forever fighting one another for nothing and killing people and rendering millions homeless. So we felt that a single community throughout the world would be a good thing."[3]

UN policies such as Agenda 21 and Climate Action generate fear, anxiety and red flags, warning of points of no return and how humanity is threatened, as they endeavor to persuade governments into adopting their agenda of a new world order through the re-alignment of economies and populations. The UN Human Rights Committee promotes worldwide access to abortion as a human right in a disguised effort to control third world population growth since 88% of all abortions worldwide occur in developing countries.[4] The WEF has proposed the Great Reset as the answer to our woes and its details are indeed alarming.

With world treaties and agreements aimed at promoting world peace and regulating world trade under increasing pressure, gaining some sense of control over world dynamics is becoming a louder and louder debate. From the impotent WTO, failed arms control treaties, a fatigued and impoverished NATO and the rope a dope UN, the world is seeking solutions to its ever growing and never diminishing problems. As instability grows and threats of World War III reverberate through the information channels, the insidious and arcane rhetoric of the UN perforates the nationalist narratives of democracies and undermines sovereignty while cloaked in benevolent and humanitarian jargon.

Underlying big business, world banking systems and the elite of the world's wealthy power structure, hints of corruption whisper on the winds of change as the deep state quietly and covertly goes about influencing every aspect of ruling the world. Mass media distorts the flow of information by acting as a propaganda machine that propagates the globalist agenda. Morality and truth were the first victims and now the sites are focused on the population itself as human lives are nothing more than expendable collateral in the generation of profit and wealth. In reality, the world is owned. Freedom is a misnomer that cannot be applied to democracies today. The only difference between the corruption of democratic governments and communist countries is the degree of openness the ruling elite willingly permit.

Just as suspicion of total control reached Orwellian proportions, the COVID 19 pandemic became the phenomenon that was exploited to disseminate fear and panic that coerced the world's citizens into relinquishing their rights and freedoms in the name of safety. Under the guise of philanthropy, seemingly benevolent non-profit foundations inject their sweet-sounding venom into the poor of the world and carry out a plan so completely and totally heinous it could only be conceived by Satan himself. By exploiting a pandemic so they could subjugate civilization, they created a nefarious facade, through which humanity is being duped into welcoming the very shackles that will ultimately enslave it. We have become the victims of subterfuge.

And just when the endgame was beginning to become apparent, the World Economic Forum gave us a glimpse of what we already suspected with the announcement of the Great Reset. Posted on their website is the statement, "There is an urgent need for global stakeholders to cooperate in simultaneously managing the direct consequences of the COVID 19 crisis. To improve the state of the world, the World Economic Forum is starting The Great Reset Initiative."[5]

There is a cloud of disinformation spreading like dry ice across the world stage, patiently waiting for its day of reckoning when its ulterior motive will be revealed. Society's complacency and lack of situational awareness have made humanity vulnerable to a charismatic and dynamic remedial awakening that will present itself as a wolf in sheep's clothing to a civilization searching for a savior. When this "savior" is revealed, it will be too late to turn back time. It will be too late to wrestle back human rights and freedoms that were relinquished to the subliminal deception and mankind will find itself wearing the mark of the beast and enslaved by the system it embraced as utopian hope.

Bible prophecy has been misinterpreted through the ages, the end of the world has been predicted by many and the second coming of Jesus has been foretold and dates set more than just a few times. These dates have come and gone and those with prophetic inclinations have been exposed as false prophets, mere swindlers, snake oil salesmen or quacks. This misrepresentation was prophesied by the apostle Paul 2000 years ago when he wrote to the church at Thessalonica. "Do not let anyone deceive you in any way, for that day will not come until the rebellion occurs and the man of lawlessness is revealed, the man doomed to destruction. He will oppose and will exalt himself over everything that is called God or is worshipped, so that he sets himself up in God's temple, proclaiming himself to be God." 2 Thessalonians 2:3-4.

So rather than trying to calculate dates and times for the return of Christ, it seems to me to be more effectual to identify the signs of the times and determine their significance on the prophetic time scale. The consequences of the volatile human condition are societal polarization, decreasing faith in political systems, stagnating economic growth, rejection of historical truths, idolizing entertainers and sports celebrities in denial of world conditions and the widespread growth in secular values at the expense of believing in God. When Jesus was asked what would be the signs that his return would be near, he answered, "Watch out that no one deceives you. For many will come in my name, claiming, 'I am the messiah,' and will deceive many. You will hear of wars and rumors of wars, but see to it that you are not alarmed. Such things must happen, but the end is still to come. Nation will rise against nation, and kingdom against kingdom. There will be famines and earthquakes in various places. All these are the beginning of birth pains.

Then you will be handed over to be persecuted and put to death, and you will be hated by all nations because of me. At that time many will turn away from the faith and will betray and hate each other. And many false prophets will appear and deceive many people. Because of the increase of wickedness, the love of most will grow cold, but the one who stands firm to the end will be saved. And this gospel of the kingdom will be preached in the whole world as a testimony to all nations, and then the end will come.: Mathew 24:4-14.

Humanity has been led down a garden path and fed a diet of secular propaganda that amounts to a compendium of lies designed to raise doubts about the existence of God and pave the way for Satan to accomplish the ultimate deception of his repertoire, having the antichrist be worshiped in the rebuilt temple in Jerusalem and control the world.

While mankind wrestles with ways to overcome what are perceived as existential threats using secular logic and man-made methodologies, the reality is our worldly values and solutions are pitted against unworldly adversaries. We are fighting with physical weapons against a spiritual enemy. Paul put it like this, "For our struggle is not against flesh and blood, but against the rulers, against the authorities, against the powers of this dark world and against the spiritual forces of evil in the heavenly realms." Ephesians 6:12.

Humanity's problem is a spiritual problem. We've put our faith in everything but the one thing that matters most. Our Creator and our Master.

While walking the slippery slope of the last century, rather than holding fast to the honorable principles that enabled the greatest procurement of wealth and prosperity in the history of humanity, society has all but abandoned the Judeo/Christian values that upheld law and order and facilitated the success of the free enterprise system that resulted in our unprecedented standard of living. Was it the complacency of wealth, or the leisure time we have afforded that allowed morality to sink to levels so depraved that the sins of Vegas and Hollywood seem almost mainstream and acceptable compared to the suspected transgressions of the wealthy and powerful? Human trafficking, pedophilia, child sacrifice, adrenochrome and Satanic worship by the wealthiest in government, business, entertainment and sports? What used to be unfathomable is now suspected to be widespread, eluded to by sane and credible sources and proven by the indictments of Jeffery Epstein, Ghislaine Maxwell and Marc Dutroux.

The fallen state of man has been exposed by the fine line that divides the innocent perspective that pornography has no victim and the degenerate dark web solicitor of a trafficked slave child. In our generation we have permitted the normalization and monetization of the sexualized abuse of innocent children through legitimate businesses such as Pornhub. Allegations of children being bred and reared for the soul purposes of trafficking, without birth certificates and untraceable are becoming more and more plausible. These children can then be abused and discarded, murdered or sacrificed in Satanic worship rituals without a trace. The harsh reality that we live in a time and place in human history that we will come face to face with the responsibility for our actions that is about to overtake us. Humanity has left the door wide open for evil to walk right in and take over the control panel while society preoccupies itself with games and pleasure.

Mankind has lived recklessly and reveled in the freedom God created us with, rather than use that freedom of choice to live upright and holy lives to glorify him. We are guilty of taking the path of least resistance and have devolved to the lowest common denominator where we rest and relax rather than endeavoring to take the high road that is less travelled. Jesus said, "Enter through the narrow gate. For wide is the gate and broad is the road that leads to destruction, and many enter through it. But small is the gate and narrow is the road that leads to life, and only a few find it." Mathew 7:13-14.

The Bible says that all will be judged and sentenced for eternity for our choices and actions in our earthly lives. Jesus offers to settle out of court and pardon our debt if we accept his offer of salvation. This is illustrated in the parable Jesus told in the fifth chapter of Mathew. "Settle matters quickly with your adversary who is taking you to court. Do it while you are still together on the way, or your adversary may hand you over to the judge, and the judge may hand you over to the officer, and you may be thrown into prison. Truly I tell you, you will not get out until you have paid the last penny." Mathew 5:25-26. Jesus has paid the price of our sentence for sin. We can simply thank him and follow him or choose to pay that penalty ourselves.

Man cannot turn back time, and we cannot get out of the boat that is headed for the waterfall, nor can we change the sequence of events unfolding before us to spare us from calamity. The plans that were set in motion at the creation of the universe must come to pass in order to reveal the perfect and just love of God. We can either choose to deny it and face the coming judgement as unrepentant people or embrace the truth of God, repent and accept his free gift of grace through Jesus Christ.

In the mean-time, the birth pains Jesus spoke of in Mathew 24:8 are getting more and more intense and closer together. Now, more than ever before, our situational awareness is of utmost importance. "When these things begin to take place, stand up and lift up your heads, because your redemption is drawing near." Like 21:28. The pages hereafter are meant to provoke thought and compel you into an assessment of our existential meaning and purpose and your individual role within it. A challenge to the axioms held by the majority of society and the truth of God revealed in the Bible.

ACKNOWLEDGEMENTS

Once again I sincerely thank God for his grace and hand upon my shoulder, guiding me and providing words and wisdom to proclaim his truth. All Glory belongs to him.

A New World Order

It seems as though the amelioration of civilization is accelerating. Digital technology has forever altered the way we do things and how we see the world. Every great invention by man has the potential to be used for good or evil. The atomic reactor is a case in point with nuclear energy and nuclear weaponry at odds with each other in purpose and application. Digital technology on the other hand is perhaps less dynamic in its destructive capabilities, however it may be much more sinister because of its insidious and covert nature.

As our comfort grows with new platforms in social media, banking and security we are gradually yielding incrementally to the erosion of our privacy, rights and freedoms and ultimately to the prospect of big brother watching us and many welcome this concept from a safety perspective. Terrorism has been the catalyst to propel mankind to the next level of acceptance as our individual rights and freedoms become of secondary importance and we accept government infringement in our lives without much resistance.

Nowhere is this more evident than in China, where ideological purity standards are dictated by the state and enforced throughout the culture. Xi Jinping has rewritten the country's constitution allowing him to remain in office for life. He has said that his "brand of authoritarian capitalism is a 'new type of political party system' that would benefit the rest of the world."[6]

The belt and road initiative is a global development strategy involving infrastructure development and investments in nearly 70 countries and international organizations in Asia, Europe and Africa. It includes 65% of the world's population and 40% of global GDP and offers capital to countries desperately in need thereby creating allegiance and the potential for control on a scale never before rationalized. As noble and tempting as the initiative is at first glance, there must be a component of wariness before jumping on board with China that can only be appreciated when we examine what happens within her borders.

China's social credit system is the first of its kind and compels thoughts of George Orwell's 1984. It monitors what you buy, where you buy it, how you behave and who you associate with. Your movements are tracked and rated to show how responsible and trustworthy you are. A score between 350 and 950 is determined and good credit scores can redeem discount hotel fees or reduced heating bills while severe infractions can result in you being blacklisted.

The system encompasses artificial intelligence, facial recognition and a web of over 200 million surveillance cameras to track everything you do. Citizens are encouraged to do hours of volunteer work to achieve social benefits and scores are docked for things like littering, gossip, a messy yard or jay walking. Additionally, scores can be affected by how many kids you have, your political affiliation, how much time you spend on social media or gaming, your faith, your spending habits and essentially all your behaviors. Video of offenders is shown on the local news. Information collectors are paid to report on their neighbors. Good social credit is rewarded with cheap loans and travel deals. Bad credit scores may prevent you from buying plane tickets, getting a good job or putting children in top schools. Over seven million people had been publicly shamed by the end of 2017.

Even dating sites post social credit scores. The system monitors what you look at on the internet, what you order online, your bank transactions and uses the GPS in your phone to track your movements. With roots in the Mao system, it gets even more sinister below the surface with the potential to ultimately determine your food ration.

The Chinese government says it will make trustworthy people benefit everywhere and restrict untrustworthy people everywhere. The system will work to enforce law and court decisions and encourage good behavior. The government can bar political opponents from obtaining housing, travel and employment. Several regional pilot projects are ongoing through some of the largest tech companies like Alibaba. The government will then base its integrated system off these pilot projects.

The mass data collection is the most ominous part. All social platforms mine your data to influence your purchasing decisions and sell data to other companies. While the global populace goes about its daily routine, there is a huge conspiracy taking place that wants you to remain unaware of its deception and hidden agenda. This is not a theory. It is the United Nation's Agenda 21 or Agenda for the 21st century.

Essentially it is an inventory and control plan for all land, water, minerals, plants, animals, construction, production, food, energy, information and all human beings in the world. It has been agreed to by 179 nations in the world since its inception in 1992 under the guise of sustainable development. It employs moving populations into concentrated city centers, in essence, clearing people out of rural areas.

Agenda 21 encompasses the ideology of communitarianism, which is a social and political construct where the individual's rights are balanced vs the rights of the community. The community being NGO's, corporations and governments that dictate and regulate everything. It begins as regionalization and progressively morphs into globalization through the standardization of all systems including water, law enforcement, education, and energy by bringing all systems into harmony in order to control them all. Through synchronization they can all be managed by a central command entity.

The goal of Agenda 21 (or 2030 Agenda) is a one world government with the ultimate objective of destroying representative government and instituting a totalitarian state. By establishing unelected boards and commissions, promoting socialism and undermining capitalism, the existing fabric of society is manipulated to accept the changes happening around it. Europe is already implementing regionalization through local Agenda 21 public/private partnerships that at their foundation work to bypass the individual.

The system is supported by three pillars. Economy, ecology and equity. Social equity is achieved by impoverishing huge portions of the world population and lowering the standard of living in the developed nations – not by raising living standards of the poorest nations. This is accomplished by restriction on wealth transfers, land use and infrastructure investment in order to collapse economies.

We are seeing this happen in Canada as Justin Trudeau pushes the U.N. narrative in his war on climate change which has crippled the Canadian oil and gas industries through unreasonable environmental regulations and emissions taxation. Additionally, corporations look to move workers around the world cheaply and without regulations which is more efficient than building factories where cheap labor can be obtained as has been the case with China, Taiwan, and Mexico in the past. The migration of refugees we are witnessing is the first great experiment in this philosophy.

A balance between the three pillars will benefit the corporations and exploit the people as "assets" or "collateral." By moving the people to tightly controlled areas, they can be monitored and managed. Today, the mainstream media is owned by 5 corporations, so there is already synchronized propaganda being projected continually. It starts with federal funding to prepare regional plans for land control through limiting development in urban areas and forcing cities to grow and populations to become more-dense. In rural areas, roads will be left to deteriorate, private water will be closely regulated, power will be restricted, school services will be reduced, police funding cut and services neglected which will make living in the country unaffordable and agriculture unprofitable. Eventually the majority will move to the city and the corporations will buy up the land at a reduced value.

In the city, the high concentration of people will be rewarded for snitching on each other and managed in the same way that China's social credit system is doing now.

Managing population growth is a discussion that seems exclusive to the world's wealthy but impacts the world's poorest citizens. With an average growth rate of 83 million people per year, world population is now predicted to hit 10 billion by the year 2057. The U.N.'s population division has expressed concern that current systems in the world generate more money, power and influence but ignore the sustainability of long-term population growth. The danger here is the advocating of abortion, assisted dying legislation and fear mongering through pseudo-science proclaiming an impending climate catastrophe in order to scare young couples out of having kids. [7]

The Population Institute of Canada's website states, "Population growth (10,000 an hour) seriously threatens global peace and stability. It is the primary cause of humankind's most challenging problems, including climate change and the greatest obstacle to overcoming them." By tying population to climate change and prosperity, they instill apprehension to raising families into the hearts of the next generation. Their website goes on to say, "PIC campaigns for smaller, environmentally sustainable populations through universal access to voluntary family planning. Numbers matter. Infinite growth on an already overcrowded planet, with finite resources and space, is impossible. Fewer feet mean smaller, less harmful footprints, and a safer, more manageable world. PIC seeks to empower women, promote sustainable development, enhance prosperity, and create a healthier, more stable planet through family planning. Children by choice not chance."

Extinction Rebellion Canada has shut down traffic across Canada, advocates the shutting down of Alberta's oil and gas industries and embellishes the climate change narrative by telling student classrooms that they are the last generation. Their website warns, "Under our current system, we are headed for disaster. Catastrophic climate change will kill millions, cause food collapse, and render many more homeless. Mass extinction of wild species will lead to ecological collapse. Destruction of natural habitats will lead to genocide of indigenous peoples and the loss of our planet's life support systems." [8]

Chemical companies Dupont and Monsanto have developed an infertility gene known as Epicute which has been spliced into GMO foods. People who consume these foods produce antibodies rendering them irreversibly sterile. In North America and Europe, birth rates are already below sustainable levels for their populations.

In Canada it is no secret the Prime Minister Justin Trudeau has been posturing for the U.N. and covets a seat on their security council. Trudeau has been governing directly from the UN's playbook since 2015, with his climate agenda and plan for migrants and his legacy will spotlight his record spending per capita with the distinguished accomplishment of increasing the federal debt more than any other Prime Minister since 1870 (not facing a world war or recession) and spent more money per capita than any Prime Minister in Canadian history. He achieved this dubious honor, not by spending on infrastructure, education or health care, but by simply giving away billions of dollars in foreign aid to developing countries. He has followed the U.N. script almost to the letter.

As Canada falls deeper into the UN's vision for the world, Trudeau annually gives hundreds of millions of dollars away as foreign aid in the support of abortion and women's health, with the plan to increase it to $1.4 billion annually by 2023 and maintain that level through to 2030. The taxes required to pay for this funding will be paid for by future generations of Canadians and may never truly be reconciled at all.

Canada has partnered with George Soros and the UN Refugee Agency UNHCR to increase the number of refugees being brought into the country as a humanitarian initiative and service to the world. Trudeau's policies have eroded Canada's sovereignty through the alienation of half the country's geography by propagating catastrophic climate change propaganda, legislation and ultimately decimating the oil and gas sector of the economy. His efforts to control the media include regulating internet content by requiring new websites and social media to obtain a government license and constitute censorship of the free press and facilitate an incremental social transition from a broken democracy to socialism and communism. Additionally, the Trudeau government announced it would be funding qualifying Canadian media companies to the tune of $600 million over five years, however eligibility will be determined by a panel including Unifor, a left leaning union representing journalists, auto workers, forestry and mining.

Trudeau has never hidden his admiration for Fidel Castro and Xi Jinping and China's communist regime and has referred to Canada as the world's first post national state. His inclinations to mirror the UN's framework as a governance model are painfully obvious yet are overlooked by a large percentage of Canadian voters at the ballot box. Despite dropping from a majority government to a minority one in 2019 he has maintained an even tighter control of power by exploiting the COVID 19 pandemic and through the support of left of center parties ensuring he won't be defeated through non confidence. The vanguard of conspirators under the umbrella of the UN have duped the nation of Canada into acceptance of the framework that will see their wealth transferred to third world countries and leave the country bankrupt and at the mercy of the IMF and the new world order.

The Canadian implementation of these government policies and NGO rhetoric are the foundation of the regionalization of Agenda 21 as it creeps into Canadian society and is gradually accepted as truth by a young generation that has enjoyed the highest standard of living in the history of civilization. The same can be said in the U.S. where the acceptance of socialism by the young generations is changing the geopolitical landscape and has the country fiercely divided along political lines. The election of Joe Biden as president will further the devolution of democracy and freedom as the country returns to a global participant in the scheme to bring about a new world order.

It seems by and large that most of the populace are not critical consumers of information and don't question propaganda when it has been sugar coated in scientific sounding jargon and humanitarian extended paraphasia. Underlying the 'all for one" UN sustainable development goals to be achieved by 2030, there is the consolidation and integration of power in the hands of very few people. While this sounds necessary in order to save us from ourselves, in reality, it leaves the opportunity to abuse that power wide open for the right circumstances and the right person to seize it.

Under the guise of climate change, the UN along with the G7 and their tag along countries including China, propose to transfer wealth from the wealthy countries to the developing world. By identifying potential for a climate catastrophe without immediate action, they have created a false sense of urgency to implement the immediate cessation of burning fossil fuels in favor of green energy. Through taxation of carbon emissions and international cooperation, these groups proposed to bring about climate financing to the order of about $100 billion in 2020 and increasing per year thereafter. Essentially it amounts to developed countries paying to upgrade developing countries in reducing their carbon footprint in relation to human caused climate change.

Next, there is provision to allow developing countries to infringe upon patents held in developed countries to utilize technology and build industry at the expense of the developed nations. Nationally determined contributions are climate targets established as goals for countries to reduce their individual emissions by a set date. In reality, they are simply stepping-stones to the elimination of sovereignty and the establishment of a one world government.

As it became apparent that the world was falling off pace to deliver on the goals set for 2030, the UN and others ramped up their propaganda machine with the "climate catastrophe/emergency" message, by increasing the generation of pseudo-scientific research and parading Greta Thunberg in front of the wealthy audiences of developed nations. It was a pathetic plea to elicit guilt for "ruining her childhood," while millions of starving children worldwide have suffered at the hands of drought and famine for decades. Her sense of entitlement was appalling.

Additionally, by taking a human rights approach to sustainable development, and using a holistic strategy to achieve its objectives, it is becoming apparent that some prioritization must be implemented, or the goals are unachievable. However, a target by target approach would result in duplication, resource wastage and unintended outcomes. It has subsequently been identified that by eliminating gender inequality, progress can be made more readily in medicine and social and health sciences. It is believed that a gendered approach can "provide the dynamic to trigger the goals' working in unison." [9]

This includes providing access to reproductive services globally for women and empowering women's decision making thus reducing the risks of unwanted pregnancies and unsafe abortions. Additionally, by increasing educational opportunities for girls and women, the prevalence of early marriages can be reduced, and the use of modern contraceptives increased resulting in smaller families and more women in the workforce. This in turn increases women's input into decision making in the family and opens up borrowing and investment avenues for women who can then play an active role in promoting clean energy and securing food resources through sustainable agricultural production. Furthermore, by increasing the earning potential for women in the workforce, would increase global wealth by 160 trillion dollars U.S.

Effective participation by women in social, political and economic dynamics, can reduce violence by improving the value of female children thus reducing negative connotations of raising girls as an added expense, and reducing female feticide thereby balancing the ratio between boys and girls. Ultimately this will reduce male violence against women and between men. From the UN's perspective these goals justify population management of Orwellian proportions. In practical terms, it amounts to empowering women so their productivity can be taxed.

Human activity has resulted in the loss of 83% of the world's animals and 50% of the world's plants. Additionally, biodiversity is said to be declining at an increasing rate. Industrial development, urban expansion and agriculture are listed as contributors to changing the world's land surface by 75%. Because of their poor record in mitigating biodiversity risks through improved practices in forestry for example and emissions management, the developed nations will ultimately pay for improvements in poor countries. The perception that nations can somehow spend money on natural disaster prevention and thereby save on clean-up costs afterward is the type of ludicrous logic being fed to taxpayers, in order to save the planet.

By coupling human health with planetary health, the premise is that you cannot have human health without sustainable ecological systems. Therefore, the climate change/gender equality narrative is the most important talking point for governments tied into the UN's vision for a new world order. Once again, the end justifies the means and that means population management.

Ultimately, the climate debate is a monetary debate. "Green" companies benefit from government policies that provide tax relief, subsidies and grants for their technology development while the UN yokes up with governments in funding climate "science" data that matches their propaganda which amounts to scientists becoming hooked into the scheme in order to keep their funding flowing. The public, convinced that they are squandering their children's future, in turn vote for politicians who promise to address their fears of climate catastrophe and support "green" companies, creating fortunes for them. Many of these dollars, in turn flow back to governments through donations and lobbying which perpetuates the cycle.

When it comes to world economies, pundits like George Soros are quite open about advocating a global currency and changing imbalances of wealth between nations. Soros argues that wealth accumulation by developed nations is essentially a misuse of resources that should be benefiting poor countries. In fact, he considers the IMF's gold reserves fair game in redistributing wealth to the least developed countries. He has also opined that China must be brought into the global financial network in order to facilitate a global system. Soros suggests the current system of the U.S. dollar being recognized as the main international currency cannot continue as deficit spending remains the method of financing and the multilateral currency system is broken, but not recognized as such yet. If the U.S. economy weakens as the main driver of the world economy, then it will drag that economy down with it.

The coronavirus pandemic of 2020 is a case in point of how the world's population is being conditioned through fear, to relinquish more control. Whether the virus is man-made or not, its impact has been exploited by the media and world markets have responded in a negative manner that exudes manipulation on an epic scale. Adding to the panic, the WHO warned that the virus could be spread by banknotes since they are never washed and circulate between people constantly, facilitating a rapid transfer of bacteria and viruses over large geographical areas. This lack of sanitation is easily overlooked and as long as banknotes are used, the risk of money as a vector for disease transmission remains. Therefore, the recommendation has been made to move to a cashless society as quickly as possible since the digital technology is already widely used and COVID 19 is the perfect catalyst to encourage its implementation all in the name of "safety." And furthermore, moving to a cashless society is a huge step towards converting to a one world currency which exactly the new world order envisions. [10]

Conveniently on the stage adjacent to the COVID 19 pandemic is the announcement of ID2020 an innovation spearheaded by Bill Gates and Microsoft in partnership with a group of pharmaceutical companies that will, "get digital ID's right." By providing free vaccinations through the Bill Gates Foundation, if recipients receive an ID chip implant, people will be connected through "blockchain backed data" that will allow access to services where IG is required. By improving the standard of official identification, older "archaic" methods will be replaced as will new digital identification systems that are easy to pirate. Through the leveraging of free vaccinations, the potential to track refugees and provide identification to the poor in third world countries, it is conceivable that the goal of ID implanting every person on the planet is achievable.[11] In Austin, Texas, the homeless are being incorporated through ID2020 and the program "MyPass" to "empower homeless people with their own identity data." Simply put, they become trackable and manageable.

And what better vaccine to start with than a coronavirus vaccine which just so happens to be patented by the one and same Bill Gates, who after the SARS outbreak in 2001 developed and patented W02004092360A2 secure acute respiratory syndrome coronavirus vaccine.[12] In collaboration with the Global Alliance for Vaccines and Immunizations, (GAVI) and other partners in government, academia and humanitarian relief, another cog in the new world order gear to drive and control the world has been solidified. [13]

In addition to the UN's agenda for a one world government, bringing the world's religions into line is a goal that Pope Francis has taken special interest in and is quietly working towards. By connecting religion and governance on a global scale the pope is fulfilling biblical prophecy whether he wants to admit it or not. If he is unknowingly aspiring to achieve a one world religion, he is either completely inept concerning end times prophetic scripture or he doesn't believe the Bible.

At a recent Fortune Global Forum, he was presented with a new social compact that represented a commitment from global businesses to work together with the Pope to end global inequality. The document identified challenges to reaching their objectives which included servicing hard to reach populations, lack of financial literacy, and a shortage of accessible tools to bring women onto the financial grid. They proposed to achieve their objectives of bringing previously unbanked populations into the system by producing digital identities for the one fifth of global citizens that don't have one and are therefore shut out of financial systems.[14] While innocent and noble at first glance, it falls beautifully in line with the UN's Agenda 21 goals.

In July of 2019, the Vatican hosted a "meeting that has been described as an 'exclusive gathering of technology, corporate, finance, government, academic, ecclesiastic and media leaders… to catalyze awareness and establish the best path forward with humanity and technology in harmony.'" The Humanity 2.0 mandate is to construct the future of mankind through collaboration of these groups with artificial intelligence being a component in what is being called the TransHuman code. Ensuring humanity can continue to thrive in the "emerging tension between a human-controlled or a machine-controlled world." As this endeavor continues to take shape, it will become more evident that this is not about the welfare of humanity so much as it is about global control of the population. [15]

Pope Francis seems more interested in driving history and influencing political leaders than addressing the human "exploits" within his congregations. His lack of coherence regarding the wellbeing of the victims at the hands of his clergy and his messages of helping the poor in developing countries must raise questions of his motives and amount to little more than sound-bites. The papacy has a long history of political involvement and perhaps that is the root of the issue. The office itself began as a political appointment bestowed on the bishop of Rome (for a thorough examination kindly refer to my second book *Seeking Truth*, where this is explained in detail).

In North America, society seems more interested in entertainment and recreation than anything else. Society has become more accepting of the hypersexualization of young girls through advertising, gay pride parades and Superbowl halftime shows that have no business in front of a family audience. People shrug it off in the name of tolerance but don't recognize the subtle message we are allowing our children to absorb, that morality is personally defined. Our post-modern mentality and post-truth perceptions have left us extremely vulnerable to powers we know nothing about. The present darkness at work in humanity has been methodically developing our psyche to accept higher and higher doses of evil in a process that will culminate in true catastrophe when mankind is forced to bear the number of the beast.

The insidious and pervasive campaign to influence and control the way humans think and perceive the world through a narrative that has taken on a life of its own, has been underestimated and we fail to grasp its significance. What began as political correctness, inclusivity and respect for others has become an oversensitive hype of racism, harassment and bullying by a society that has had its speech, culture and thought funneled into a predetermined value matrix and has relinquished control of how it perceives others. The subliminal influences of how we interpret gender, for example, have transformed what is considered normal behavior. Bans on advertising depicting women doing housework while lazy men observe or of women driving poorly have been outlawed in the UK as "dangerous gender stereotypes."

Even Disney "has adopted the policy of attaching warnings about 'outdated cultural depictions' to classic films and cartoons."[16] The danger in this is that by condemning the relevance of historical values, society gets pigeon holed into accepting the new cultural narrative through the fear of contamination from what is deemed to be outdated. A self-conscious population then becomes more malleable and can be manipulated into denying historical events, tearing down memorial statues and distancing itself from uncomfortable truths from the past, like slavery and defining what is proper. Front and center in this cultural battle is transgenderism with its ridiculous insistence on using transgender people's chosen pronouns. Those who refuse can lose their jobs as was the case with Dr. David Backereth who refused based upon his Christian beliefs. "An employment tribunal ruled that his views were 'incompatible with human dignity.'"[17] In another case, the ruling stated that the accused's "views do not have the 'protected characteristic of philosophical belief.'" In essence, it has become acceptable to criminalize someone's belief that there are only two biological sexes.

This war of words threatens our ideals and undermines our freedom of expression that is most evident on social media where sensitivity police can land you in Facebook jail for sharing ideas deemed inappropriate. This not only includes the usual suspects of sexually graphic images or content, criminal activity or hateful posts, but also encompasses what would be considered benign religious posts. The thought police have now become part of our culture.

Any post on Facebook mentioning COVID 19 is automatically highlighted by an attachment making readers aware of the "official" narrative and effectively censoring the post. Freedom of speech has succumbed to corporate power and the agenda of wealthy media owners, who have even suspended the Twitter account of President Donald J. Trump indefinitely. When one voice is perceived to threaten the well-being of the entire population and is therefore silenced, many more rights and freedoms than freedom of speech are at risk of being lost.

In a bold counter move to Trump's quest for freedom of speech and an act of solidarity to the deep state, Amazon shut down Parler, which had become a popular social media platform for conservatives and anyone tired of the censorship on Facebook and Twitter. Apple and Google followed suit announcing they would suspend Parler from their app stores. Not only was this a slap in the face to freedom of speech but also a blatant disregard for anti-competition trust.

Politicians offer platitudes to appease a populace that too readily accepts the information it is fed and doesn't take the time to gain an understanding of the implications and underlying motives of government policies because of their preoccupation with media hype over climate change and other intentional smokescreens designed to conceal the true strategy of a new world order. Those who advocated climate change initiatives, while being robust users of social media and even taking part in protests, made little to no effort to park their cars or shut off their furnaces and lights in winter and in doing so have a personal stake in "un-saving" the planet.

This hypocrisy, combined with a political leader in Justin Trudeau, operating directly from the UN playbook, resulted in an chaotic economic climate that saw Teck Resources scuttle the $20 billion Frontier oil sands mine, Warren Buffet withdraw his support of $4 billion that effectively killed the proposed Energie Saguenay LNG plant in Quebec and B.C.'s capitulation to first nations creating the conditions that allowed a small group of hereditary chiefs with no political representation to effectively shut down the national railway over a natural gas pipeline all in one month. The haughty rhetoric of climate action advocates continues even after the loss of thousands of jobs, livelihoods and careers and won't end until they themselves lose the things they value. Just think of all the everyday products derived from petroleum- based ingredients like plastic, waxes, asphalt, Vaseline, nail polish, fishing lures, bicycle tires, rubbing alcohol, umbrellas, linoleum, ice cube trays, etc. The complete list contains over 6000 products. [18]

In Canada, we have swallowed the bait and tolerate the hoax of a carbon tax that is somehow supposed to magically reduce green-house gas emissions or the sham of targeting "net zero" emissions by 2050 despite Canada only contributing 1.6% to global GHG emissions. By skewing the statistics into an expression per capita, a sparsely populated country becomes one of the top ten emitters globally, resulting in 38 million people being guilted into playing a major role in saving a global population of

7.7 billion (2019). Even if every Canadian ceased to drive or take a bus or any mode of transportation that used carbon based fuel and shut off their fossil fueled heating today, Canada could not have a significant impact on global GHG emissions or make a measurable contribution to reducing man made climate change.[19]

The globalists have used this type of disproportionate mathematics to cleverly disguise their agenda as sustainable, equitable and inclusive, ensuring peace and safety for all people. However, when scrutinized under a microscope, the details translate into a dark and covert plan to incrementally destroy personal rights and freedoms. With creative language that includes redistributing wealth to end poverty when in fact it is simply transferring wealth from the middle class both to the poor and upwards to corporations and the super-rich.

Ending hunger, improving nutrition and food sovereignty through sustainable agricultural practices, meaning use of GMO, patented crops that earn tidy profits for corporate suppliers and force producers into legal agreements requiring strict adherence to protocols and licensing that locks them into a cyclical servitude that dictates crop inputs and production contracts that ensure perpetual reliance on the corporations to stay in business. Dovetailed into this will be the sustainable management of all water resources, including rivers and wells on private land through licensing and quotas controlled by the corporations in conjunction with government at all levels.

Additionally, the surreptitious scheme calls for dictating energy consumption and the type of energy consumed in order to reduce the carbon footprint of civilization through increased taxation on carbon fuels and incentives to use green energy owned by the corporations. Conservation of marine resources through severe restrictions on ocean fishing and usage through licensing and trade agreements including sport fishing and fishing for personal consumption. Creation of sustainable ecosystem habitats and management areas that are no go zones for the public in an effort to reverse deforestation, desertification, loss of biodiversity and climate change. This will require mass migration into cities.

The blueprint also promotes a sustainable workforce by providing guaranteed incomes, equal employment access through migrant workers maneuvered into jobs by government and through mortgage relief in exchange for affordable government housing, creating protected rural spaces and forcing people into cities where they can be continuously monitored in the name of safety. Private homes and gardens will be outlawed so that only government controlled food will be available making society captive to corporately produced food. Overconsumption will be penalized and rationing will be implemented.

The plot thickens with coordinating affordable and equitable education systems that in reality socially engineer children to conform to the new world order without questioning it. This will include empowering women to achieve higher education thereby securing better paying jobs which keep them taxable and reduce family size through greater access to abortion so the world population can be held in check.

The strategy also includes implementing universal healthcare systems that offer health and well-being for all classes of people equally, which really means mandatory vaccinations, digital branding of identification to ensure total surveillance and control over the movement, employment and quarantine if necessary of all people for the greater good. All of this will require increased policing, government oversight and result in greater national debts, triggering greater taxation on the population and the loss of national sovereignty as countries become chastened to the IMF. This will open the door for the natural progression to a one world government and totalitarian new world order.

In our eagerness to implement the latest technology, we become governed by our smartphones, digital watches, fitness trackers, and headphones. Everything we do, from our purchasing and banking, the way we obtain information and even the way we date has become digital to the point where our devices are an extension of our bodies. The development of RFID microchips that can be implanted in people's wrists or hands is the next step in a very real progression on the path to the capability of continual monitoring of citizens. Your driver's license, house keys, wallet and passport are all contained in the chip and become part of your body. While the chip which is about the size of a grain of rice, has some beneficial applications like providing emergency room doctors with your name, address, birth date, blood type, allergies, medical history, insurance plan and medication you are on, and can save your life, it represents an incremental progression and infringement on individual rights and freedoms that will eventually culminate in the mark of the beast. While our technology worshipping society rushes to get chipped and have their children implanted as well (just think how you will be able to track your kids' whereabouts) under the impression of novelty and convenience, civilization is taking one of the final steps towards surrendering total control to government authority. This technology is in use today.

Facial recognition technology is already being implemented by police forces to match suspects from crime scenes with known offenders. This system has the power to drastically reduce the time to identify and locate suspects.

"Universal Biometric Identification" has been implemented among refugees arriving in Europe and has been touted as the model for the "New World Order." "The system collects the face, the iris, and the biometric data from the fingerprints, settling in the only official documentation for refugees."

Originally a project of the World Bank, the goal is to have this kind of technology in place to identify every man, woman and child on the planet. Refusal to accept the microchip will potentially disqualify the person from getting a job, opening a bank account, obtaining a credit card or a mortgage or receiving any kind of government payment, etc. Ultimately you would not be able to buy or sell without the chip. This truly has biblical implications.

Do our smartphones provide a mechanism for governments to build a control grid so our lives can be managed by the state? Or are they just the beginning as technology like the Oculus Rift signal the end of normality where users can take virtual holidays, play virtual sports and have virtual relationships. Will the next generation, wear virtual masks instead of staring at cell phones as they walk down the sidewalk? The insidious potential of digital technology is at the heart of the new world order's implementation of an authoritarian state where big brother can monitor your every move.

The ulterior motives of sinister spiritual forces are becoming more and more visible and clearer and will one day be revealed fully when the man of lawlessness emerges as the leader of the deep state. He will be so confident in himself and have garnered so much support from the elite and have so much control over the masses that he will not find it necessary to conceal his network of corruption, influence and power. In fact, the deep state itself will be held captive by a deeper state. A much deeper state with much deeper evil. A much darker state with a much darker objective.

The malevolent nature of the spirit of antichrist combined with the manifestation of Satan incarnate as the man of lawlessness will soon grasp the inhabitants of the earth in a horrific death grip never before seen and never to be seen again. The new world order has as its premise and foundation to rebel against God. It has its power in darkness through clandestine operatives and dark spiritual forces. Its ultimate leader is the prince of darkness and Bible prophecy predicts that he will establish his son of perdition as the ruler of this world and he will subject all humanity to his tyranny.

Yet there is hope on the breeze. While we can only dare to think the unthinkable or speak the unspeakable, the secretive interest groups who seek to manipulate the world, the hidden powers that are all too real, these principalities and empires are about to crumble. While civilization shudders with anxiety at the roaring of the sea, signs in the sun, moon and stars, and world events, their heats will fail them. Luke's gospel records. "People will faint from terror, apprehensive of what is coming on the world, for the heavenly bodies will be shaken." Luke 21:26. What most of humanity sees as an approaching game changer will simply be prophetic fulfillment for true believers in Jesus Christ. Jesus said we should not be alarmed by these things and that they mark the advent of his return. God is going to right the wrongs, straighten the paths for the righteous, prevail against the empires of man, the secret cabal that is running this world and ultimately put an end to evil and Satan himself.

If you listen intently, you can hear the sound of faint hoof beats. There are horsemen approaching and their time is near. They represent the extent of God's patience for mankind. His final invitation and last call. Their nostrils are flaring, their lungs are filled to capacity, and their necks are lathered with sweat. Their riders are death and destruction. Jesus is about to take earth's land title back from the deceiver who usurped it in the garden of Eden. The time for Satan's self-glorification will soon be at an end. The horsemen are coming, and it is going to be one wild ride. Are you ready?

The Deep State

William Guy Carr was a Canadian naval officer and author who was labeled as a conspiracy theorist and accused of antisemitism. He has been described as being the most influential source of creating the American Illuminati demonology. In 1931 he started giving conferences on international conspiracy and how the Illuminati controlled world events with international banking through the Rothschilds and the Rockerfellers. In his book *Pawns in the Game*, he postulated that World War I was orchestrated by the Illuminati to overthrow the Russian tsar and create a communist, atheist regime in its place. He believed that World War II was fought in order to create the nation of Israel by bringing about the clashing of the forces of fascism and Zionism. He also thought that World War III would be fought between Russia and the United States in a final social cataclysm with Israel remaining neutral. His perspective pitted Christianity vs atheism and secularism.

In his book *Satan, Prince of this World*, he expounded on the Illuminati and their link to Satanic secret societies like the Freemasons. He wrote of the "Synagogue of Satan," referencing Revelation 2:9 and 3:9. Carr did not finish this book and died in 1959. Circumstances surrounding his death were considered mysterious. [20]

Involvement with illicit drugs, and human trafficking as well as initiation rites such as murdering a whole family are alleged to be common within secretive cults that operate incognito, while society goes about business as usual, and are typical of the far reaching and corrupt tentacles of the dark powers that make up the deep state. From dark back alleys right on up to the shadows in the corners of billionaire boardrooms, there lurks the ever-present hidden agenda of the principalities and powers that secretly rule the world. Their caviar spoons are covered in blood and their hearts of darkness know no limits as their pursuit of money at the expense of everything humanity holds dear drives them to crush the spirit of man to satisfy their lust and thirst for power. Their influence over governments, intelligence agencies, and corporations is both prevalent and extensive from the bottom to the top.

They operate based on the premise that mankind is inherently evil by nature and that the best way to govern is through terrorism and violence as opposed to academic reasoning. Therefore, they play both sides against the middle, creating chaos by stimulating riots and racism and then subsequently influencing government to employ law enforcement crackdowns which can then be hailed as victories for liberty and freedom. By instilling fear and apprehension among citizens and then removing it through force, society is desensitized to the presence of military or police in their back yards to maintain law and order and at the same time is drawn in to accept the usurping of their rights and freedoms incrementally in exchange for safety and security. Their role as the devil's advocate is not just mere allegoric, but intimately literal, as Satan himself stirs up their lust and greed for control and wealth. To the deep state, political freedom is a misnomer.

Furthermore, under their philosophical cupidity, citizen rights don't exist and are fluid by definition, depending on who is interpreting laws and thereby confusing the laws and ultimately renders them useless therefore, it becomes the right of the ruling class to usurp the rights of the populace. The key is to do it covertly, so society has no idea it is happening. Little by little, in the name of safety, security and sovereignty, through allowing freedoms and then pulling back cyclically and incrementally, through laws and regulations, restricting and impeding, followed by periods of relaxation and free trade, the ruling class gains control. The true power is always kept hidden and must continue to be hidden until it is so absolute that it cannot be stopped.

Mob psychology is used to stir up causes that people are passionate about and that dominate the discourse of the day. The mass media fans the flames of the pre-arranged global agenda as they have with the catastrophic climate change debate and the COVID 19 pandemic. Entire economies are brought to their knees and multi-generational wealth is lost as was the case with the Alberta oil and gas industry being vilified and destroyed by a combination of foreign capital behind protestors and lobbyists, and a federal government bought and paid for by the world's elite through the UN. Mob thinking is illogical and unreasonable, and it is easily manipulated.

Mexico is an example of how creating chaos and domestic violence through drug cartels, the citizens are caught in the crossfire between law enforcement and the criminal elements. By corrupting the police, the war on drugs becomes a perpetual chess match that nobody can win. While appearing to defend the people, the government allows innocent bystanders to become collateral damage and they are simply the cost of doing business. Liberal justice systems apply lenient sentences and day parole conditions are designed to quickly return convicted criminals to the streets where they can continue to terrorize society. When the public outcry becomes loud enough, these criminals are deemed expendable and executed in a gun battle with police. The resulting surrender of a few more rights and freedoms in the name of safety and security is then welcomed by the people.

In the same way, the deep state supports both sides of war efforts and manipulates peace conferences to ensure any territorial gains harmonize with their secret agenda. Both sides incur debt, which the deep state has financed, therefore they can install and uninstall governments at will. It is no coincidence that 50% of the world is communist and 50% is democratic. The massive build-up of armaments has been carefully orchestrated to maintain a constant threshold of fear. It is a classic thesis, antithesis, synthesis arrangement where political and historical progress move forward in a zig zag pattern rather than a straight line as civilization reacts for and against the political forces of communism and democracy, much like the swinging of a pendulum.

There is a prominent postulation that the deep state is steeped in Free Masonry and uses a system based on the old school Masonic warfare platform. It treats all people as collateral, free for exploitation by the commander general who is Great Britain. The world court system is applied to people from a global perspective and all countries of the world are involved. The world's financial systems are a key component to the structure of this system through the Rothschild banks and the Vatican, as well as international trade and commerce.

The monarchy in England assumes authority and exercised that clout when North America was settled by prevailing over France and Spain for control of the new world. In the same way, the colonial period was used as a conduit to transfer wealth to England much like the game of Monopoly where properties are acquired and pay dividends to their owners. Complicit in this clandestine scheme is the Vatican with its own bank and the Jesuit intelligence agency within it that is concentrated on the objective of setting up a new world order through the UN with Lucifer at the top.

The corruption this power struggle has precipitated is evidenced in the USA by the CIA's involvement with illicit drugs and money laundering through the Rothschild and Vatican banks to bankroll their covert activities without the approval of congress. This was recognized by John F. Kennedy who spoke out against it as well as global secret societies and the existence of the deep state and its all-encompassing sphere of influence. Ronald Reagan also spoke out against the hidden powers of the cabal that secretly controls the world and emphatically promoted the concept of freedom and its fragility. Furthermore, he connected this battle between good and evil with the war between Christianity and atheism including communism.

According to a popular supposition the constitution of the United States expired in 1999 and was replaced by the Quantum Global Construct implemented by its architect Russell – Jay: Gould. His Linkedin profile lists him as the Lodial-Owner/Chief-Postmaster-Bank-Banker/Director of the Planet-Earth: Whether real or imagined, this claim to power will never be realized because it counters biblical prophecy.

The deep state reportedly pushed back and has portrayed this hypothesis as a conspiracy theory leaving it deep in the rabbit hole, denied its authority and forged ahead with their new world order plans. They continue to manufacture crisis after crisis to ensure chaos, encourage globalism, and in turn create the environment that will precipitate a one world government. The 9/11 acts of terrorism in New York were instigated from within the USA to create an ongoing fear of a fabricated enemy that justified their invasion of Afghanistan and Iraq, which had nothing to do with weapons of mass destruction and everything to do with oil. This constituted an orchestrated act of fraud against the world and it continues today with the next manufactured crisis of a global pandemic.

Throughout the last couple hundred years, as civilization gained in material wealth, the world economy played into the hands of the cabal. People became more materialistic as standards of living rose and faith in God waned as society embraced money and wanted for little, so they didn't feel the need for faith. Freedom was taken for granted and the yearning for more of the good life left the population vulnerable to manipulation through advertising. Today the corporations have society eating out of their hands, purchasing whatever is new and flashy with no regard for cost as personal and household debt has skyrocketed to unprecedented levels. Saving for the future is no longer in the vocabulary as young families enjoy immediate satisfaction and live the dream at younger and younger ages. North America has become an insatiable consumer of anything and everything that has resulted in a generation of overweight, self-absorbed, materialists with a sense of entitlement never before seen on such widespread levels of deplorability.

Dishonesty in politics has come to be accepted as standard fare and honesty is often seen as detrimental to popularity. Justin Trudeau is a case in point. He is the only Canadian Prime Minister to be found guilty of breaking the law through conflict of interest (repeatedly) and attempted obstruction of justice by the ethics commissioner, yet his popularity remains high. He not only stepped over the line with regards to influencing the Attorney General Jody Wilson-Raybould during the SNC Lavalin scandal, his alleged sexual abuses were disregarded as differences in interpretation of the same events and his blatant disregard of ethics in the WE controversy had little effect on his approval rating. Politicians make promises during election campaigns that they never intend to keep and skillfully serve up word salads of philosophical jargon never even attempting to answer for their actions.

All the while, through funding lobby groups and campaign donations the wealthy procure malleable candidates that once elected can be manipulated from behind the scenes to cultivate ideologies within government that will facilitate the ideals of the wealthy elite to rule the world. Joe Biden is a case in point. Our democratic governments are literally "owned" in every sense of the word by the deep state.

By making it legal to seize property for nonpayment of taxes, governments have grasped control where they have no justification. Income taxes were introduced as temporary measures one hundred years ago but somehow, they have managed to endure no matter which party is in power as politicians have become addicted to taxation as a form of revenue. Goods and services taxes, excise taxes, luxury taxes and ultimately succession taxes amount to taxes upon taxes that keep the working class enslaved to the wealthy elite. And as if not to be outdone, Prime Minister of Canada Justin Trudeau has now introduced a carbon tax upon a carbon tax to finance his war on the climate. The rationale that the safety provided to the populace through sovereignty overrides any guilt for the subjugation of citizens to their exploitation by the ruling class is the vindication they adhere to.

During COVID 19 emergency measures, through legislation and restrictions, unfair competition in the form of favoritism to huge corporations like Walmart as essential services, small mom and pop businesses have had their equity eroded and eventually they go bankrupt and become a thing of the past. By encouraging higher wages to reduce the profit of small businesses these drivers of the economy are brought to financial ruin, leaving the middle class in poverty. This created high unemployment and financial panic which will ultimately transferred significant wealth to the elite wealthy with huge gains made by the likes of Amazon and Microsoft due to increased use of Zoom meetings. The middle class, meanwhile fall below the poverty line and are then provided with social assistance and become enslaved to the government. On the other side of the coin, the giant corporations are given massive bailouts in times of economic collapse and governments are applauded for their support and rewarded through campaign donations from the super-rich.

Through liberal ideologies, tolerance and acceptance are epitomized while alcohol and drugs are promoted to the youth through legalization of soft drugs, provisions for safe injection sites and lowering the legal age of drinking. By encouraging sexualization at younger and younger ages and by facilitating gay rights and transgender agendas, the youth are corrupted and conditioned to accept the untruths of the government and the ruling class of elites who pull the strings. They exchange the educational curriculum for a "socially acceptable" template designed to deceive and corrupt kids by teaching principles known to be false. The entire education system has been revamped to allow for mediocre performance and society gets "dumbed down" through tolerance of lower grades and acceptance of lower standards. Today the majority of the population accepts evolutionary thinking as second nature because it was introduced to them at a very young age. They will even argue until they are blue in the face defending it showing how deeply the lie has become embedded in their worldview. Critical thinking has become a relic of the past.

The deep state proclaims liberty and equality to mislead the population to follow their agenda. Since neither liberty or equality are tangible, they become moving targets that compel followers into allegiance to the cause. By using a series of half-truths to conceal their true motives, they promise whatever society wants to hear in order to achieve their objectives.

The mainstream media never acknowledges these underlying and ulterior motives because they are owned by the perpetrators themselves, therefore, they distribute fake news that corroborates with the narrative the hidden powers dictate. Ultimately society is programmed to believe exactly what the deep state wants them to believe. Anyone challenging the official narrative is ruled a conspiracy theorist and dismissed by the public, thereby exonerating the canned mainstream media rendition of events. This has become so blatant that a press conference video was shown by main stream news without sound, with subtitles conveying the exact opposite of the press secretary's comments denouncing the violence at the U.S. capitol on January 6th 2021.

In the words of author Saul Alinsky, "True revolutionaries do not flaunt their radicalism. They cut their hair, put on suits and infiltrate the system from within." This is the methodology of the deep state that desires all of the wealth and power the world has to offer. The cabal are truly wolves in sheep's clothing.

In 1954, the most powerful men in the world met in Oosterbeek, Netherlands and discussed the future of the world. They included the top representatives from the European Royal families, the Council on Foreign Relations (CFR), IMF, World Bank, Trilateral Commission, EU, Federal Reserve, the ECB and the Bank of England, NATO, the Pentagon, and the world's wealthiest corporations. They maintained a high level of secrecy with no agenda, no press, and no public discussion of the meeting details. These reticent meetings continue to be held regularly and those who are invited to attend are sworn to secrecy. The Bildergerg Group since that time has evolved into a shadow world government with the goal of supplanting sovereign nations with an "all-powerful global government, corporate controlled, and check mated by militarized enforcement." [21]

Their strategy was and is to maintain an "Aristocracy of purpose" between major players in Europe and the U.S.A. and therefore control the world. NATO was identified as a key component in maintaining "perpetual wars and nuclear blackmail," as they raped the planet and accumulated vast wealth and power. Controlling the world's money was identified as crucial to maintaining absolute power. In the words of Amschel Rothschild, "Give me control of a nation's money and I care not who makes its laws." [22]

A steering committee decides who is invited each year. Those invited must come alone. One third of those who attend are political figures, while the balance, are from industry, finance, academia, labor and communications.

The ultimate plan is for a one world government, operating in a global market, policed by a one world military, financed by a one world bank using one global currency. Underlying components supporting the design include: centralized policy, centralized control of populations, centralized laws, eliminating the middle class, all progress and prosperity would benefit the ruling class, manufactured crises and perpetual wars, the majority of the population would fall into a class of serfs with little or no rights and the UN would be the frontal organization of this global entity.

David Rockerfeller (Trilateral Commission) wrote on page 405 of his memoirs, "Some even believe we are part of a secret cabal working against the best interests of the United States characterizing my family and me as 'internationalists' and conspiring with others around the world to build a more integrated global political and economic structure – one world, if you will. If that's the charge, I stand guilty, and I am proud of it." [23]

Behind the scenes, the expertise and technologies of the CIA, FBE, NSA and other leading government agencies are at their disposal through connections in the top brass. The Council on Foreign Relations controls the Whitehouse no matter who is president. Both Republicans and Democrats essentially work for the CFR with the only dissenting presidents being Abraham Lincoln, John F Kennedy and Donald Trump. The fact that Trump cannot be bought explains Trump's efforts to drain the swamp and the incredible extremes his opponents have gone to in order to remove him from office. There have been several attempts on his life which of course are never reported by the mainstream media.

In 1992, Henry Kissinger commented, "Today, Americans would be outraged if UN troops entered Los Angeles to restore order; tomorrow they will be grateful. This is especially true if they were told there was an outside threat from beyond, whether real of promulgated, that threatened our very existence. It is then that all people of the world will plead with world leaders to deliver them from this evil.... Individual rights will be willingly relinquished for the guarantee of their well-being granted to them by their world government."

The CFR's influence over government is so extensive that it includes 14 members who served as U.S. Secretary of Defense since 1947, every Secretary of State since 1940 with the exception of James Burnes and virtually every U.S. National Security advisor over the last 80 years. Top generals, admirals, presidential candidates, CIA directors and many Treasury Secretaries have been members of the CFR. This influence propagates the CFR agenda in government by creating perpetual tension in order to manipulate the populace to accept a particular climate of opinion that is dictated by the CFR.

Playing a major role in the propaganda machinery is the mass media, which is controlled in large by the Rockerfeller family, that provides the narrative they decide to provide. This is how citizens are drawn into the ideologies of globalism, climate change and pandemic induced government control. This is why Donald Trump's rhetoric over "fake news" has been so violently opposed. As the world's most-wealthy grow stronger, their self-preservation comes at the expense of democracy. Today's youth's support of socialism at an all-time high, thanks to the ideologies perpetuated by the education system, which has largely been indoctrinated by plutocratic influences through donations and appointments.

The Trilateral Commission's founding goal is a "New World Order" governed by the elite from the U.S., E.U. and East Asia. Much like the Bilderberg Group, their agenda is secretive, and its members bring expertise to the table in the fields of business, finance, military, academia, media and politics. Ultimately the elites of one group do not want to compete with the elites of another group therefore their members often work together for the common good of global dominance. The Bilderberg Group, TC and CFR collaborate against democracy in their quest to rule the world. By eroding sovereignty incrementally, they have the power to change the landscape of world politics in their favor forever.

By running the world as a business, these elite, wealthy, tycoons seek to eliminate competition by pulling the rug out from under the feet of the middle class and eventually eliminating it completely. This is accomplished by manipulating world markets and causing destruction of the economy in order to facilitate the transfer of wealth to the most-wealthy. When middle class families lose their jobs and fall below the poverty line they wind up on social assistance or welfare programs and the gap between the wealthy elite and the rest of the population widens.

Through proposals like Universal Basic Income or a guaranteed minimum income, governments provide hope in the form of bribery to relinquish employment in times of distress such as in the case of the COVID 19 pandemic where businesses were forced to close to contain the spread of a man made virus or job losses to robotics or artificial intelligence. The resulting welfare state usurps all ambition and power from the newly created ex-middle class and leaves it at the mercy of government control.

The North American Union was formed in 2005 when the leaders of Canada, Mexico and the U.S. created a secretive task force to circumvent the legislatures of the three governments, suppress public knowledge and integrate secretive working groups to influence political, economic and social dynamics to promote a borderless North America, giving the corporations access to Mexican labor, Canadian oil and fresh water. Indeed, as the collective influence of the elite has land locked Alberta's oil and gas sector, decimating Canada's economy and syphoning investment south of the 49th parallel it is only Donald Trump's immigration policies and desire to build a wall along the southern border of the U.S. that prevent the NAU agenda from succeeding, much like the united Europe.

As these secret initiatives become exposed, tarnished or identifiable, they simply change their names and remain one step ahead of the public until it will eventually be too late in the game to matter. The deep state recognizes that it must move in slow, "measured" increments in order to create enough chaos to cause economic hardship for the middle class and mitigate the risk of having their exploits spin out of control so they themselves don't become overwhelmed by world events and even lose control of the globe in the process. This exact scenario that the elite would like to avoid, will be their ultimate downfall and precipitate the conditions that only someone with extraordinary capabilities of financial, political, social and even religious talents will be able to calm the storm and create a cohesive ruling entity that even the elite will find themselves subject to. He will emerge as a hero and humanity will place him on a pedestal and ultimately worship him. This has been prophesied in the Bible.

When we examine this plutocracy, it is truly mind boggling to comprehend the vastness of their wealth and the extent to which they control the world we live in. People like George Soros, the Rockerfellers, the Rothschilds, Bernard Arnault, Bill Gates, Jeff Bezos, Warren Buffet, Mark Zuckerberg, the Clintons and the Obamas plus the rest of the elite own a disproportionate amount of the world's wealth. While the top 1% own over fifty percent of the global wealth, the ultra-rich top ten billionaires have a net worth exceeding the wealth of Saudi Arabia, Switzerland, Turkey, Taiwan, Poland, Sweden, Belgium, Thailand and Iran.[24] According to the Forbes and the IMF, they own over $800 billion in combined wealth which is greater than the total goods and services most nations produce in a year. The disparity between us and them is growing as well. In 2009, the combined wealth of the world's richest 380 people equaled the wealth of the bottom half. By 2018, just 26 billionaires held as much as the bottom 50%.

They own the world's banks, the food supply, technology, medical systems, universities, research and the media. They control what we see, hear, consume and are interconnected with each other on so many levels through marriage and business partnerships that it would make your head spin if you knew. The organizations they own aren't here to serve the public, they are here to serve the agenda. That agenda is a new world order with tighter controls and greater authority over every one of our lives.

The extent of their corruption and grip on world affairs is as spine chilling as is their involvement with secret societies like the Illuminati, the Bilderberg Group, shadow governments, the CIA and a host of other clandestine organizations that surface periodically and briefly only to fade back behind the curtains of the global stage. The Rothschilds alone own the Federal Reserve and the International Monetary Fund with an estimated net worth of $500 billion. They have financed both sides of nearly every war since Napoleon and even financed the Nazis in WW II. The national debts of virtually every country are held by the Rothschilds.

The Rockerfellers' fortunes came from oil and industrialization, which led to ownership in banking, pharmaceuticals, hospitals and universities, while they control the International Health Foundation, the American Cancer Society, the Drug Trust, the American Medical Association and the Food and Drug Administration. Together with Bill Gates they own millions of dollars-worth of shares in Monsanto and Bayer. They are heavily involved in eugenics and vaccine development.

In the midst of the COVID 19 pandemic, just when society seemed to be coming to grips with the loss of certain rights and freedoms, George Floyd, a black lawbreaker known to police, was killed in the hands of Minneapolis police officers during his arrest for allegedly passing counterfeit bills. The ensuing protests, commanding center stage news coverage, quickly erupted into well-orchestrated violence, rioting and chaos. It soon became apparent that there was much more to the BLM demonstrations than racism as the discord between ethnicities, political affiliations, social stature and law enforcement became exploited and manipulated in ways that were much more precise and effective than simply organic upheaval expressed through modern media.

With the memories of Russian interference in the 2015 U.S. election, the Chinese hacking into American corporate databases and foreign intelligence trolls insidiously undermining social media disguised as domestic online posters polarizing the narratives, fresh in recent history, the fakeness of the BLM agenda quickly became evident. Why, only weeks earlier was law enforcement touted as essential to ensuring the successful flattening of the curve through their role in propagating restrictions on the population, suddenly deemed the enemy of the state and targeted for defunding? Why were average family members arrested and fined for walking on a secluded beach or playing catch in an empty park only to be replaced in the mainstream media narrative by masked gang members being allowed to loot and destroy private property and take over several city blocks of Portland Oregon seemingly without retribution? Who was controlling the agenda and manipulating the narrative? How was ANTIFA so quickly and seamlessly injected into the fray as the unlikely ally of BLM?

Who was paying for pallet loads of bricks strategically placed prior to every protest – turned – riot? And who was paying for busloads of paid protesters being delivered to demonstrate and create havoc and even paying their bail money after arrest?

Rather than a misguided noble philanthropist bleeding heart black celebrity, genuinely sympathetic and supportive of black Americans exercising their rights of assembly and free speech in order to voice legitimate grievances, there was an influential well informed and well-funded adversary of the United States and democracy in general, waiting patiently to pounce on the next opportunity to create civil unrest. George Soros and his Open Society Foundations openly positions itself at the front of the protest movement amid donations $220 million to achieve racial equality in America. George's son, Alexander Soros gave the following statement that the dollars were a response for urgent and bold action.

"These investments will empower proven leaders in the black community to reimagine policing, end mass incarceration and eliminate the barriers to opportunity that have been the source for inequity for too long." [25]

The manufactured crisis of the migrant caravan that threatened to flood the southern U.S. border with illegal aliens and overwhelm immigration enforcement, complete with paid families traveling with full makeup and no visible luggage, day after day, was funded by "dark" money funneled through Soros funded organizations which happen to be the same people who called for the defunding of the police forces. You cannot make this stuff up. By sowing discord and calling for the overthrow of law and order these groups constitute an ongoing assault on the democratic freedom and destabilization of the United States and other countries as well. By intentionally harming the economies of the world, manipulating the narrative to align with their agendas, subjugating the media through ownership and propaganda, Soros has become one of the front men for the cabal that seeks total control for the elites because of his blatant arrogance and brash disregard for civilized negotiation. He remains unapologetic for his exploits and justifies his position with the logic that if he didn't do it, someone else would.

George Soros was implicit in the systemic dismantling of the Stephen Harper government by the Liberal party through influencing the outcome of the 2015 Canadian federal election by facilitating exchanges between U.S. Democratic backroom operatives and the Liberal Party of Canada campaign team and by channeling OSF funds into Tides Canada with whose support, "the organizations Leadnow and Dogwood spent millions of dollars and mobilized thousands of campaign workers to defeat Harper's Conservatives in a total of 40 ridings." [26]This has been well documented through the research of the Canada Decides report as well as investigative reporter Vivian Krause. The Canadian government's subsequent commitment to global environmentalism, capitulation to the OSF funded anti-oil campaign that spread misinformation and crippled Alberta's oil sector and ultimately the unbridled spending on the coronavirus pandemic effectively sabotaged the Canadian economy and the mountain of new debt in excess of $1 trillion will have to be financed by international bankers, leaving Canada open for exploitation by billionaires like Gorge Soros.

Justin Trudeau has followed the globalization template exclusively with little regard for the welfare of Canadians or for Canada itself for that matter. The thought that the federal government is indeed "owned" by foreign powers is front and center in the minds of many politically astute Canadian citizens. What is apparent on the surface is similar to an iceberg floating in the Atlantic Ocean. 70% - 80% remains hidden beneath the surface and only our imaginations can fathom the deep dark secrets and decisions arrived at behind closed doors. Justin Trudeau's adversity to the truth is evidence that he is hiding the fact that he has sold out Canada. What remains to be determined is to whom?

Looking back at the "terrorist" attack on the U.S.A. on September 11, 2001 that saw planes crash into the twin towers in New York, the Pentagon and a field in Pennsylvania and the uncertainties and contradicting narratives surrounding the supposed hijackings, it is highly likely that this event was a catastrophe orchestrated by the deep state in order to initiate a fear response and create a conflict with middle eastern terrorists. The events and actions surrounding the 9/11 attacks are both intriguing and alarming. The main stream media were complicit in maintaining the official narrative despite substantial evidence suggesting that this was indeed an inside job. It wasn't long until G.W. Bush ordered that the U.S.A. invade Iraq under the guise of liberating the people from their dictator Saddam Hussein and as an excuse to find weapons of mass destruction that never existed.

Cover ups and conspiracies have accompanied the rich and powerful throughout human history and death has been the common denominator to many who have tried to break into the inner circles of the elite or expose them. Were presidents Abraham Lincoln and John F. Kennedy assassinated for what they knew or for who they would implicate in their plans to right the wrongs of previous administrations or for disrupting the wealthy corporate profitability complex? Those who dare to speak the unspeakable, those who endeavor to expose the custodians of silence, the secretive underlying manipulators of all things that generate profit, are inevitably doomed so the charade can continue.

The following quote by John F. Kennedy is from a speech given seven days before his assassination, and it testifies to the present darkness at work in the world. "For we are opposed around the world by a monolithic and ruthless conspiracy that relies primarily on covert means for expanding its sphere of influence – on infiltration instead of invasion, on subversion instead of elections, on intimidation instead of free choice, on guerrillas by night instead of armies by day. It is a system which has conscripted vast human and material resources into the building of a tightly knit, highly efficient machine that combines military, diplomatic, intelligence, economic, scientific and political operations. Its preparations are concealed, not published. Its mistakes are buried, not headlined. Its dissenters are silenced, not praised. No expenditure is questioned, no rumor is printed, no secret is revealed. It conducts cold war, in short, with a war-time discipline no democracy would ever hope to match." [27] One week later JFK was dead. What did he know that compelled him to be so bold as to speak these words and what did the deep state fear by his very mention of this conspiracy?

The covert evil behind so much of postmodern presuppositions and even values stems from the subliminal manipulation generated over time disguised as goodness. This methodology is apparent when you examine the alleged Masonic Creed of John D. Rockerfeller. Vowing to keep the wealthy a superior class at the expense of the common people by "keeping their lives short and their minds weak while pretending to do the opposite." Using science and technology in subtle ways, adding soft metals, aging accelerators and sedatives to food, water and the air. Through their power and influence via big pharma they continually promise to find cures for diseases yet they manufacture and propagate more poisons infused into vaccines and drugs. "Chemical poisons and will be absorbed through the skin of idiots who believe that certain hygiene and beauty products presented by great actors and musicians, will bring eternal youth to their faces and bodies, and through their thirsty and hungry mouths, we will destroy their minds and systems of internal organs." Whoever it is that wrote these words, it is evident that their cupidity is deep rooted and the ruthlessness they endorse is as nefarious and ominous as their apparent lack of scruples.

The creed goes on to say, "The poisons will be hidden in everything around them, in what they drink, eat, breathe and wear." It doesn't get more blatant than this language that demonstrates the lengths the cabal will go to secure their hold on world power. The alleged rant continues, "When their ability to learn has been affected, we have created drugs that will make them sicker and cause them other illnesses, for which we will create even more drugs. We will make them docile and weak before us, by our power. They will grow depressed, slow and obese, and when they come to us for help, we will give them more poison." I've always said that fiction holds nothing over reality and these words are a case in point. You cannot dream this stuff up.

As if these concepts aren't disturbing enough, there's plenty more. "We will use fear as our weapon. We will establish governments and we will establish opposition within them. We will own both sides. We will always hide our goal, but we will continue our plan. They will do the work for us and we will profit from their toil." As insane as this rhetoric sounds, it is exactly what society has been victimized by.

What was openly done by the ruling class in the middle ages is the standard operating procedure for the elite wealthy of today's cabal. Their covert manipulation sows the seeds of dissention within populations to keep all the advantage in their court. These intentions are conveyed within the creed with the words, "We will keep them separate from unity through dogma and religion. We will control all aspects of their lives and tell them what to think and how. We will guide them kindly and let them think they are guiding themselves. We will instigate animosity among them through our factions. When a light shines among them, we will extinguish it by mockery or death, which suits us best. We will make them tear their hearts apart and kill their own children. We will accomplish this by using hatred as our ally, anger as our friend. Hatred will completely blind them and they will never see that in their conflicts we will be their leaders. They will be busy killing each other. They will bathe in their own blood and kill their neighbors...."

"We will benefit greatly from this, for they will not see us, for they cannot see us. We will continue to prosper from their wars and their deaths. We will repeat this until our ultimate goal is achieved. We will continue to make them live in fear and anger, we will give them images and sounds. We will use all the tools we have to achieve this. The tools will be provided by their own work. We will make them hate themselves and their neighbors."

"When we ban them together, we will accuse them of murder and present a different story to the world because we will own all the media. We will use the media to control the flow of information and their feelings in our favor. When they rise up against us, we will crush them like insects, because they are less than that. They will be helpless to do anything about it." While most certainly not written by John D. Rockerfeller, the creed, which was posted anonymously to the website of BankIndex.com in 2002, and its nefarious theme should not be taken lightly since it so accurately reflects the dark forces evident, yet hidden in civilization.[28] It's as if the creed was spawned from the pen of Satan himself.

Today we can feel a subtle chill in the air as we witness the erosion of our rights and freedoms as governments that claim to act on behalf of citizens, institute greater and greater controls over our lives. In the name of safety, we are increasingly restricted through taxation, health protocols, increased surveillance, the impending introduction of cashless currencies, pseudo-science paid for by those who will profit from the resulting green economies, coming mandatory vaccinations and digital identity micro-chip implants. The darkness of the human heart and its capacity for greed, lust for power and deception to achieve it are evident in the secretive ruling class in our civilization. Past history reminds us of the corruption of the Roman Emperors, the Mafia organized crime chronicles of the last century, and the temptation of Jesus Christ himself.

In the fourth chapter of Mathew, we are told that Jesus was led by the Spirit into the wilderness to be tempted by the devil. In verse 8, the devil took him to a very high mountain and showed him all the kingdoms of the world and their splendor. "All this I will give you if you will bow down and worship me." It gives one pause, in light of the covert powers that pull the strings of world rulers, just who else has the devil tempted in such a way. Jesus did not capitulate. Others have not been so resilient.

The apostle Paul wrote, "Those who want to get rich fall into temptation and a trap and into many foolish and harmful desires that plunge people into ruin and destruction. For the love of money is the root of all kinds of evil." 1 Timothy 6:9-10. The material focus of civilization today has made society vulnerable to manipulation through advertising, entertainment and coveting the wealth and lifestyles of celebrities. Sports heroes and movie stars draped in expensive jewelry captivate their fans as they bask in the limelight of luxury, lavish treatment and affection. Lotteries continually dangle golden carrots with astronomical jackpots, and many become addicted to gambling in hopes of striking it rich. The elite of the super-rich however, take the immorality of money worship to an entirely different level. Rather than the outward appearance of wealth they prefer the secluded cloak of mystery and blend into the crowd with their business suits and dark glasses. The covert nature of their empires is unknown to most and the multiplicity of their holdings would stagger the average person's imagination.

The alleged depravity of the plutocracy is of such a loathsome, repulsive, and detestable nature it cannot be fathomed by anyone with intrinsic goodness. The magnitude of its cupidity is so colossal that most could not even begin to describe it let alone quantify it. It is rooted in the practices of the Illuminati and Free Masons, and is historically anti-Christ. From trafficking drugs, guns, nuclear weapons, people and even body parts, the sheer depth of its turpitude is of Satanic proportions. It is no small wonder that this power structure is envisioned as a beast in end times prophecy.

In the seventh chapter of the book of Daniel, the prophet had a dream in which he was shown the great kingdoms of the world, depicted as beasts. An angel interpreted his vision and disclosed that the beasts represented Babylon, Medo-Persia, Greece and Rome. The fourth beast was different from the others and the most terrifying one. It had ten horns on its head and a little horn that came up later and before which three other horns fell.

The angel gave this interpretation, "The fourth beast is a fourth kingdom that will appear on earth. It will be different from all the other kingdoms and will devour the whole earth, trampling it down and crushing it. The ten horns are ten kings who will come from this kingdom. After them another king will arise, different from the earlier ones; he will subdue three kings. He will speak against the Most High and oppress his saints and try to change set times and the laws. The saints will be handed over to him for a time, times and a half time.

But the court will sit, and his power will be taken away and completely destroyed forever. Then the sovereignty, power and greatness of the kingdoms under the whole heaven will be handed over to the saints, the people of the Most High. His kingdom will be an everlasting kingdom, and all rulers will worship and obey him." Daniel 7:23-27.

Since this fourth and final kingdom is derived from the Roman Empire yet is different insofar as it is portrayed as a coalition of nations, many have equated it with the European Union. While this is plausible, I see its difference and uniqueness as being a covert power that transcends borders and is sinister in its nature to the degree that it can spawn the antichrist, which is the little horn that comes later. He will be different from the earlier kings insofar as he will be Satan's protégé and reign for three and one half years during the second half of the great tribulation which will be followed by the return of Jesus Christ and the destruction of the antichrist. Jesus will then install his millennial kingdom in which the saints or true believers will rule with Christ.

Since the man of lawlessness remains surreptitious until he is "revealed," (2 Thessalonians 2:3) it is logically consistent that he emerges from a covert power structure. The cabal that secretly controls world governments through its iniquitous "behind the scenes" methodologies, is the ideal breeding ground to develop and groom the devil incarnate. It is the consummate entity for him to rise through the ranks to a position from which he can assume ultimate global authority and control. I believe he will be unknown from a political perspective and seemingly come out of nowhere to assume the reigns of the final one world government. He will be no stranger to power however, as he will emerge from obscurity well versed in backroom deals, corrupt negotiating tactics, and coercion skills learned while ascending the hierarchy of the deep state.

Deep State Manipulation

The COVID 19 (Certificate of Vaccination Identification) pandemic of 2020 gave rise to an abundance of conspiracy theories and fear, in response to sensationalized media coverage and a seemingly pre-written script that closely followed the UN's playbook for managing populations and controlling the world. It seemed apparent that by creating a problem and subsequently offering a solution, civilization was manipulated towards a predetermined outcome and incrementally surrendering rights and freedoms it has taken for granted, in the name of safety and for the greater good. Underlying the obvious pandemic, the question that begged to be asked was, who would benefit from a crippled world economy and who was promoting a cashless society, a one world currency, mandatory vaccinations and individual digital identification implants for the entire population? Ironically, the conspiracy suspicions appear to be far more than theory and much more insidious and heinous than the public could ever imagine.

The World Health Organization (WHO), established in 1948, plays a major role in the global governance of health and disease response by influencing governments and other stakeholders to coordinate their efforts toward common goals. The global health landscape requires effective global action to manage the complexities created by globalization. World travel, trade, business interactions and ultimately diseases dictate a global response when challenges such as pandemics arise. This is the narrative that directs us toward the conclusion that the WHO is the leader that must implement a global mission that we in turn are to accept and follow.

On the surface these are noble and admirable aspirations since the organization can facilitate the transfer of medical and health knowledge and technology, health promotion and disease prevention strategies, best practices and medical treatments. Since globalization has accelerated the spread of infectious diseases like SARS, H1N1 and COVID 19, with the potential to quickly exacerbate health system deficiencies and impact social, political and economic well-being, the end justifies the means. The WHO works closely with the UN to monitor and deliver their values and vision to all peoples and nations thereby keeping the world safe.

On May 24, 2018, the WHO teamed up with the World Bank to "strengthen global health security through stringent independent monitoring and regular reporting of preparedness to tackle outbreaks, pandemics, and other emergencies with health consequences."[29] With the introduction of a major money stakeholder, as with all things, the money became what dictated the game plan. Today the organization is responsive to dollars and that has had an impact on its recommendations.

When you look at the progression from how SARS was handled in 2003 and H1N1 in 2009 to how the 2020/2021 COVID19 pandemic has been handled, it quickly becomes apparent that the role of the media has evolved to that of propagating fear and apprehension to justify drastic government restrictions and surveillance that simply isn't supported by the statistical data. It is estimated that the death rate of H1N1 was 0.001% to 0.007%, compared to the mortality rates observed with COVID19 of an estimated 3.4%. However, there were major differences in the way cases were counted and governments were strongly advised to list the coronavirus as the cause of death even when the actual reason for the fatality was another factor, so long as there was suspicion of COVID 19 as a health concern.

In the U. S. this was supported through increased funding for COVID deaths vs. deaths of other causes, which misrepresented the number of COVID deaths and the subsequent mortality rate. These overinflated statistics were propagated widely, creating apprehension and frustration in the public. Ultimately, the programmed perceptions and pre-arranged narratives distributed by the mass media supported the surrender of individual rights and freedoms on a scale never before seen. It amounted to exploiting humanity's fear of death to induce a response that favors the agenda of the principalities and powers that stand to profit from it.

The world's drastic reaction attempted to imitate China's apparent success in controlling the spread of the virus through the lockdowns of its cities and controlling the movement of its citizens. Following that model, Canadian Health Minister Patty Hajdu issued a stern warning to Canadians defying self-isolation orders, that failing to follow public health guidelines could "put our civil liberties in jeopardy."[30] It is nonsensical to think that isolating an entire population from a virus it would develop an immunity to once they are exposed, is a better long term solution than simply isolating the high risk element of society, which in this case were the elderly and those with otherwise compromised health. However, that does not serve the purposes of those who promote vaccinations for protection, nor does it harmonize with the WTO and UN goals for population management. The hidden agenda's premise is money. This is the wolf dressed in sheep's clothing.

People's survival instincts will welcome any solution that claims to prolong life to the point where humanity will accept tyranny in order to feel safe. And patiently waiting in the wings is Bill Gates with his global immunization strategy, ready and willing to guilt the population into accepting vaccine injections so the elderly will not be put at risk. Interestingly, surrendering oneself to the greater good conveniently is coupled with the RFID micro-chip that allows for you to be monitored for "the greater good."

While China was exalted for its response, the rest of the world, by implementing similar human tracking initiatives such as utilizing people's cell phones to monitor activity in the name of safety and protection for high risk populations, effectively places the population under surveillance 24/7. This includes fines and /or imprisonment for noncompliance to lockdowns and curfews. In fact, Canada's legislation included fines of up to $500,000 for corporations and $1000 for individuals not implementing social distancing guidelines. And this was implemented after only 19 deaths. The Northwest Territories banned non-essential travel into the territory after its first case was identified, which is punishable by law and up to a $10,000 fine and six month's imprisonment. China was the testing ground and the rest of the world will capitulate.

As democracy becomes neutered and vilified because communist regimes were more effective at containing the pandemic, and voters are manipulated to accept authoritarian rule, the elite wealthy will profit from the chaos. Mainstream media broadcasts the rhetoric, the WHO asserts its influence and governments fall into line. While politicians come and go, there is a hidden power structure dictating every move. It is a heinous, unscrupulous force that controls and runs the world behind the scenes and its only morality is money. It is the cabal.

Pharmaceutical companies succeed by keeping people sick. The cure for cancer will never be publicized because it's bad for business. Right around the corner in the fallout from pandemic pandemonium is mandatory vaccinations. Funded through a cycle of corrupt government grants and contracts to those whose donations swing elections and pull the puppet strings of the faces in parliament. Big pharma is an insatiable manipulator of world policy that controls our food supply and has us consuming GMO foods produced with chemicals that are known carcinogens and then supplies the drugs to treat the cancers they created. On the heels of genetically modified foods that are patented so farmer growers cannot retain seed for production, the reality of GMO viruses has become plausible as research and development of new strains and more lethal viruses continues in an effort to produce vaccines capable of creating immunity to these more virulent organisms. And of course, these GMO viruses are patented and include the coronavirus. Largely owned by the wealthy elite, big pharma systematically determines world health and misrepresents drugs as medicines.

History shows us that mass vaccination programs can result in compromised immune systems. As far back as 1796 when Edward Jenner developed the first vaccine for smallpox, complications arising from vaccination interference with immune response have been documented. In 1853 vaccinations became mandatory in England and by 1857 fines and imprisonment were applied to those who refused the vaccination for smallpox. According to the Register General of England, between 1857 and 1859, there were over 14,000 deaths from smallpox. Then between 1863 and 1865, there were over 20,000 smallpox deaths. Between 1870 and 1872, there were almost 45,000 smallpox deaths.

It was only after massive demonstrations like the Leicester rally of over 80,000 people that became known as "The Great Demonstration," that the freedom to choose not to vaccinate was provided. Over the next eight years, the percentage of citizens vaccinated dropped to 5% and the death rates and outbreaks dramatically decreased as well. [31]

In the case of the flu or coronavirus that is usually only fatal when those infected have compromised health and immune systems, there is absolutely no need for immunization of 100% of the population, since exposure to the disease acts as immunization in and of itself and produces herd immunity. Implementing a mass immunization program for something like COVID 19 will only result in immune system interference putting the high-risk populations at even greater risk of succumbing to the disease. Some doctors even recommend getting a flu shot, however, a 2017-2018 study published in "Vaccine" found that flu vaccines may increase the risk of infection from other respiratory viruses, including coronavirus. This condition is called "virus interference."

The media has played a pivotal role in propagating fear with their sensationalizing of COVID 19 statistics regarding the spread and fatalities associated with the "pandemic." The pre-packaged pseudo-science and narrative of the WHO has been systematically generated on a timeline that has induced the highest fear response attainable with massive hoarding, panic selling of stocks, business closures, travel shutdowns and ultimately the lockdown of entire cities and delivered on que by the media. You would think it would give one pause to question why a "novel" virus from a common family of viruses with a prevalence and mortality rate as that of COVID 19, would justify such extreme measures. We don't quarantine from the flu despite the fact that the seasonal flu kills up to 646,000 people per year worldwide, or Tuberculosis which killed 1.4 million people in 2019.

Furthermore, the tests used to identify coronavirus infections have been brought into question since they are based on unproven methodology and have high incidences of false positives. The PCR test looks for RNA and doesn't prove the presence of a virus. According to David Crowe (an expert in global infections such as SARS, EBOLA and flu), the data is being interpreted to support the viral theory, and there is zero concern for false positive results.[32]

Once the pandemic began there was virtually no news about the issues that had dominated headlines for months. No news about catastrophic climate change or Greta Thunberg. No news about the oil price war between Russia and Saudi Arabia or the trade war between the U.S. and China. Just 24/7 coverage of the COVID 19 pandemic, complete with death count updates, graphs depicting the number of new cases and their hourly changes, commentaries on the shortfalls of medical systems and speculation on what the origin of the virus was. There were countless articles published that added to the hysteria with messages ranging from why it is essential to act immediately to control the spread to long term suggestions to flatten the curve. The media truly took the fear mongering narrative to unprecedented levels. It was like all other problems mysteriously fixed themselves or weren't problems in the first place.

China was simultaneously elevated as the epitome of containing the spread of the virus while being blamed for hiding its knowledge of it at the beginning of the pandemic. The media sowed the seeds of discord by directing the coronavirus focus onto Chinese scientists and health systems suppressing and withholding information about the contagion. China's communist regime was portrayed as corrupt yet effective in their draconian response to the pandemic and became an example of what other countries were encouraged to mimic in order to successfully reduce the prevalence of the virus.

In the City of Wuhan, China, less than 1% of the population was clinically infected and 3% of that 1% died. [33]

Inevitably, governments restricted travel, closed schools and restricted gatherings of more than 10 people. The news was filled with press conferences of health ministers issuing the latest warnings and regulations as if they were war time measures. This behavior is not supported by the epidemiology of the disease and focuses on the unknown. News reports suggesting the virus was man-made added to the apprehension as well as suspicion that communist regimes had under reported their case and death numbers. Anything that could potentially increase anxiety surfaced in the media, for example, Prince Phillip was quoted as saying, "If I were reincarnated, I would wish to be returned as a killer virus to lower human population levels."

The COVID 19 pandemic has been unprecedented in shutting down the world economy and terrorizing humanity. As the economy crumbled and small businesses ceased generating income, governments introduced emergency funding in the form of loans that essentially handcuffed these businesses into capitulating and accepting the government agenda. When the businesses finally fail, the employees and business owners alike, become dependent on welfare and are therefore at the mercy of the government and the UN agenda. When the wealth of the middle class disappears, they slip below the poverty line and become enslaved to the wealthy elite.

As poverty increases, desperation grows along with violence and crime, therefore law enforcement responds accordingly, resulting in a police state. This strengthens the position of the deep state and justifies continued control and surveillance. It becomes a cycle of demonstrations and civil disobedience followed by police crackdowns similar to what was experienced in Hong Kong in 2019.

In a mock exercise to determine just how societies and governments would react to a worldwide pandemic, the John Hopkins Center for Health and Security partnered with the World Economic Forum and the Bill and Melinda Gates Foundation on October 18, 2019. Event 201 was a simulation of a coronavirus pandemic with potentially catastrophic consequences. In his 2015 TED talk, Bill Gates expounded on the need for such an exercise and how humanity's next biggest threat would most likely be a highly infectious virus. He identified five major points to enhance global readiness, including, strengthening health systems, establishing a medical corps similar to the army reserves, pairing medical responses with the military, creating pandemic simulations and investing in research and development. [34]

Interestingly just a month later, that scenario began to play out in real time in Wuhan, China. It was first suspected of originating at a raw food market and the mainstream media postulated the theory of cross-contamination between animals and humans. No mention was made of the Wuhan Institute of Virology, the largest lab of its kind in Asia containing over 1500 viruses and highly pathogenic micro-organisms. Also falling through the cracks of mainstream media was Harvard's Chemistry chair, Charles M. Lieber who was charged with lying about a China contract called "Thousand Talents" which paid him $50,000/ month salary, $158,000 in living expenses and $1.74 million to set up a research lab in China.

Was the coronavirus intentionally placed in Wuhan or did it accidentally escape the Wuhan Institute of Virology? Doesn't it seem odd that the 2019 World Military Games were held in Wuhan from October 18-27 bringing in nearly 10,000 athletes from over 100 countries? That would be a pretty good distraction for some covert activity. Was China used as a pawn to evaluate their response and ability to contain the spread of the virus? Was everything planned in advance to generate a desired outcome? Who would potentially profit? Why did over 1300 CEO's step down in 2019 prior to the pandemic (a record number)? Were they tipped off that something was about to happen that would crash world markets? Why did Bill Gates step down from the board of directors of Microsoft when he did? Was China used as a distraction so the real agenda could be carried out without attracting attention to its implementation?

Or did the Chinese government develop and intentionally release the virus to bring the world to its knees in order to provide an economic advantage to China? A Chinese virologist came forward in September, 2020 claiming she had proof that the virus had originated at the Wuhan Institute of Virology. Dr. Li-Meng Yan, a research scientist who has been in hiding for fear of her safety, and worked on some of the earliest COVID 19 research, has claimed she has evidence that the virus was man made and the narrative that it came from a wet market in Wuhan was a smokescreen. She fled China for the U.S.A. in April. [35]

The hysteria generated by the COVID 19 pandemic left all rationality behind. Just as fire drills focus on staying calm and reacting in an orderly fashion, the absence of calm resulted in disorder on a worldwide scale. When the government steps in and imposes self-isolation and introduces a military presence to reinforce what is essentially house arrest during the lock down of cities, citizens become desensitized to the sight of the military in their neighborhoods and will eventually accept martial law. In the Philippines, President Duterte issued a shoot to kill order to police and military personnel in response to anyone caught breaching quarantine measures. This included protests over the government's lack of relief response to the pandemic.

In Canada, the Trudeau government enacted emergency legislation that would enable cabinet to raise taxes without approval of parliament and bail out companies without limitations, purchase or hold a company's shares, guarantee new pools of debt without the need for new legislation and break patents on medical technology that might be urgently needed.

Not only does this represent an unprecedented infringement on individual rights and freedoms and facilitate government monitoring and detaining citizens, it also amounts to potentially adding over $1 trillion to the Canadian national debt through its stimulus response to COVID 19 based on the promises made by Trudeau.

The country may never recover from his "leadership." After half a million Canadians had lost their jobs through company cutbacks, losses and closures, Trudeau opened the UN playbook to the chapter on immigration once again, relaxing the health protocols to allow more foreign workers into the country to assume jobs left vacant by Canadians who were in isolation because of infection. These foreign workers did not require testing nor the standard 14-day isolation to enter the country.

In both Canada and the U.S. numerous violent criminals were released from prison because they couldn't be provided with social distancing minimums and were deemed at risk of spreading the disease. Essentially a "get out of jail free" card, judges are now faced with a growing number of applications from prisoners seeking to be released. The knowledge of their release into the public generates additional fear and the increased police presence acts to desensitize communities even further to added surveillance.

In the U.S. the Trump government announced a $2 trillion stimulus package to bail out small businesses, while implementing regulations and restrictions on the movement of people both domestically and internationally. The CDC was tasked with the development of a surveillance and data collection system to track movements of people and the spread of the virus which may include using personal smartphones to monitor people. Trump approached the Canadian government with a plan to position the U.S. military along its' northern boundary, an irrational move considering the pandemic was much less prevalent in Canada than in the United States. No sane person sneaks from the frying pan into the fire.

In California's bay area, "shelter in place" orders and other restrictions even included plans to prohibit the sale of firearms. What do guns have to do with disease? Rep. Thomas Massie, R-Ky warned that American liberties were at stake, adding that "the greatest harm to society will have been the public's unquestioning acceptance of the unchecked authority of governments to force private behavior and disrupt economies."[36] In the face of such enormous implications on businesses and the world economy, the World Bank estimated global wealth would drop by $3 trillion from the pandemic.

As the economy shifted to freefall, the government's stimulus package included the establishment of a digital dollar which it defined as, "a balance expressed as a dollar value consisting of digital ledger entries that are recorded as liabilities in the accounts of any Federal Reserve Bank.... An electronic unit of value, redeemable by an eligible financial institution (as determined by the board of governors of the Federal Reserve System)."[37] It also introduced the digital wallet or account maintained by the Fed on behalf of any person. There is also provision to help unbanked people and/or individuals without proper ID to establish their identity to be provided with a digital dollar account. The pandemic turned out to be just the catalyst needed to upgrade the financial infrastructure to facilitate phasing out the green back.

Sweden was the first country to adopt bank notes in 1661 and is leading the world by introducing digital currency in 2021 and targeting being a cashless society by 2023. Cash already accounts for less than 1% of all transactions in Sweden and most merchants do not accept cash. While reducing bank robberies and counterfeiting, the system also minimizes tax evasion, giving the government surveillance capabilities that previously didn't exist.[38]

Whether the COVID 19 pandemic was caused by man or nature, the ruling class of the world are exploiting it to further their agenda. Media, WHO and government narratives maintain a specific message that involves centralized control of information and censorship of what is considered misinformation. The demonizing of cash as a vehicle complicit in spreading the virus and the opportunity to take the next big step towards a cashless society in which governments gain control of every aspect of the lives of individuals through digital tracking is just too convenient. China has already identified cash as a culprit in spreading coronavirus and is recommending that paper money must be taken out of circulation because of the possibility that it could contain traces of COVID 19.

Mandatory vaccinations have always been on the agenda of proponents of a new world order and coincidentally (or not), China passed a law on June 29, 2019 introducing a national mandatory vaccination program that came into effect December 1, 2019. Furthermore, the leveraging of vaccinations to establish digital identification through ID2020 that promotes itself as a "trusted and reliable way to fulfill a fundamental and universal human right – safeguarding your identity both online and in the physical world."[39] It is recognized that the design of digital identification systems carries far reaching implications of individual's access to services and livelihoods. The COVID 19 pandemic turned out to be the ideal catalyst to make digital identification implants and mass mandatory vaccination programs a really attractive management tool for global safety. The digital implant will contain not only all of your personal identification, banking, health, taxation and driver's license, it will also reveal if you've been vaccinated for the coronavirus thereby rating your risk level as a potential asymptomatic carrier.

The potential for abuse of control of what an individual will be permitted or not permitted to do will become public knowledge with the swipe of your hand. Just as China's social credit program rewards and penalizes citizens based on points, your digital ID will be able to allow you to buy or sell or be denied if the implant is missing. Already China has introduced thermal scanners at various locations to identify individuals with fevers. Alphabet Inc's Google has released location data for 131 countries from users who have enabled the location history feature on their devices, revealing violations in quarantine parameters and tracking traffic at retail venues, recreation spots, train and bus stations and workplaces.

When you realize that the deep state that runs the world is simply operating a business, then you can grasp the concept that there is no empathy or compassion involved in its decision making. Old people become expendable since their productive contribution to society has expired and they become a burden on the system. Italy was a case in point. They openly discussed the ramifications of a coronavirus pandemic during Event 201. In the first six months after the lockdowns and subsequent crash of the world economy, Canada's 20 wealthiest people increased their net worth by an estimated $37 billion collectively while millions of people lost their jobs and businesses. [40] At the same time, the U.S.'s billionaires became $637 billion richer.[41]

They knew in advance that thousands of young people would view the closure of schools as a unique opportunity to gather and socialize at beaches, ski hills and parks. They knew the arrogance and cavalier attitudes of youths would lead them to disobey isolation protocols as was evidenced by a disgraceful video of a heavily tattooed man touring through a Walmart while claiming to have tested positive for COVID 19 and sharing his disdain for others as his commentary declared his insubordination and mocked the elderly and those with health issues. They knew that thousands of people would die. They knew all of this and proceeded to exploit it so they could justify the imposition of greater controls and less freedom for citizens. The evil of the wealthy elite is incomprehensible to the average person. George Soros said in an interview once, that he felt absolutely no guilt for making money at the expense of others, potentially ruining lives, rationalizing his perspective by adding that if it wasn't him doing it, someone else would.

The deep state maintains an advantage over humanity because it ultimately controls what the population thinks. By dictating the narrative of the education system, the media and governments, they manipulate what we see, hear and process in our minds. The secular perception of society that death is the end of existence creates a fear response. Fear looks for protection and there is no grater fear than the fear of death. Individuality succumbs to uniformity and as a result people accept tyranny as an escape from anarchy.

Gordon Brown, former prime minister of the UK stands out as calling for a temporary global government in response to the COVID 19 pandemic. He advocated for a bureau of world leaders, health experts, and leaders of international organizations that would be given executive powers to execute a world response to mitigating the impact of the coronavirus. The group would in turn give more power to the IMF and the World Bank. What is alarming about his comments is the fact that he has been a member of the Bilderberg Group and his past comments that give context to his perspective. In 2009, at the London Summit for the G20. He said, "I think the new world order is emerging, and with it the foundations of a new and progressive era of international cooperation."[42] It's easy to predict the outcome of this proposal by looking back at how income tax was introduced as a temporary measure. Once that line has been crossed, its proponents will never rescind that decision and will never surrender territory they have occupied.

While vaccines are being hailed as the key component of a global health response, there is little talk of a natural immune response triggered by the generation of antibodies from within. While countless parasites, bacteria, weeds and most organisms including humans adapt and become resistant to the immune challenges they face, in typical scientific reaction, the medical community will treat the symptoms without concerning itself with the causes. Furthermore, death statistics from COVID 19 have become skewed since the Center for Disease Control began recommending hospitals attribute even suspected deaths related to COVID 19 as the result of the virus. This data is then being used as justification for the draconian measures introduced and the resulting social control attained.

Hindsight is 20/20 and with a little investigation it is possible to connect some of the dots in the world pandemic "create a problem and supply the solution" agenda. Under the guise of philanthropy and his investments in vaccines, Bill Gates has become a "credible" voice in world health discussions despite never being elected to public office and receiving no formal training in human medicine. He arguably has more influence over world health policy than any other single person. Why is that?

When you investigate the history and connections of the Gates family, you soon discover that the same names so heavily influencing the deep state are prevalent in the Gates family historical record. His father, William Gates II, was a lawyer and contemporary of George Sorros and the Rockerfellers through his political activism and a board member of Planned Parenthood before Roe vs Wade.[43] His mother, Mary Maxwell Gates, came from a wealthy banking family with connections to the Federal Reserve.

The Gates foundation was established with Bill's father, his wife, Melinda and Warren Buffet. It is the largest private foundation in the world. Bill's personal wealth was gained through the growth of his company Microsoft which he held as shares in the company. Since these shares were not taxable until sold, he donated them to the Gates Foundation as a charitable organization and avoided paying capital gains, making him one of the wealthiest and influential people in the world. He is now heavily invested in drug companies who manufacture contraceptives and vaccines. The Gates foundation collaborates with the CDC, WHO, UN, etc., to ensure there is a cohesive agenda and the wealth is maintained within the elite players.

As a public advocate of reducing the world population in order to combat poverty, infant mortality, and deficiencies in women's health (abortion), as well as reducing the global carbon footprint through reduced energy usage from a smaller population, Gates has conflated the rhetoric of catastrophic climate change with the language of the potentially devastating consequences of global pandemics. Together, they have become a powerful engine to drive legislation and regulations for the future. What has happened is a dramatic acceleration of policies that will facilitate a one world government, a totalitarian state and ultimately lay the foundation for the man of lawlessness to assume power and control the world as a fulfillment of biblical prophecy.

Philanthropy is the disguise that masquerades as benevolence yet manifests as capitalization of the pandemic. We are witnessing a systemic scare tactic to keep the public focused on the potential of billions of people dying from a virus. As global vaccination programs that are coupled with digital ID implants, are implemented in the name of safety, billions of dollars will be generated for their manufacturers and other stakeholders of which Bill Gates plays a significant role.

What was learned in the COVID 19 pandemic will result in pressure to introduce legislation to permanently implement laws to enable a quick intervention by governments similar to China's and other communist regimes. In the same way that increased security measures introduced after the 9/11 terrorist attacks remain in place today, there will be plenty of resolve not to relinquish control once it has been obtained. This will include plugging the holes identified in the free democratic systems that prevented the intervention in restricting the movement and tracking of people. Traceability of contacts will be identified as a key component in response management which will be remedied by digital tracking and identification of individuals.

Fitting like a puzzle piece into the UN's plans for a new world order, the agenda will be to raise the living standards of third world countries so people can be provided better health care, access to abortion and employment for women so they will have fewer children thereby reducing population growth which will result in a smaller global carbon footprint with the added bonus of greater tax revenue from women in the workforce. Wouldn't it be more cost effective to invest in clean water, combat malnutrition and starvation and fight corruption in poor countries? This would have a profound effect on child mortality rates much more than vaccines.

Corruption is made possible by wealthy global enablers. To put it in perspective, natural resource exports out-weigh aid cash flows by 19:1 in Africa, Asia and Latin America. Through the use of anonymous shell companies that are used to transfer money out of poor countries in order to benefit wealthy elites at the expense of average citizens. It's all non-traceable and the world turns a blind eye as the international banking systems such as the Cayman Islands and Swiss bank accounts facilitate exchanges.

The government spending to bail out the world economy has been morally irresponsible because it will burden future generations with debt that funded a lifestyle but didn't generate wealth and increased dependency on government support that isn't sustainable. When the government can no longer service the debt, it becomes insolvent and prints more money to fuel the economy which only results in high inflation, devalued currency and makes it vulnerable to losing control of its sovereignty to a one world government and one world currency.

Belarusian President Aleksandr Lukashenko admitted that he was offered a bribe by the World Bank and the IMF to the tune of $940 million USD, packaged as "COVID Relief Aid" if he was willing to impose an extreme lockdown, including strict curfews, implement a police state, force his citizens to wear masks and crash his economy. He declined. Regardless of the amount of truth behind his claim, it exposes the underlying coercion the world financial system is willing to employ to subjugate society. The pressure placed upon governments, corporations and NGO's to adhere to strict protocols like wearing face masks, trickle down to regional and local companies who are subsequently guilted into following suit.

Threats of mandatory vaccinations, tax penalties for those who refuse, higher insurance premiums, and denying many government and private services have become considerations the medical community has permitted to be within the realm of possibilities to win the war on the coronavirus. "Private businesses could refuse to employ or serve unvaccinated individuals. Schools could refuse to allow unimmunized children to attend classes. Public and commercial transit companies – airlines, trains and buses – could exclude refusers. Public and private auditoriums could require evidence of immunization for entry." Wrote Dr. Michael Lederman, Dr. Stuart Youngner and Maxwell J. Mehlman. They advocate a "registry of immunization" documenting citizens who have received a vaccination, who would receive "immunization cards."

Bill Gates has advocated the use of digital identification of individuals who have received a vaccination or show immunity to COVID 19. The doctors mentioned above have compared the pandemic to fighting a war, equating those who refuse to draft dodgers during WWI and WWII.[44] Not only are these measures extreme, they are blatantly insincere, since known, inexpensive therapies such as using hydroxychloroquine have been successfully employed against COVID 19. However, there is not the profit upside in generic therapies so the elite have pushed back fighting common sense with big pharma.

French doctor and virologist Didier Raoult who promoted the malaria medication for patients with COVID 19, found himself at the center of controversy when the WHO declared the drug dangerous and suspended all trials with it. Raoult, who is the head of the infectious diseases department at the university hospital in Marseille, also believes that natural immunity is likely in populations exposed to the novel coronavirus. Voices that have echoed his regarding using hydroxychloroquine have also been discredited by the WHO and big pharma will not be denied their profits from vaccine sales. [45]

It certainly sounds like a conspiracy theory, but when you really dig into the details, the word theory seems to disappear from the equation. Back during World War II a pharmaceutical company conducting certain experiments, named IG Farben, was run by George Sorros. He later broke up IG Farben and formed another pharmaceutical company called Moderna. Moderna's first CEO was Anthony Faucci who had attended Cornell University and who's roommate while at Cornell just happened to be a young Bill Gates. As if this wasn't incredulous enough, one of Moderna's main financial investors up until his death in 2019 was Jeffery Epstein. Fiction has nothing on reality. Is it any coincidence that Moderna is at the forefront of developing a vaccine for COVID 19? How long do you think they had it develcped ahead of the pandemic but just held it back to make it seem legitimate? [46]

The wealthy elite want you to believe they are concerned for the welfare of society. They maintain a strong presence in politics, speak of fresh new ideas and claim to represent the grass roots however they are cut from the same cloth as the establishment, come from wealthy backgrounds and use the rhetoric of controlled opposition to convince young voters they actually represent change. However, once in power, all roads lead back to the cabal and the same old wealth dictating policy that protects the deep state and discriminates against the middle class.

Will we be confronted with mandatory vaccinations, or will the clever wording of government programs coerce our voluntary capitulation? Will it begin with a tax exemption to vaccinate your children? Will you receive an offer from your financial institution offering a reduction in your payments with proof of vaccination or a reduction in life insurance premiums with a proof of vaccination? Or perhaps you will encounter roadblocks that hinder your ability to get a job or book a holiday without proof of vaccination. Will governments take away your ability to earn a living, go to school or take your child to daycare if you don't have proof of vaccinations? While they claim that vaccinations are not mandatory, will they force you into a corner where its either get vaccinated or don't eat? Or will they blatantly rule that vaccinations are mandatory by law?

How quickly the world forgets the botched attempts to implement a Polio vaccine regimen in India that saw nearly half a million children paralyzed from 2000 -2017 from Gates Foundation vaccinations and the complications in Africa that resulted in the sterilization of young African girls as well as many deaths from malaria and meningitis vaccines. Gates has used his money and influence to produce deceptive research and propaganda and coerce governments and NGO's into furthering his vaccination agenda.

He has set the standard for other philanthropists to mimic his benevolent leadership in the environment of COVID 19 fear. Jack Dorsey, co-founder and CEO of Twitter announced that he would be donating $1 billion of his own money for COVID 19 relief and progressive political programs such as population control and universal basic income. Operation Drawdown proposes to educate girls and thereby influence them to, "have fewer and healthier children, and actively manage their reproductive health." [47]

In Canada, the Trudeau government issued a Request for Proposals (RFP) to build coronavirus internment camps across the country to isolate people with the virus. Industry service providers are being solicited for feedback and information regarding whether "Federal Quarantine/ Isolation sites" can be used for other purposes in addition to COVID 19 internment. Requests for information were posted on the Government of Canada's buyandsell.gc.ca website, and list every province and territory as potential regions for delivery. In his usual nebulous response, or outright circumvention when questioned, Trudeau's failure to deny the plans has added to the suspicions of Canadians that his ambitions are less about health and more about politics. Given his affinity for the UN, this is seen as one more example of his sly approach to tip toe toward the model of a new world order, which he has fully endorsed.[48]

By the end of January 2021, Trudeau had implemented greater travel restrictions, requiring people returning from other countries to enter mandatory quarantine in hotels at their own expense until they could provide negative COVID test results. They would then be permitted to go home and be expected to self-quarantine for the remainder of the fourteen-day period. Once at home they could expect to receive phone calls from the government, or even visits from private investigators hired to surveille them. Those with positive results would be required to complete their quarantine at a designated quarantine facility.[49]

It didn't take long for the worst case scenario to play out. Edmonton resident Nikki Mathis was detained when she returned to Canada from the USA on January 28, 2021 and was told the negative COVID test she received before leaving for home was being rejected and she was quickly whisked away to an undisclosed detention facility and kept under guard. Her husband Chris tried unsuccessfully to find out where she had been taken, who the police officer was and the name of the health official authorizing the detainment. Terrorizing citizens in the name of health and safety officially became government protocol.

Additionally, a RFP from the Canadian Department of National

Defense for 36,000 canisters of the riot control agent "tear gas" delivered to the Canadian Forces Ammunition Depot at Dundurn Saskatchewan by March 31, 2021 was posted on the buy and sell website on September 15, 2020. When you listen to what the government isn't telling you, the road ahead is filled with civil unrest as governments attempt to exercise authority where they have none and are willing to embrace nefarious control in order to subjugate society.

The WHO made a deal with China to allow Chinese scientists to investigate the origin of the COVID 19 virus however, China's government has ensured this investigation is mostly symbolic and the truth may never be uncovered. In the face of a more severe second wave and the talk of a longer and more restrictive lockdown in 2021, the fear and apprehension have yet to give way to a more positive nuance moving forward.

What is most amazing about the COVID 19 pandemic and civilization's response to it is how quickly it advanced humanity's course on the trajectory to a new world order. What only months before the end of the second decade of the twenty first century seemed like a near impossibility to achieve the UN's Agenda 21 goals by the year 2030 suddenly became plausible and much more. In a matter of weeks, the world economy ground to a halt, the free world submitted to shelter in place regulations and restrictions on movement of all non-essential goods and services, and the wealth of millions of people evaporated overnight. E-commerce exploded throughout the world as governments vilified cash and shut ins relied on Amazon and online shopping to meet their needs, expediting civilization down the path towards a digital single world currency. Unprecedented fear and apprehension gripped civilization in a way that no one had predicted. No one except for a carpenter's son from Nazareth.

The COVID 19 pandemic is an event that should awaken your situational awareness. Was it sanctioned by God? Did the deep state use it as a vehicle to manipulate the world economy? One can lose a lot of sleep contemplating the reasons and causes, however if you are a believer in God, you shouldn't experience the anxiety and apprehension that non-believers have had. This is a warning shot over our heads to alert us to our place on the prophetic timeline and to call non-believers to come to Jesus. If your perception of the implications of these world events leaves you with unanswered questions, seek the truth of scripture and the peace that Jesus Christ offers. There are a great many signs present today that indicate we are living in the last days. Take comfort and understand that these signs are proof of the fact that Jesus is coming, and he is coming soon. Remember that God would rather that none of us perish and all come to full repentance.

Is Bill Gates intrinsically evil? I don't believe he is, however, his actions are influenced by something greater than even he can imagine. He is in favor of vaccinating all 7.5 billion people on the planet. Using a very modest estimate of $100 for a dose of vaccine, there is a potential $750 billion dollars to be made if everyone is vaccinated. Big pharma is all over this, with dollar signs in their eyes, trying to capture the lion's share of this market. This means that companies are rushing to produce their vaccine first and are forging ahead while potentially overlooking safety concerns and health risks. There is no downside to cutting corners to speed up the timelines due to a 1986 law that protects vaccine manufacturers from litigation from complications and side effects experienced by users of their products.

The official narrative maintains that life will not return to normal without the widespread use of a vaccine despite the fact that the virus has a 99.76% survival rate without a vaccine. The fears driven by the word pandemic alone are based on misinformation since the total number of deaths per year did not increase from 2018 to 2020. In Canada, total deaths from Jan.-Sept. 2018 were 186,825, Jan.-Sept. 2019 were 185,200 and Jan.-Sept. 2020 were 186,690. These statistics don't lead one to believe there was a pandemic in 2020. [50]

Similar results were documented in the USA and when broken into categories for cause of death, heart disease saw a significant decline as a cause of death while COVID 19 was listed as a cause of death displacing heart disease in the statistics. Meanwhile the total numbers weren't indicative of a pandemic induced increase in mortality rates. The discrepancies in reporting and categorizing deaths left a lot to be desired as coroners were incentivized to allocate COVID 19 as the cause of death even when it was proved to be nothing more than a contributing factor.

While most governments maintain that vaccines will not be mandatory, there is growing anticipation that a vaccination will allow freedom of movement for those who obtain credentials such as a health pass card or digital receipt of vaccination. Already the Australian airline Qantas has indicated that proof of vaccination will be required to fly. The province of Ontario's health minister Christine Elliott has stated that while the vaccine will not be mandatory in Ontario, "There may be some restrictions placed on people that don't have vaccines for travel purposes, to be able to go to theatres and other places."[51] Speculation that proof of vaccination will also be required to obtain insurance, drivers licenses, and other government services has caused apprehension and added tension to the atmosphere.

Bill Gates has warned that the possibility of another pandemic is almost inevitable in an increasingly globalized world. He goes on to assert, "If anything kills over 10 million people in the next few decades, it is most likely to be a highly infectious virus rather than a war."[52] Dr. Mark Ryan, head of the emergencies program of the WHO admitted that the COVID 19's case fatality rate is reasonably low compared to other emerging diseases, and warned that "we need to get ready for something which may be more severe in the future." There are already coronavirus variants being reported around the world.[53] Rest assured that if the COVID 19 pandemic fails to bring in a new world order, another more severe pandemic will surface to drive home the message that civilization must fall into a new world order to sustain the human race.

We are at a pivotal junction in the history of humanity at this moment. The dark forces of the evil, plutocracy have been working for centuries to get to this point where they can sway world governments toward their agenda of a new world order. The pandemic has been instrumental in compelling society to accept the narrative that only governments can keep citizens safe. Statistics have been openly manipulated, institutions have been coerced through the monetization of deaths to ensure the outcome and the media has been complicit in promoting the propaganda. This is much larger than conspiracy theories and is epically biblical in its proportions.

Plagues play a significant role in the Great Tribulation and the pouring out of God's wrath onto an unrepentant world. It should come as no surprise that these developments are indicative of our current position in the time-space continuum and the prophetic timeline for the last days.

The entire world has been coerced into believing that COVID 19 requires that society must submit to house arrest and close small businesses to combat the pandemic, while corporate stores like Walmart remain open and profitable. That the world economy must be destroyed in order to be reset for the greater good. That vaccines are required before we can safely implement the new normal (of complete control). That new variants of the virus will require continued draconian control measures like wearing masks and cause society to live in constant fear. Why are criminals let out of prison so they don't get coronavirus thereby enabling them to terrorize society in the name of safety? Why were bars allowed to stay open while Churches were barred from holding worship services?

The dilemma with the vaccination strategy governments have adopted is that by developing a very specific vaccine to act against the COVID 19 virus, it becomes counterproductive when the virus mutates. In the same way that bacteria have developed resistance to antibiotics, the virus is capable of reacting to the vaccine and mutating to circumvent its effects. Complicating the situation is the vaccine's antibodies interfere and outcompete our body's natural, non-specific antibodies that protect us from all the other viruses we get exposed to. Combine this with the fact that we are already in a pandemic and our immune systems are already at war, which negates the preventative protection a vaccine is intended to provide and you have a perfect storm of compromised immunity when we need it most. The results of this oversight will in all likelihood be catastrophic.

When you compare the annual deaths for COVID 19 to those from tuberculosis they are almost identical at 1.4 million, yet society has never been forced to shut down over TB. Why has a population that aborts 73 million babies per year suddenly become so concerned about the elderly?[54] Why does a pandemic require the media to suppress the truth and propagate a predetermined narrative, governments to incentivize death reporting to increase COVID numbers, and manipulate statistics by including all positive tests as confirmation of infection despite a high rate of false positives? Does that sound like a legitimate, genuine pandemic or does it point to massive interference in human rights under the guise of a health emergency?

Above The Law

Canadian Prime Minister Justin Trudeau exemplifies the persona of someone who through his sense of entitlement considers himself above the law. He has blatantly disregarded ethics rules by accepting a vacation on the Aga Khan's private island in the Bahamas in 2017, attempting to influence his Justice Minister Jody Wilson-Raybould to overrule a decision not to grant a deferred prosecution agreement to SNC-Lavalin and approving a $912 million grant to a charity with links to his family.[55] His expectations are that the law applies differently to him than it does to others and he has proven to be ethically challenged.

His willingness to sidestep the truth in order to manipulate the outcome was apparent in his response to allegations of sexual misconduct when he said, "Part of this awakening we're having as a society, a long awaited realization, it is not just one side of the story that matters. That the same interactions can be experienced very differently from one person to the next."[56] With the abundance of sexual assault accusations against men in the past five years he must have been the only one not found guilty. In fact, he was never even charged. Was it his incoherent mumbo jumbo word salad that implied his ignorance of guilt or was it his money that exempted him from the application of the law?

George Soros has been connected to controversy through funding groups like Black Lives Matter, ANTIFA, the North American Man/Boy Love Association and movements to legalize transsexuality and pedophilia. He has also been connected, through his funding, to the alien caravan that sought to invade the United States through Mexico, where he allegedly supplied busloads of paid "migrants" whose clean clothes, sandaled feet, polished nails and full make up did not emulate people who had been walking for weeks and sleeping wherever. George Soros operates behind the scenes creating anarchy and defying law and order. He plants seeds on contention that divide the population so he can promote solutions to the problems he creates that align with his own aspirations. His wealth is what facilitates his influence while providing protection from blame. He is not alone in his ability to function with apparent impunity as the extremely wealthy seem to get away with murder in society today.

After the death of George Floyd, calls to defund the police reverberated across the globe as protests turned to riots and riots to looting and eventually the burning of police stations and the takeover of several city blocks in Portland Oregon. Racial protests dominated the 2020 news for seven consecutive months. The sheer number of laws that were broken and the lack of a punitive response defies rationality in what is supposed to be a civilized society. While a few mercenary protesters have spent a few nights in jail, serious legal retribution has been lacking. While Soros and his accomplices sit back and watched the bedlam in the weeks leading up to the US presidential election and rioters and looters pillaged the neighborhoods, business owners and middle class workers payed the price with their loss of equity and wealth.

Society has been coerced into believing the American dream of being rich justifies the actions of the wealthy. They earned their fortunes and so will we one day. We accept that inequality in wealth, power and prestige is not only inevitable but necessary to facilitate the progression from lower and middle class into the upper class of society. Celebrities and wealthy personalities are epitomized, celebrated and worshiped as if they are superhuman or that their opinions carry extra credibility because of their prestige. Despite the dark side of wealth disparity, some of the most oppressed by it are its greatest advocates because of their reverence for the rich and famous.

The paradox that wealth inequality is both justified and legitimate is underscored by the thinking that the wealthy got that way by pursuing the greater good of humanity. After all it was their inventions and innovations that resulted in our standard of living being the highest in human history. It was their corporations and companies that supplied the jobs we all require in order to live the dream. The populace has bought into the premise that the wealth of the rich trickles down to the rest of society in the form of opportunities for the rest. In reality though, wealth inequality has grown over the past several decades.

At the forefront of this inequality is the failure to exert law and order to everyone fairly. This reality is nothing new in human history as kings of the past exercised their power to exempt their close acquaintances and friends from legal obligations and due processes. This is perhaps more evident in the system of taxation than anywhere else. And despite the legal loopholes that allow tax savings for the rich there is enormous tax fraud through the use of shell companies and off shore accounts to hide money from governments, all conveniently overlooked by governing bodies.

It became apparent during the financial crisis of 2007-08 that Wall Street was guilty of "egregious criminality – acts which destroyed the economic security of millions of people around the world – without experiencing the slightest legal repercussions."[57] To make matters worse, these acts of fraud were shielded from legal consequences by the Obama government and bailed out from the US Treasury with the dollars from taxpayers, of the victims themselves.

It doesn't stop there either. The elite wealthiest people, through the power of their lobby dollars and influence take an active role in writing laws and reduce the constraints that stand in the way of profits. So rather than being subject to the law, the elite plutocracy "control the law and exempt themselves from it."[58] The corruption and lawlessness practiced at the top to protect the wealth of the elite, is also propagated at the grassroots level through the funding of anarchy, perpetrated by groups like BLM and ANTIFA in an effort to divide and conquer the population and achieve their desired political results.

Additionally, this oligarchy owns and controls the media, therefore they control the narrative and define how society will respond. We see mobs of looters smashing windows, burning cars and buildings, toppling statues and beating up bystanders or those trying to protect their property and are told these are "peaceful protests." Anyone calling these events riots are immediately condemned as racists and are categorized as part of the problem, while the "peaceful protests" are applauded as part of the solution.

When a St. Louis couple brought out their guns in order to protect their home in the face of a reckless BLM mob of rioters who were trespassing, being violent and broke their iron gate, only to be the ones charged by police, the hypocrisy reached ludicrous levels. The angry protesters, some of who also carried guns, threatened their lives and threatened their house would be burned down.[59] The news networks portrayed the protesters as the victims while the home owners were exploited as evidence for gun restrictions on social media. The absurd official narrative of the BLM riots of 2020 is evidence of the systematic brainwashing of America.

The gas lighting continues as we are told that inner city crime in the form of gang violence, drive by shootings, murder, drug trafficking and armed robbery are not the problem and it is the police that are the issue. We are fed propaganda daily from what used to be unbiased news reporters who are now little more than puppets, dictated a narrative by those who control their bosses and the world.

The Clinton foundation has been linked to human trafficking through sourcing children from Haiti after the devastating earthquake in 2010 in which 250,000 people died. Under the guise of international adoption agencies and organizations like the Boys Club Network, The Clinton Foundation and a circle of allies like the Ratcliff Foundation, The Pierre Elliot Trudeau Foundation, and EAPIDA, all run by close friends, many of whom are convicted pedophiles, are suspected of operating a global human trafficking ring. Interestingly, whenever there is a leak of incriminating information or an arrest and potential trial, the witnesses or whistleblowers have a mysterious habit of committing suicide or being found dead.

When Laura Silsby-Gayler, and nine other Americans were arrested trying to smuggle 33 Haitian children out of the country on January 29, 2010, Hillary and Bill Clinton quickly intervened on her behalf. While she was found guilty, her sentence was drastically reduced, and the other nine Americans were released. Her lawyer, Jorge Puello, was found guilty of international human trafficking involving women and minors from Haiti and Central America. Since 2015 she has been employed as the vice president of marketing for AlertSense, a role that includes issuing Amber Alerts during kidnappings. Sadly, the corruption underlying the evil in Haiti claimed Monica Peterson, a young and talented Research Fellow and former Assistant Director of the Human Trafficking Center, who was in Haiti investigating human trafficking and was found dead of apparent suicide by hanging.

International charity, Oxfam, was exposed in February 2018 for its aid workers' participation in the sexual exploitation of underage girls in Haiti and a culture of impunity at the highest levels. As horrifying as that sounds, it is indicative of what is recognized as worldwide sexual abuse by NGO and UN peacekeepers and foreign aid workers. There have been a multitude of incidents by UN peacekeepers "of rape, pedophilia, prostitution and other forms of sexual exploitation of children, girls and women." [60] For those who donate money with the hope of improving the lives of the poor in the world, disappointment at this news is a huge understatement.

Outspoken senator Nancy Schaefer, who was critical of the corruption within Child Protective Services and the exploitation of children in their care as well as connections to child trafficking, and her husband Bruce were found dead in 2010. A retired police detective of Scotland Yard, John Wedger, uncovered an extensive and well-established child prostitution network as well as corruption of senior police officials and endured severe bullying for his efforts. While most of us go about our mundane and benign lives, we live right next door to the most repulsive evil the imagination can fathom.

The depravity extends to the highest offices in the land. Former president George H. W. Bush has been implicated in child sex trafficking as well as illegal gold mining in Africa and the trafficking of illicit drugs. During the 1980's children from orphanages would be given tours of the Whitehouse and selected boys and girls would be invited to State Dinners. After hours the children would be drugged and abused in the sex parties. This Congressional Blackmail Child Sex Ring was known as Operation Brownstone, named after the condo where the cocktail parties would take place.

Perhaps the most recognizable name in the global human trafficking and pedophilia scandal is that of Jeffery Epstein whose arrest and subsequent "suicide" while in prison remains a mystery. Epstein claimed to know "an astonishing number of rich, famous and powerful people.... Including details about their supposed sexual proclivities and recreational drug use."[61] Epstein, a convicted sex offender and alleged trafficker of underage girls owned an island in the Virgin Islands named Little St. James Island, where he held invitational orgies and parties with many elite personalities.

The extremely wealthy have been suspected of having integral roles in the trafficking of drugs and people on a global scale. The perversity goes much deeper than dollars and cents as elite pedophile rings operate right under the nose of authorities while the media is silent and law enforcement is blind to them.

Pizza Gate is one example of how a modest restaurant that sold pizzas and enabled kids to play ping pong on several tables in the basement has been implicated as a front to widespread sexual perversion among Washington's elite. The owner of Comet Pizza, James Alefantis, somehow went from a virtually unknown college dropout to being listed as one of Washington's 50 most powerful men in just six years. His elite clientele included the Clintons and Obamas and the artwork that adorns the walls is dark and provocative depicting pedophilia and pain that borders on the demonic. The artist, Kim Noble is known for her Dissociate Identity Disorder and her multiple personalities each have their own distinct artistic style.

Hollywood has been described as a "pedophilia den" and a "den of parasites" who feast on the blood of children. In a Rolling Stone article, Corey Feldman describes how the entertainment industry is hiding the abuse of children right up to the very top and "that the number one problem in Hollywood was and is.... pedophilia." His close friend and frequent co-star, the late Corey Haim, was a victim of rape in 1985 and he has been wanting to disclose the name of the man for many years, however, fear holds him back. He goes on to say that he's even had his life threatened more than once.[62]

Lord of the Rings star, Elijah Wood, has echoed those sentiments that Hollywood is dealing with a sexual abuse epidemic where victims are drowned out by the people in power. A documentary was made entitled "An Open Secret" that put a spotlight on a Hollywood pedophilia ring that included convicted sex offenders.[63] Kevin Spacey's career was derailed when he admitted to sexual assault involving 15 underage boys. I am compelled to make mention that these examples in no way are meant to overshadow producer Harvey Weinstein's sexual transgressions against women that spawned the "Me Too" movement that opened the can of worms of sexual misconduct in Hollywood.

This is just the tip of the iceberg though. The practices of Hollywood's elite are presumed to be so dark and so reprehensible it is truly hard to believe. There are reports of alleged satanic ritual, cannibalism and child sacrifice. The perversity that accompanies wealth and privilege has been evident throughout history and stories of Roman emperors come to mind of scandalous behavior, including indulging in orgies, incest, homosexuality and pedophilia. And of course, there were the fertility deities and rites as well as the perverse practices of the Canaanites that Moses was told to warn the nation of Israel about including the atrocity of child sacrifice to Molek as described in Leviticus 18:21.

These very things are spoken of in Hollywood today, including the harvesting of blood from children used in satanic rituals to capture its "life force." The more stress and suffering the child endures before dying, the greater the "life force." The blood of sexually abused infants is considered highly "enriched" and is highly prized. Adrenochrome (adrenaline/epinephrine) does not last long post-mortem, therefore it is obtained before the child is killed or the subject may be kept alive and captive for repeated extractions. It is often referred to as "walnut sauce" referencing the pineal gland that produces it. This intoxicating substance produces a high similar to cocaine and causes the user's own adrenalin production to shut down therefore they quickly become addicted and willing to pay handsomely for another dose. The price is so high that babies are considered currency in these cultic elite groups.

Human trafficking and in particular that of children has become an increasingly lucrative and widespread problem that law enforcement agencies have trouble penetrating because of the overwhelming corruption generated by the extreme wealth involved. The powers of persuasion are exceedingly irresistible when the value of the bribe or kickback are higher than what average people earn in their lifetimes. Just as the poachers who are willing to kill the only remaining white rhino or the only albino giraffe and her calf, law enforcement and justice will turn a blind eye to the atrocities committed right before them.

In the months and weeks leading up to the 2020 U.S. presidential election, hundreds of children were discovered and saved from human trafficking. More than 100 victims were rescued by the FBI and at least 67 arrests were made in the summer months. Officers set up "fake dates" on social media and enticed pedophiles to respond and be captured.[64] The U.S. Marshals Service rescued 13 missing children and found an additional 26 endangered children in Georgia that resulted in nine people being arrested on charges that included "sex trafficking, parental kidnapping and custodial interference, as well as registered sex offender and weapons violations."[65] These children were part of "Operation Homecoming" that 72 was comprised of children across Indiana, Ohio and Georgia in the second half of August and early September 2020.[66] Despite the negative portrayal of Trump by the press, his focus on human trafficking saved many, many lives.

In other parts of the world, similar stories echo the same horrific narrative. In Wales, in the first half of 2018, nearly 150 children from the age s of 2 -17 were identified, some destined for the sex trade. Most of the victims were female and the majority of offences they were brought to Wales for were sexual exploitation. {https:www.bbc.com/news/uk-wales-44807348) In Nigeria, 230 people including children were rescued in "Operation Sarraounia" that included "46 children who had been sexually abused or forced to beg and hundreds of Ghanaian men who had been recruited online and then enslaved," according to Interpol. 18 suspected traffickers were arrested. Similar headlines around the world attest to the evil in men's hearts, willing to exploit children for money and to satisfy the perversion of their souls.

Anneke Lucas was sold into sex trafficking at the age of six and confirms the allegations of pedophilia among the wealthy elite are not simply conspiracy theories. The perpetrators are VIP's with influence and wealth and go about their business without the fear of punishment right under society's collective nose, fully visible to the public. Her observations reveal the deepest and darkest realities of the human condition. What makes a man with wealth, power, influence and stature in society feel the need to have sex with children to be satisfied in life? What is this gaping hole in the hearts of men that provokes them to go to such depraved length to fill it? She now is an advocate for child sex trafficking victims and founder of Liberation Prison Yoga a non-profit organization.

Cassandra Diamond gave a Ted-x talk in Toronto where she explained the coercion and blackmail that kept her silent about her abuse and the massage parlor/brothels that controlled her which operated in full view as legitimate establishments on the outside while facilitating degrading and unimaginable acts on the inside. They take advantage of the naïve and vulnerable, and manipulating them into thinking they are in need of protection while exploiting their bodies for money. Police look the other way while the legal system and creative wording on business licenses permit the sale of sex even it is officially outlawed. Why? Because the influential, powerful, "upstanding" holders of high offices are among the clientele. While the legal framework exists to bring justice, the political will does not. Cassandra founded BridgeNorth, a charitable organization that provides medical assistance, support, food assistance, mentorship and education to sex trafficking victims.

The arrest of Clare Bronfman, wealthy daughter of the late Edgar Bronfman of the Seagram empire made headlines for her financing and therefore complicity in the operation of the NVIVM cult that brainwashed "slaves" to allow Keith Rainiere, aka "Vanguard" to have sex with them and brand his initials on them. As part of a plea agreement, she paid $6 million US from her $200 million fortune. Additionally, her sister Sara Bronfman was also implicated and actress Allison Mack pleaded guilty for her role in the scheme. [67]

In the case of Jeffery Epstein, his accomplice Ghislaine Maxwell, the daughter of publishing tycoon Robert Maxwell, was arrested for her involvement in his sex trafficking business. She allegedly groomed underage girls to have sex with him as well as well-known celebrities including British Prince Andrew and former US president Bill Clinton, and has been portrayed as "the real monster" in the abuse.[68] Again, one must ask the question, why do people living in luxury and supposedly in want of nothing, resort to illegally exploiting minors for sex?

Underlying the atrocious depravity of child trafficking and sexual exploitation is the sad reality that an estimated 55% of sex trafficking victims seek abortions and approximately 30% have had more than one. In situations where underage girls require abortions, the pimps are permitted to sign as guardians, with no questions asked, in order to bypass mandated reporting laws.[69] When you combine these two revenue streams with that of the porn industry and its support of the abortion business, you can see how extensive the entanglement and how deep the transgressions of human lust are and their ripple effects upon society. It is a brutal, vicious, tragic circle that has the love of money at its core. Huge profits are generated by the porn and sex trafficking industries of which abortion companies are the chief benefactor, and in turn generate huge profits of their own.

All of this profiteering would not be possible of course, if morality was considered a valuable attribute in society. Sadly, mankind's depravity and pursuit of carnal pleasures is at the root of the problem. It is easily demonstrable that our culture today is much more liberal in its acceptance of behavior that only a generation ago was considered taboo. Even within the Christian community, roughly half believe that casual sex between consenting adults is sometimes or always acceptable according to a Pew Research Center survey.[70] In California, laws have been passed that reduce penalties for adults who engage in sex with a minor if the minor is within ten years of age of the offender. The law is justified as an attempt to reduce discrimination against LGBTQ people and illustrates just how far morality has plummeted in the state. [71]

Today's justice system is nothing more than a legal system and there is no justice in it. It is filled with loopholes and provides more rights to the offenders than it does to the victims. Essentially it is failure in action. Law enforcement has become exasperated as hard working policemen deliver criminals before judges who politely slap them on their wrists and release them to offend once again. Politicians appoint judges sympathetic to their cause and justice becomes a commodity that is paid for by those whose pockets are the deepest. And those deep pockets belong to the likes of Soros, the Rockerfellers, the Rothschilds, the Clintons, and Bill Gates who effectively dictate the narrative and direction of law and order (or the lack of it).

There is a growing feeling that the game is rigged when the elite continue to grow their wealth by double digit percentages while the average person's income remains stagnant, the cost of living steadily increases putting the middle class between a granite ceiling of potential and a quartz basement floor. A system that facilitates the world's 2200 billionaires increasing their wealth by 12% in 2018 and permitted the lower 50% of people to become 11% poorer simultaneously is a playing field that is incredibly tilted. This is not about to change since it is these wealthy elites who pull the strings of governments that write the laws governing the game.[72] Racketeering has become so commonplace in government that it is not only tolerated, it is accepted as normal and in fact encouraged.

As the angry mobs grow in intensity, the elite, in an effort to defend their position, default to rebranding themselves as leaders in the fight to save humanity, offering solutions that ultimately benefit themselves while promoting the perception that they are interested in social change and righting the wrongs in the system. With creative language and crafty "green" initiatives, they play on the sensibilities of the middleclass, vilifying governments and proposing private sector solutions through the free market, influenced by the corporations they happen to own. Thus they pit the two sides against the middle and appoint themselves as adjudicators thereby ensuring their perpetual societal status as the elite.

They give back to society with one hand, just enough to make headlines through hundreds of millions of dollars in the form of donations to causes that "align" with their commitment to making the world a better place, only to hoard billions more in profits with their other hand, while the average person's life never changes for the better. Inevitably this plutocracy amounts to nothing more than loyalty to each other rather than genuine compassion for humanity and sacrificing for the common good is something left to the middle class. It amounts to double speak, proclaiming social change in an effort to maintain the status quo and the prevailing elite posture.

Rather than organic reform, change from the top cannot be trusted, as the self-interested oligarchy will stop at nothing to maintain control of the world's power. The cabal has sown discontent and divided society to the point where democracy seems doomed and voters are questioning its efficacy. Acceptance of socialism is on the rise and many young people are seeking a redistribution of wealth from the top to the bottom. By fueling this dissension, the likes of George Soros and his plutocratic comrades inch the world toward more socialism, communism and ultimately a new world order.

As liberal thinking continues to permeate our culture, pedophiles are now calling themselves MAPS or "minor attracted persons" and seek to be accepted into the mainstream as LGBTQ members of society. The normalization of pedophilia under the guise of "love is love," is indicative of the covert, systemic undermining of the Judeo-Christian values western civilization was built upon. By controlling the media, the extreme left controls the narrative and slowly and steadily erodes the foundation of any sense of moral responsibility.[73] And we wonder why so many children are victimized through sex trafficking.

Perhaps the most notable entertainment headline in 2020 was the Netflix release of the French movie "Cuties" which created controversy over the sexualization of underage girls and resulted in the indictment of the network for its "lewd visual material depicting a child."[74] This isn't the first time Netflix has pushed the boundaries of acceptability on moral grounds. Their January 2020 release of the film "The First Temptation" portraying Jesus as gay, met with stiff opposition, was temporarily banned in Brazil before having the decision overturned by the supreme court. Despite the parody of the film, its poor taste demonstrates how broken society's moral compass has become. [75]

In the midst of all this darkness, rather than being a light to the world, the church is embroiled in its own lack of moral awareness. Archbishop of Melbourne, Peter Comensoli, was quoted on July 1, 2020 as saying, "I'd rather go to jail than report a pedophile priest who confesses his crimes." He was echoed by Bishop William Wright who said "that he would never break the seal of confession, even if a pedophile priest confessed to raping a child."[76] This has been an ongoing tragedy for hundreds of years within the clergy that was explored thoroughly in my book *Seeking Truth.*

In his third encyclical, entitled "Fratelli Tutti" or "Brothers All," released October 3rd, 2020, Pope Francis commented on the brokenness of humanity and the fragmentation of society. "Other cultures are not 'enemies' from which we need to protect ourselves, but differing reflections of the inexhaustible richness of human life." However, by focusing on the political side of humanity's problems he noticeably steered clear of any mention of the degradation of morality and was silent on the church's struggles with pedophilia. In essence, his message amounted to an impotent appeal for societal peace and acceptance without divine inspiration. It neglects the root cause of civilization's moral decay and declining spiritual health. Ultimately one has to wonder if the gospel ever crossed his mind while writing. What does Pope Francis believe repentance is?

It brings to mind the words of Charles Spurgeon who wrote, "I do not believe that any man can preach the gospel who does not preach the Law. Lower the Law and you dim the light by which man perceives his guilt; this is a very serious loss to the sinner rather than a gain; for it lessens the likelihood of his conviction and conversion. I say you have deprived the gospel of its ablest auxiliary (its most powerful weapon) when you have set aside the Law. You have taken away from it the schoolmaster that is to bring men to Christ. They will never accept grace till they tremble before a just and holy Law. Therefore, the Law serves a most necessary purpose, and it must not be removed from its place. The Law cuts into the core of evil, it reveals the seat of the malady and informs us that the leprosy lies deep within. They must be slain by the Law before they can be made alive by the gospel." [77]

Indeed, deep inside each and every one of us there exists a rebellious spirit that inclines us to disobey our conscience's good judgement or inherent intuition of right and wrong. Even those of us who love God and earnestly endeavor to walk in obedience to his commands contain this spirit of rebellion or sinful nature as the apostle Paul describes it. Those who relinquish control to their sinful nature, lust for the fulfillment of the desires of their flesh and are capable of tremendous evil. Most of us keep it under control and temper it to societal expectations and standards. Paul wrote: "Those who live according to the sinful nature have their minds set on what that nature desires; but those who live in accordance with the Spirit have their minds set on what the Spirit desires. The mind of sinful man is death, but the mind controlled by the Spirit is life and peace; the sinful mind is hostile to God. It does not submit to God's law, nor can it do so. Those controlled by the sinful nature cannot please God." Romans 8:5-8.

An old Cherokee chief was speaking to his grandson one day. He was telling him about a battle that goes on inside on people. He said, "My son, the battle is between two wolves inside of us all." One is evil. It is anger, envy, jealousy, sorrow, regret, greed, arrogance, self-pity, resentment, inferiority, lies, false pride, superiority, and ego. The other is good. It is joy, peace, love, hope, serenity, humility, kindness, benevolence, empathy, generosity, truth, compassion and faith. The grandson thought about it for a minute and then asked his grandfather: "Which wolf wins?" The old Cherokee chief simply replied, "The one you feed."

At some point in the lives of criminals and those who sit in ivory towers manipulating outcomes to favor their pursuits of power and wealth, a line is first crossed. When money becomes more important than integrity, honesty and legitimacy it has become your God. Have you ever wondered why the war on drugs is such a losing battle? Have high level bureaucrats been bought off and granted indemnity to the drug cartels? Are government officials in bed with the drug lords? Have world leaders signed a deal with the devil? The answer is yes.

When people are willing to go the lengths that the deep state, or the plutocratic elite go to in order to protect their wealth empire, their cupidity causes them to cross a line from which there is no recovery, apart from the saving grace of Christ. The darkness in their hearts that provokes them to traffic, exploit, abuse and murder the children of the world testifies that their souls were either sold to the devil a long time ago or are so hideous and nefarious that they are beyond redemption.

Memories of old Mafia movies where hitmen go to confession and are forgiven for their sins by the priest only to immediately go back to the streets and kill again come to mind when I think of the cabal. Obviously these people possess intelligence beyond that portrayed on movie screens, yet there still seems to be this denial of their own mortality. They seem to remain untouchable. Hidden by layers of corporate subsidiaries, protected by their obscurity and elevated by their wealth which makes them insurmountable to prosecute. From this hidden power structure will emerge one man who will redefine the term totalitarian. He will fear no one, his empire will encircle the globe and he will introduce the culmination of globalism in an all-encompassing new world order. He will even seem to have conquered death.

There has never been legal action taken against the Clintons or Obama for the destroyed evidence in emails or phones and servers. There has never been any investigation into their alleged spying and wiretapping, their lies to FISA or the lies of the FBI and CIA or to Comey, Brennan and Clapper or George Soros for that matter. Why are there never any charges brought forward against the left yet even right leaning representatives in government tolerated their pursuit of the Russian collusion scam and the phony impeachments of Trump. Why was Hunter Biden never charged for possession of child pornography? Why were his China connections never investigated nor his Ukrainian involvement? Why was the mainstream media so biased and social media so quick to censor alternative points of view? How did a career politician with a 48-year record of problematic governance and dementia, who never aggressively campaigned and lacked cognitive engagement in the election, receive more votes than any other presidential candidate in the history of the USA?

In a coordinated, systemic effort the deep state ensured the right of center ideologies and nationalist platform of the Trump administration never succeeded. COVID 19 was weaponized, economies were shut down and the U.S. 2020 election was commandeered in order to remove the power of democracy from the American people. All these things happened in broad daylight and any attempts to resist were squashed by AG Barr and the SCOTUS whose allegiance wasn't to democracy but to the establishment.

The ripple effects of what happened in America will be felt worldwide and accelerate the agenda of the cabal. The will of the people will be crushed and the path to a new world order will have been paved. The dark power structures of the plutocracy believe they have won the war. They may have won the battle but the war is far from over.

Jesus Christ will have the final say and the deep state will be held accountable for their abuse and exploitation of the world. Their crafty obfuscation of the laws of the land and their secretive manipulation of all things to satisfy their insatiable cupidity will be fully exposed. Jesus is the only name that can accomplish this delivery of justice. "Therefore God exalted him to the highest place and gave him the name that is above every name, that at the name of Jesus every knee should bow, in heaven and on earth, and every tongue acknowledge that Jesus is Lord, to the glory of God the Father." Philippians 2:9-11.

The Man of Lawlessness

Big brother is more than a complex or a collective of factors on different levels precipitating an environment for government surveillance, regulation and control. It is much more totalitarian than that. With the elite ruling class entertaining the notion of a new world order, a one world government and one world currency, there is grave potential for abuse of a system that places control of the entire world in the hands of a few privileged individuals, families or corporations. In fact, it is easily plausible that one person can commandeer this power structure and seize control of every detail of running the planet. The Bible foretells of this usurping of our rights and freedoms as one man is destined to rule the world and demand to be worshipped as a god. Let's look at what scripture says about this man.

The Bible comprises literal history and not an allegoric story. Its prophetic predictions have all been fulfilled literally thus far and the same will be true with those that foretell of the man of lawlessness coming to the world at the end of the age. The Bible says he will be "revealed" intimating his true identity will be concealed until world conditions facilitate the appropriate opportunity for the divulging of his purpose. The book of Revelation or Apocalypse, translates more accurately as "Unveiling," meaning the debut of the devil's emissary is a disclosure of things that have been hidden and not just merely a tale of metaphorical religious mysticism predicting a symbolic power struggle and judgement. It is a prophetic description of actual events preceding the end of the world and the judgement of God. The intentional mystique is in harmony with Daniel's instructions to, "Go your way, Daniel, because the words are rolled up and sealed until the time of the end." Daniel 12:9. At that time, he will drop all pretense and allow his previously hidden wickedness to be fully disclosed. He will head a one world government and a one world religion, and his totalitarian rule will make Stalin's legacy look passive.

He will be highly intelligent, charismatic and possess a magnetism that will captivate the populace and draw people into his circle of influence, yet he will be conceited and corrupt and possess a nefarious side, making him capable of extreme evil. I believe the antichrist will appear on the world stage as a political or influential figure with the abilities to mediate diametrically opposed parties to form consensus, provide decisive leadership and compel nations to follow him through the troubled waters of a political landscape that has been floundering to reconcile population growth, ecological concerns, the climate conundrum, solve world trade challenges and most importantly negotiate world peace. He will be a counterfeit Christ that will appear to have all the answers to save the planet from destruction and save humanity from itself and ultimately desire and in fact demand to be worshipped as Christ.

It has been suggested that the antichrist refers to a movement or a nation-state such as the Roman Empire rather than a human figure, however, the language of scripture, while eluding to a spirit of antichrist already at work in the world, refers to the antichrist as an individual person. Scripture interprets scripture and Daniel wrote, "the ruler who would come," inferring this entity is a man. Paul tells us he is the man of "lawlessness." Both Daniel and John wrote this man would be like a beast, referencing his malevolent nature. Revelation 13 tells us the number of the beast is the number of a man. Daniel confirms this by saying, "He will confirm a covenant with many for one 'seven.' In the middle of the 'seven' he will put an end to sacrifice and offering. He will set up an abomination that causes desolation, until the end that is decreed is poured out on him," Daniel 9:27. The antichrist is a man and he will coerce humanity into idolatry by setting up an image of himself and those who worship it will be doomed to desolation where souls cannot be saved.

It has also been hypothesized that the prophecies regarding the antichrist were fulfilled in A.D. 70 when the Romans destroyed Jerusalem and general Titus defiled the temple. This interpretation is not compatible with the prediction of the antichrist setting himself up in the temple and demanding to be worshipped as God, which Titus failed to do, therefore it must be ruled out as a possible fulfillment of this prophecy. Furthermore, Revelation was written in AD 95, twenty-five years after Jerusalem fell and John penned these events as future occurrences.

The paradoxical personality of the antichrist will be displayed by his drive for prominence in the forum of world politics and he will be the one person to finally get the peace process correct in the middle east and will orchestrate a seven-year peace accord between Israel and the Arab nations or maybe even many other nations as well. This treaty will facilitate the building of the third temple in Jerusalem. This will mark the beginning of the great tribulation, the final seven years of Daniel's prophecy. The seventieth week. Halfway into the peace treaty, he will set up the abomination that causes desolation which will be a statue of himself, and demand to be worshiped as God (Revelation 13:5-8). Interestingly, the UN's goal of achieving a one world government by the year 2030 suggests the antichrist is already quietly at work in the background of today's political and corporate framework. Perhaps he doesn't even know his own fortune and may not until Satan takes possession of him.

The identity of the antichrist has been the subject of much speculation, with fingers being pointed at Pope Francis, Barack Obama, Emmanuel Macron and Jared Kushner who happens to own 666 Fifth Avenue in Manhattan and has been working on a peace plan for Israel. I would rather not speculate who the man of lawlessness actually is because as was revealed with the ministry of Christ, hindsight is 20/20 and it's easy now to see how Jesus literally fulfilled all the prophecies written about him but this insight was not apparent while he walked with the disciples. The Jews were looking for someone entirely different. Speculation has pointed to the pope, with his vision of one world religion and the same God for all as a new world order, as the false prophet, appearing gentle like a lamb, yet speaking like a dragon.

The man of lawlessness will work together with the false profit, amalgamating church and state together in a one-world religion-government that will seem to unify all the nations of the earth under one umbrella of peace. Together they will hold immense power until they will meet their doom together (Revelation 19:20). Complicit in their power is the corrupt religious system portrayed as a mysterious woman, guilty of many adulteries with the kingdoms of the earth. She is also depicted as holding great wealth, she was "dressed in purple and scarlet and was glittering with gold, precious stones and pearls." Revelation 17:4. It has been speculated that she represents the Catholic Church whose misdeeds are contained in the golden cup she holds. She is "drunk with the blood of God's holy people, the blood of those who bore testimony to Jesus." Revelation 17:6, meaning those martyred for heresy at the hands of the institution of the oldest church. The antichrist will grow to hate the woman and will bring her to ruin and leave her naked, eat her flesh and burn her with fire (Revelation 17:16). He is the embodiment of evil.

What clues are provided in the Bible to help identify the man of lawlessness? Daniel said he would come out of the Roman Empire or one of the peoples from that empire. In Revelation 17, John sees a beast which represents all of the major earthly empires in Israel's history or seven kings, five of which had already fallen, one that is, and one that is to come. The five that had already fallen when John wrote were, Egypt, Assyria, Babylon, Medo-Persia, and Greece. Rome was in power at the time and the last king is still yet to come and will only be in power for a short time.

Daniel's vision only had four kingdoms that were all future empires when he wrote, therefore Egypt and Assyria were not in his prophecy since they were already in the past (more on this later). The visions describe these kingdoms as beasts and in fact they were monsters in both size and ruthlessness in their day and age. The final kingdom is said to suffer a mortal wound however it miraculously is brought back to life in the last days. Even though the Roman Empire fell in 476 AD attempts to revive it have continued right up until the European Economic Community became established in 1958. Since that time the EU has morphed into a larger and more powerful entity and may play a key role in the antichrist's progression to global dominance.

Today's EU struggles to maintain unity and lacks strong leadership. It is an arena ripe for a charismatic, powerful leader to emerge as the answer to all of Europe's concerns. As a counterfeit Christ, the antichrist will be capable of miracles and portray himself as the savior of a dying world. With his accomplice, the false prophet and Satan they are the counterfeit trinity. The false prophet will have the power to produce counterfeit miracles also and will deceive people, so they worship the antichrist. Everyone will be forced to receive the antichrist's mark so that no one can buy or sell without it. Those who refuse are killed. (Revelation 13:11-18).

As the previous chapter illustrates, the conditions and technology of the world today are ripe for exploitation by someone with vision and aspirations that align with the personal attributes of the man of lawlessness. There is apprehension among people everywhere. World violence and terrorism have created a sense of fear that is allowing authorities to incrementally erode individual rights and freedoms on a scale that is comparable to sci-fi movies. The COVID 19 pandemic has illustrated how easily civilization will panic and become lost and follow those who claim to have the answers. How quickly and how vulnerable people become when the media narrative is focused on fear and destruction and how the world economy can grind to a halt overnight when the right conditions are manipulated. How easily one man with the right message will be able to gather the masses into a captive audience so they will follow him wherever he will lead them.

When Jesus said there will be wars and rumors of wars in the last days, he was speaking of this past century which has witnessed more wars and more bloodshed than the previous nineteen put together. With the discarding of nuclear arms reduction treaties in the last year, there is now potential to blow the world to smithereens and the doomsday clock sits at one hundred seconds to midnight, the closest it has ever been. Only three years have been registered at 2 minutes to midnight since it first appeared in 1947: 1953, 2018 and 2019. All eyes are focused on the middle east now as the saber rattling and posturing has the world on edge. Currently there are even more Christians being killed through persecution than there were during the Roman empire.

Jesus foretold what signs would reveal the last days preceding his return at the end of the age. He said, "Watch out that no one deceives you. For many will come in my name, claiming, 'I am the Messiah,' and will deceive many. You will hear of wars and rumors of wars, but see to it that you are not alarmed. Such things must happen, but the end is still to come. Nation will rise against nation, and kingdom against kingdom. There will be famines and earthquakes in various places. All these are the beginnings of birth pains.

You will be handed over to be persecuted and put to death, and you will be hated by all nations because of me. At that time many will turn away from the faith and will betray and hate each other, and many false prophets will appear and deceive many people. Because of the increase of wickedness, the love of most will grow cold, but the one who stands firm to the end will be saved. And this gospel of the kingdom will be preached in the whole world as a testimony to all nations, and then the end will come.

So when you see standing in the holy place 'the abomination that causes desolation,' spoken of through the prophet Daniel – let the reader understand – then let those who are in Judea flee to the mountains. Let no one on the housetop go down to take anything out of the house. Let no one in the field go back to get their cloak. How dreadful it will be in those days for pregnant women and nursing mothers! Pray that your flight will not take place in the winter or on the Sabbath. For then there will be great distress, unequalled from the beginning of the world until now – and never to be equaled again.

If those days had not been cut short, no one would survive, but for the sake of the elect those days will be shortened. At that time if anyone says to you, 'Look, here is the Messiah!' or, 'There he is!' do not believe it. For false messiahs and false prophets will appear and perform many signs and wonders to deceive, if possible, even the elect. See, I have told you ahead of time.

So if anyone tells you, 'There he is, out in the wilderness,' do not go out; or, 'Here he is, in the inner rooms,' do not believe it. For as lightning that comes from the east is visible even in the west, so will be the coming of the Son of Man. Wherever there is a carcass, there the vultures will gather.

Immediately after the distress of those days

'the sun will be darkened, and the moon will not give its light;

The stars will fall from the sky, and the heavenly bodies will be shaken.'

Then will appear the sign of the Son of Man in heaven. And all of the peoples of the earth will mourn when they see the Son of Man coming on the clouds of heaven, with power and great glory. And he will send his angels with a loud trumpet call, and they will gather his elect from the four winds, from one end of the heavens to the other.

Now learn this lesson from the fig tree: As soon as its twigs get tender and its leaves come out, you know that summer is near. Even so, when you see all these things, you know that it is near, right at the door. Truly I tell you, this generation will certainly not pass away until all these things have happened. Heaven and earth will pass away, but my words will never pass away." Mathew 24:4-34. The fig tree here represents Israel. In the same way, when Jesus cursed the fig tree (Mathew 11:13-14) because it had no fruit, it signified the nation of Israel which was a religious society with plenty of foliage and no fruit.

To illustrate just how precise Jesus' words were, he had earlier in Mathew stated as he and the disciples were leaving the temple, "'Do you see all these things?' he asked. 'Truly I tell you, not one stone here will be left on another; every one will be thrown down.'" Mathew 24:2. In AD 70 when the Romans laid siege to Jerusalem the fires were so hot that the gold of the temple melted and ran into the cracks between the stones. The Roman soldiers literally pried every rock apart to get at the gold.

When Jesus references the prophet Daniel with the caveat, "Let the reader understand," in verse 15, he is speaking of the detailed prophecies of Daniel which predicted the coming Messiah as well as the timing of his return after he was crucified and the antichrist appearing on the scene in end times Jerusalem. Daniel's prophecy was given when the nation of Israel was in captivity in Babylon in the first year of the reign of Darius in 539 BC. While Daniel was praying, he was visited by the angel Gabriel, who revealed the timeline for the coming Messiah and Israel's destruction and rebirth.

"Seventy sevens are decreed for your people and your holy city to finish transgression, to put an end to sin, to atone for wickedness, to bring in everlasting righteousness, to seal up vision and prophecy and to anoint the most holy place.

Know and understand this: From the time the word goes out to restore and rebuild Jerusalem until the Anointed One, the ruler, comes, will be seven 'sevens,' and sixty-two 'sevens.' It will be rebuilt with streets and a trench, but in times of trouble. After sixty-two 'sevens,' the Anointed One will be put to death and will have nothing. The people of the ruler who will come will destroy the city and the sanctuary. The end will come like a flood: War will continue until the end, and desolations have been decreed. He will confirm a covenant with many for one 'seven.' In the middle of the 'seven' he will put an end to the sacrifice and offering. And at the temple he will set up an abomination that causes desolation, until the end that is decreed is poured out on him. Daniel 9:24-27.

The timeline given by Gabriel was divided into three sections, one of seven 'sevens,' one of sixty-two 'sevens,' after which the Messiah was to be killed and the city destroyed once more, followed by the final one 'seven'. The context of the 'seven' implies years since Daniel was praying about the 70 years of captivity in Babylon, therefore the first time period is 49 years, the second is 434 years and the last is 7 years.

The final 'seven,' or seven years begin when a covenant is made with many by the ruler who will come. Three and one-half years into the agreement, this ruler will stop the sacrifice and offering, therefore, rebuilding the temple in Jerusalem must be a component of the treaty. He then sets up an abomination that causes desolation in the temple.

In the first year of Cyrus king of Persia, the Lord stirred his spirit to issue a decree (Isaiah 44:24, 28 and Ezra 1:1-4). This happened in 538 BC, however king Cyrus stopped short and only decreed that the temple be rebuilt and not the city. It is important to note that Darius was a Mede and Cyrus was Persian. At this time Babylon was being ruled by both the Medes and the Persians which is why there seems to be overlap in their reign. It wasn't until Nehemiah lamented before king Artaxerxes in the twentieth year of his reign (444 BC) that Jerusalem still laid in ruins, which resulted in Nehemiah travelling to Jerusalem to begin the rebuild. So in order to calculate Daniel's seventy weeks, 444 BC is the correct starting point for determining the time that would elapse during the 69 weeks of years (seven 'sevens' and sixty-two 'sevens') to when the "Anointed One" would be cut off.

Beginning at 444 BC and adding 483 years, but remembering that the Jews used the lunar calendar of 360 days in a year, the math looks like this: 483 x 360 then divide by 365 and you have 476.34 years. Add 476.34 to 444 and then add 1 year, for the year zero which isn't counted and you arrive at 33.34 AD or Easter of 33 AD, which is the exact time of the crucifixion of Jesus, when he was "cut off and had nothing." The people of the ruler who will come were the Romans who destroyed Jerusalem and the temple in AD 70 and that end came like a flood resulting in the Jewish diaspora.

Some scholars have argued that since Daniel's prophetic predictions were so detailed that they were written after the fact and their literal style made them sound prophetic, however a very powerful substantiation of their authenticity was made by the Jewish historian Josephus as well as being recorded in the Talmud. When Alexander the Great arrived at Jerusalem with his conquering army in 332 BC, the high priest, Simeon the Just, showed him the Book of Daniel with its prophecy regarding the Greek kingdom whom Alexander fought for, and their prophesied conquest of Persia in chapter 11. Alexander made the connection and surmised himself as the mighty king, therefore decided not to attack Jerusalem and instead marched on to Babylon and victory there.

The people of the ruler who will come were the Romans, who destroyed Jerusalem and the sanctuary in A.D. 70 and the ruler who will come is none other than the antichrist that John speaks of in Revelation and Daniel prophesied about in Daniel 9:26-27 and11:36-45. In fact, Revelation 19 dovetails perfectly with Daniel 12 when the Messiah returns. Both Jesus and the apostle Paul speak of him as the man of lawlessness and refer to him in future tense, confirming the last 'seven' was yet to be fulfilled. When Jesus spoke of the signs of the end, he said, "There will be great distress in the land and wrath against this people. They will fall by the sword and be taken as prisoners to all the nations. Jerusalem will be trampled on by the Gentiles until the times of the Gentiles are fulfilled." Luke 24:23-24. Israel remained trampled by the Gentiles from AD 70 until 1948.

Both Daniel's description of the beast and John's in Revelation have many similarities and share the same underlying theme throughout. The Great Tribulation will be a time of great distress upon the world and "If those days had not been cut short, no one would survive, but for the sake of the elect those days will be shortened." Mathew 24:22. I believe "the elect" being referred tc here are the citizens of Israel that have accepted Christ and are now walking in obedience to God. The implication here is that salvation is still attainable in the second half of the Great Tribulation, although it will be a difficult time to follow the Lord.

If you've ever imagined the world during the Great Tribulation, I believe it will be horrifying. A kind of chaos more terrifying than we can fathom. Once believers in Christ are taken out of the world in the rapture and evil is allowed free reign, the lawlessness alone would be petrifying. However, add to that the pouring out of God's wrath on mankind and things become mystifyingly hysterical.

The pandemonium coming upon the earth will be so severe that people will beg to be killed. In Revelation 6:16-17 we are told, "They called to the mountains and the rocks, 'Fall on us and hide us from the face of him who sits on the throne and from the wrath of the Lamb! For the great day of their wrath has come and who can withstand it?'" Jesus said, "If those days had not been cut short, no one would survive, but for the sake of the elect those days will be shortened." Mathew 24:22. This kind of bedlam will make things easy for the antichrist to dominate the world stage with all the answers to humanity's problems.

2 Thessalonians 2:1-12 also describes him, and the end times, "Concerning the coming of our Lord Jesus Christ and our being gathered to him, we ask you, brothers and sisters, not to become easily unsettled or alarmed by the teaching allegedly from us – whether by a prophecy or by word of mouth or by letter – asserting that the day of the Lord has already come. Don't let anyone deceive you in any way, for that day will not come until the rebellion occurs and the man of lawlessness is revealed, the man doomed to destruction. He will oppose and exalt himself over everything that is called God or is worshipped, so that he sets himself up in God's temple, proclaiming himself to be God." (Again, this was not fulfilled in AD 70).

"Don't you remember that when I was with you I used to tell you these things? And now you know what is holding him back, so that he may be revealed at the proper time. For the secret power of lawlessness is already at work; but the one who now holds it back will continue to do so until he is taken out of the way. And then the lawless one will be revealed, whom the Lord Jesus will overthrow with the breath of his mouth and destroy by the splendor of his coming. The coming of the lawless one will be in accordance with how Satan works. He will use all sorts of displays of power through signs and wonders that serve the lie, and all the ways that wickedness deceives those who are perishing. They perish because they refused to love the truth and so be saved. For this reason God sends them a powerful delusion so that they will believe the lie and so that all will be condemned who have not believed the truth but have delighted in wickedness."

The restrainer eluded to here is referred to as "'what' is holding," "the 'one' who holds" and "will continue to do so until 'he' is taken out of the way" which in the original Greek is expressed as both a neuter gender and a masculine form of speech. There have been many hypotheses concerning the identity of the restrainer, including the Jewish state, Paul, the gospel, the Church but the only logical solution is the Holy Spirit. The Holy Spirit matches the description of holding (present tense) and will continue to, as well as until he is taken out of the way (future tense), which encapsulates the personality of the Holy Spirit. Only the Holy Spirit could be both present in Paul's lifetime and continue to be present until the antichrist is revealed. [78]

It has also been suggested that if the Holy Spirit is what holds back the revealing of the antichrist until he is taken out of the way, then his removal must mean the removal of believers in the rapture since the Holy Spirit is indwelling in all true believers. However, this view loses credibility when the first verse in this chapter of Thessalonians is reexamined, "Concerning the coming of our Lord Jesus Christ and our being gathered to him… that day will not come until the rebellion occurs and the man of lawlessness is revealed…", which rules out the possibility of a pre-tribulation rapture. The word apostasy translated from the Greek apostasia, which can also mean defection, departure or revolt, is where the word rebellion is derived in the Paul's second letter to the church at Thessalonica. Some have tried to imply this verse refers to the departure of the Church, however, that is a nonsensical observation since apostasy in the biblical context used by Paul in the original Greek means to express abandonment of the faith. So, the apostasy Paul is referring to here is a "falling away" or a "withdrawal" which is what North America and Europe are experiencing today.[79]

The advent of the man of lawlessness is being "restrained" by the Holy Spirit until such time as God's plan will allow. "At the proper time" illustrates God's sovereignty and signifies a time when God will allow mankind to prove just how evil their hearts are thereby condemning themselves and justifying the wrath that will be poured out upon them. It will be impossible to mistake the fact that prophecy is being fulfilled and that the end the Bible predicts is close at hand, however, nonbelievers will be deluded by the fantasy they have bought into that was served up as fine food on a silver platter by the antichrist.

Russia (Magog), Iran (Persia), Turkey (Rosh, Meshech and Tubal), Sudan (Cush), Germany (Gomer), Egypt and Libya (Put) and their allies will be the nations that become embroiled in what will likely be World

War III when they are drawn into battle against Israel (Ezekiel 38). "Son of man, set your face against Gog, of the land of Magog, the chief prince of Meshech and Tubal; prophesy against him and say: 'This is what the Sovereign Lord says: I am against you, Gog, chief prince of Meshech and Tubal. I will turn you around, put hooks in your jaws and bring you out with your whole army – your horses, your horsemen fully armed, and a great horde with large and small shields, all of them brandishing their swords. Persia, Cush and Put will be with them, all with shields and helmets, also Gomer with all its troops, and Beth Togarmah from the far north with all its troops – the many nations with you. Get ready; be prepared, you and all the hordes gathered about you, and take command of them. After many days you will be called to arms. In future years you will invade a land that has recovered from war, whose people were gathered from many nations to the mountains of Israel, which had long been desolate. They had been brought out from the nations, and now all of them live in safety." Ezekiel 38:2-8.

This will happen when Israel is living under the peace treaty negotiated and brokered by the antichrist, probably 3.5 years into it at about the same time he sets up the abomination that causes desolation in the rebuilt temple. Even today, Iran does not hide her contempt for Israel and would love to destroy her. Turkey and Russia are allies with Iran today, just as Ezekiel predicted 2600 years ago. Syria is noticeably absent in this prophecy which was puzzling until civil war and ISIS virtually crippled the country over the last few years. Especially prophetic was the decision by the U.S. to pull its troops out of Syria in October of 2019, leaving a power vacuum that was immediately filled by Russia and Turkey.

So much of prophetic scripture focuses upon the nation of Israel that it is at the very center of end times world events that are predicted in the Bible. The fact that there is even a nation called Israel today is a miracle in itself because without divine intervention it would not exist. In Ad 70, the Romans overran Jerusalem, destroyed the Temple and the Jews were dispersed throughout the nations for nearly 2000 years. Despite the Jewish Diaspora the people maintained their religion and followed the Torah diligently. They flourished wherever they went, and eventually anti- Semitism began to raise its ugly head in a response to their prosperity and their religious practices that set them apart from the mainstream population. Any other culture would have been assimilated into the countries they went to, but as God's chosen people the Jews have been preserved and restored to their land in the fulfillment of prophecy.

"'The days are coming,' declares the Lord, when the reaper will be overtaken by the plowman and the planter by the one treading grapes. New wine will drip from the mountains and flow from all the hills, and I will bring my people back from exile. They will rebuild the ruined cities and live in them. They will plant vineyards and drink their wine; they will make gardens and eat their fruit. I will plant Israel in their own land, never again to be uprooted from the land I have given them,' says the Lord your God." Amos 9:13-15. Today the desert is green and fruitful as the Jews have irrigated and transformed the land into a productive paradise. What no other people could accomplish in this particular geographical location, God's chosen people have, illustrating the prophetic truth regarding the nation of Israel.

We are called to pray for Jerusalem. The Bible says those who bless Israel will also be blessed and the United States has received these blessings more than any other country. Pray that Jews will have the gospel preached to them and seek God through the New Testament. Pray they accept Jesus as their Messiah and that any obstacles are removed out of the way to building the third temple. God will make all prophecy come to pass and we are the generation who will witness it.

Paul explains how the blessings of the Messiah that were intended for Israel were given to the Gentiles because of the unbelief of the Jews in the eleventh chapter of Romans. "I do not want you to be ignorant of this mystery, brothers and sisters, so that you may not be conceited: Israel has experienced a hardening in part until the full number of Gentiles has come in, and in this way, all Israel will be saved. Romans 11:25-26. As the full number of Gentiles coming into the kingdom of God approaches fullness, we are witnessing Messianic Jews accepting Christ and beginning Christian ministries all over the world, including Israel and in Jerusalem itself.

The Middle East has been a time bomb waiting to explode ever since Israel became a nation after World War II, erupting into chaos in the 1948 Arab – Israeli war, the Six Day War in 1967, the Yom Kippur War in 1973, the 1982 Lebanon War and the 2006 Lebanon War. Israel's tenuous peace seems always just a degree or two below the boiling point, every now and then erupting into exchanges of missile fire and air raids. Today it is a pressure cooker that is only a miscommunication or misinterpretation away from letting loose into a raging regional conflict. Continual infractions by the nation of Iran have kept the Israelis air force and army busy engaging in confrontations on Syrian soil. With the Biden administration's restoration of America's participation in the Iran Nuclear Deal and the lifting of sanctions, there is increased potential for conflict between the two nations.

As Israel's biggest supporter, the U.S.A. maintains a significant presence in the area as a deterrent to the Arab nations who would love nothing more than to destroy the Jews. The oil rich region plays a huge role in world stability with Europe, Russia, China, and the west all having significant stakes in the game, therefore aligning themselves as allies with the powers in the mid-east. When you add religious differences into the ingredients, the political soup becomes a recipe for disaster, that at any time threatens the stability of the entire world. If the U.S.A. were to fall or lose world dominance it would create a power vacuum that would precipitate a new world order with a malicious hidden agenda.

There have been several attempts to generate a consensus that would result in lasting peace in the middle east however, a meaningful and comprehensive template has proven to be elusive. Violence is commonplace in our world these days and terrorism seems to be in the news on a daily basis. Iran has displaced North Korea as the evil rogue state that potentially could ignite WW III with or without the nuclear weapons that are coveted so vehemently by her militant Islamic governing regime. Whoever successfully brokers a peace deal between Israel and her inhospitable neighbors will become a celebrity hero on an epic level.

Jared Kushner seems to be the one to attempt the impossible and bring together the diametrically opposed actors. As 2020 progressed three peace treaties were signed between Israel and the UAE, Bahrain and Jordan (1994) and President Trump claimed 7-9 more countries were seeking peace agreements with Israel, including Saudi Arabia. As more treaties are signed there will be increased pressure placed on Palestine to capitulate within the framework of the Arab Peace Initiative.[80] When this happens the stage will be set to turn the temple mount in Jerusalem back into the home of the Jewish Temple.

Preparations are already being made to build the third temple. The temple Institute has re-created all of the works of art that will go in the temple, including the golden lampstand or "menorah". They also believe they know the location of the Ark of the Covenant. It is believed that much of the temple walls have been prefabricated and can be moved at a moment's notice so the temple can be completed quickly. Most of the priestly garments are already made and ready. As well, the 4000 harps required for the Levites to play are almost completed. This is no small undertaking and just one obstacle stands in the way for it to proceed. The Muslim dome of the rock sits on the temple mount and no construction can take place until it is taken down. The antichrist will facilitate this as a component of his Israel-Arab peace treaty. The temple must be built in order to be desecrated by the abomination of desolation, when the man of lawlessness sets himself up in the temple to be worshiped as God.

The antichrist is a false Christ and as such, he will endeavor to be the mirror image of Christ, and mimic Christ, only he will endeavor to succeed where he perceives that Christ failed. However, what he will consider as success, God will use as his downfall. His actions will be a reflection of Christ's actions. He will imitate the gospels with false signs and wonders. Jesus performed true signs and wonders. Jesus was obedient to the laws of the land and to authority. The man of lawlessness will position himself above the law and will be a totalitarian leader.

While Jesus was humble, the antichrist will be arrogant. Where Jesus associated with the lowest of society, the man of lawlessness will rub shoulders with the elite. Jesus was without sin and the antichrist will be the man of sin. Jesus was the light and the antichrist will be darkness. Jesus was spiritual nourishment and the antichrist will be spiritual poison. Christ was the truth and the antichrist will be the lie. Christ was the man of miracles leading to life and the antichrist will be the man of deception leading to death. Jesus was God incarnate and the antichrist will exalt himself as the abomination that causes desolation, through self-deification.

Just as Christ's death on the cross was celebrated as victory by the Pharisees but was used by God to proclaim victory through the resurrection, the antichrist's rule will be limited by the return of Jesus to make the victory complete. The significance of 3.5 years is intentional insofar as that was the length of Christ's ministry therefore it will be the allowed length of the antichrist's tenure as supreme ruler throughout the earth.

The man of lawlessness literally means the man without law. "This person will be the consummate lawless one; a blasphemous sinner, who will live in open defiance of God's law. Of all the billions of godless, evil, lawless sinners in human history, his evil influence will be greater than any other's. Even in the end times, when "lawlessness is increased" (Mathew 24:12), this Satan-energized leader will stand out as the one whose depraved, wicked, lawless leadership sweeps over the whole world – with influence never before seen." [81]

Satan lives vicariously through the hidden cabal as the spirit of antichrist spoken of by the apostle Paul. Manifested as pride in the human intellect, expressed through scientific efforts to explain away the need for God, like evolutionary misinformation, religion in the form of diminishing God's word through the exaltation of traditions and rituals, materialism, hedonism and worldly values, and through other religions like Islam that act diametrically to Christian truth. Mankind will cling to these worldly values and resist the truth of God's word because the spirit of antichrist resists being exposed and openly displayed for all to see. Man would rather not confront the truth because it reveals his sinful nature. Jesus said, "This is the verdict: Light has come into the world, but people loved darkness instead of light because their deeds were evil. Everyone who does evil hates the light, and will not come into the light for fear that their deeds will be exposed. But whoever lives by the truth comes into the light, so that it may be seen plainly that what they have done has been done in the sight of God." John 3:19-21.

Throughout the last 2000 years, theologians have put forth an abundance of propositions of who or what the antichrist may be. Will he be the personification of evil? Could the antichrist even be a woman? Is the antichrist nothing more than a position opposing Christ? The pastiche contained in the book of Revelation referring to Satan, the antichrist and the false prophet as an imitation trinity versus the Father, Son and Holy Spirit has inspired imaginative interpretations of the book of Revelation.

Ever since the beginning and Satan's deception of Adam and Eve in the garden of Eden, he has made it his mission to drive a wedge between man and God. I believe Satan was jealous of the loving and open relationship between God and Adam and Eve which compelled him to destroy that relationship. Satan will also seek to place himself between man and God through the antichrist as his agent of evil in controlling the world and all who dwell upon it. Based upon incomplete information and sensationalized, overdramatic misrepresentation through movies and books, fear has created a boogey man and without the gospel as an anchor, most will be subject to mass hysteria which will play directly into the hands of this man of lawlessness. The panic witnessed over the COVID19 pandemic illustrates humanity's tendency to knee jerk reactions which snowball and create widespread irrationality.

In order to recognize a counterfeit, you must first be able to identify the authentic original. In a world where apostasy is increasing and ambiguous Christianity leaves believers without solid knowledge of scripture, the vast majority of people do not know Christ. How then, will they discern the illusions the man of lawlessness will display to deceive them are not of God? Even Christian leaders shy away from the difficult questions and prefer a vague analogy to explaining what the Bible clearly states. Father Patrick Keleher believes the "label of antichrist is metaphorical language used when people get paralyzed and that there is too much emphasis on apocalyptic visions that embody evil." This complacency is dangerous in the face of deception by the son of perdition empowered by Satan to perform false miracles. Keleher states, "Instead of labeling somebody on the outside for their heresy which is the original thing, or their sense of evil, wouldn't it be nice if we could use some self-examination in our meditation in the morning, or before we go to bed at night," before adding, "Was I antichrist today somehow in my attitude, or in my heresy? My beliefs in my attitude toward people? So in that way it could be healthy?" [82]

Scripture is precise for a reason. God wants Christians to have his word written in their minds and in their hearts so we can possess discernment when hard questions require answers. Paul illustrated this precision when he wrote, "The promises were spoken to Abraham and to his seed. Scripture does not say, 'and to seeds,' meaning many people, but 'and to your seed,' meaning one person, who is Christ." Galatians 3:16. In the same way that the book of Daniel prophesied the coming of Christ in pinpoint accuracy, the scriptures about the man of lawlessness must be interpreted as exact, literal depictions of who and what to expect.

The antichrist is more than an essence or spirit. While the spirit of antichrist was already at work in the apostle Paul's day, the persona or personal manifestation of antichrist in the man of lawlessness is a distinctly identifiable fulfillment of the abomination that causes desolation spoken of by Daniel and Jesus Christ which will take place in the future. The thirteenth chapter of Revelation describes how the antichrist and the false profit are truly beasts in their character. The text tells us that Satan gives the antichrist his power and that he is permitted to have authority over the world for forty-two months. He will slander God, heaven and the angels, persecute all believers and rule over every nation. The false prophet will be given power to exercise the authority of the antichrist and he will perform great signs and even cause fire to come down out of the sky. He will set up a statue of the antichrist in the rebuilt temple in Jerusalem and even cause it to breath and speak. Anyone who refuses to worship the statue will be killed. The false prophet will force everyone to receive the mark of the beast, without which they are not permitted to buy or sell. The mark of the beast is the number of his name (666). Revelation 13:18 warns, "This calls for wisdom. Let the person who has insight calculate the number of the beast, for it is the number of a man." The man of lawlessness.

There is much more that will be disclosed in my upcoming book *Revelation of Truth.*

One World Religion

Underlying the challenges mankind is facing is the need for collaboration and acknowledging the problems we face are too big to handle unless all of humanity works together. The world's secular belief systems fail because they leave God out of the equation. Without God, the world's people are spiritually dead. Without God, the world's wealth will continue to be acquired by the elite wealthy plutocracy while the rest of the population struggles for equality, food, shelter, security and dignity. Without God, this imbalance will erupt in violent, revolutionary protest. Without God, we are all doomed.

Humanity's problem is a spiritual problem. We've put our faith in everything but the one thing that matters most. Our Creator and our Master. As flesh and blood, we can never address the spiritual nature of our sin or the spiritual battles happening all around us. God speaks to us in Spirit. He speaks to our hearts and to our souls. When the Holy Spirit enters us and takes up residence within us our blindness leaves us and we begin to understand the truth that was present all along.

Christianity is unique because it is based on faith in Jesus Christ that is credited to the believer as righteousness. It doesn't require the observance of religious dogma, ritual, ceremony or tradition and is the only belief system that offers forgiveness of sins. The Bible is the inspired word of the one true living God and is infallible (the authenticity of the Bible is given in my first book *Truth Cries Out*). The Bible is unique in its claim to be the only true word of God. Knowing what the Bible says about our generation is critical to understanding the signs of the times.

Today it is popular to embrace religious pluralism and interfaith concepts that all religions are equal. These views are a foreshadowing of the predicted global religion of the Book of Revelation that will witness the entire world uniting under one religion and one government. The Bible says that God is a jealous God (Exodus 34:14) and as Christians we are betrothed to Christ as his bride (2 Corinthians 11:2) therefore, we are called to be faithful to the one true God. The church of the end times is depicted in the seventeenth chapter of Revelation as drunken and adulterous, having committed adultery with the kings of the earth. Furthermore, she is "drunk with the blood of the saints, the blood of those who bore testimony to Jesus." Revelation 17:6.

This religious entity is guilty of both compromising the truth of the gospel with political ambition for power and money as well as murdering true believers in Christ as martyrs for their faith. The vision in Revelation is explained for John by an angel. The institution the woman represents has close ties to the beast who is the antichrist and she sits on seven hills yet she also sits on many waters, meaning she is international in nature as well as headquartered in Rome (the seven mountains of Rome). Revelation 18 goes on to detail her evil exploits, her wealth, power and arrogance. "Give her as much torture and grief as the glory and luxury she gave herself. In her heart she boasts, 'I sit as queen; I am not a widow, and I will never mourn.'" Revelation 18:7

The fear and anxiety being displayed by humanity today have more people searching for answers than ever before and the multitude of world religions creates confusion and an environment of naivety that leaves society vulnerable to deception. The lack of a solid foundational understanding of God combined with an abundance of half-truths and "spirituality" perceptions has set the stage for many false teachers and finally the ultimate deception of a one world religion to satisfy every desire for acceptance without judgement. In an age where it isn't in vogue to mention hell as a physical place of punishment and it is popular for everyone to be tolerated and accepted, we are witnessing the salesmanship of a smooth talking, sincere looking, humble acting elderly statesman in the person of the pope.

Pope Francis called for global leaders to come together and develop a global compact on education on May 14, 2020. A reeducation of our youth to teach a universal solidarity and a new humanism. Essentially this was an invitation to rewrite the way we think and constitutes a heavy-handed influence or programing and dictation of what will be tolerated and what won't be by the new world order. His message was sugar coated in honorable proposals like addressing climate change in a meaningful way, caring for the earth, education to bring about peace and justice and openness between all peoples and dialog between all religions. He called for the formation of a global village where everyone has the same values, the same respect for others, the same commitment to the global society, one global family worshipping one global god. This all-encompassing pact will include religion, politics, economics, education and progress. Those invited included international organizations and "the great ones of the earth" in helping to "heal the fracture between man and the Absolute."

Recently, Pope Francis and Imam Sheikh Ahmed al-Tayeb signed "A Document on Human Fraternity for World Peace and Living Together" which intends to foster peace between nations, religions and ethnic groups while combating extremism and violence. Promoting peace is one thing but selling out God in the process is unacceptable for a Christian entity like the Roman Catholic Church. The language of the agreement is vague and essentially equates God with Allah and intimates that God allows for hundreds of different religions that are all equally valid. In 2016, Pope Francis declared that all world religions "are seeking God or meeting God in different ways."[83]

The document proclaims, "Freedom is a right of every person: each individual enjoys the freedom of belief, thought, expression and action. The pluralism and diversity of religions, color, sex, race and language are willed by God in his wisdom, through which he created human beings. This divine wisdom is the source from which the right to freedom of belief and the freedom to be different derives. Therefore, the fact that people are forced to adhere to a certain religion or culture must be rejected, as too the imposition as a cultural way of life that others do not accept."[84]

In an all-inclusive, warm and fuzzy, human effort affirming, inter faith covenant, every group of people is dumped together along with good and evil and an imaginary image of an all-encompassing, sin tolerating, morally flexible God. While sounding noble and humanitarian on the surface, the devil is in the details, concealed in linguistic smoke and mirror logic. This language is nearly indistinguishable from the compatibility rhetoric of the advocates of a new world order.

It continues, "While recognizing the positive steps taken by our modern civilization in the fields of science, technology, medicine, industry and welfare, especially in developed countries, we wish to emphasize that, associated with such historic advancements, great and valued as they are, there exists both a moral deterioration that influences international action and a weakening of spiritual values and responsibility. All this contributes to a general feeling of frustration, isolation and desperation leading many to fall either into a vortex of atheistic, agnostic or religious extremism, or into blind and fanatic extremism, which ultimately encourage forms of dependency and individual or collective self-destruction." [85]

"The Second Vatican Council teaches that Muslims 'adore the one God, living and subsisting in himself, merciful and all-powerful, the Creator of heaven and earth, who has spoken to humans. They take pains to submit wholeheartedly to even God's inscrutable decrees.'"[86] Jesuit Father Tom Michel adds that, "Islam and Christianity are two different religions and have different teachings, and God is able to save both Muslim and Christian if they faithfully follow their respective paths." These statements are contrary to what God says about himself in the Bible.

Jesus said, "I am the way and the truth and the life. No one comes to the Father except through me." John14:6. There is a tremendous risk in seeking global religious unity. As with any consensus and collective collaboration, compromise is an integral component of success and one thing that God does not do is compromise. He is the same now as he was at the beginning and as he will be at the end. God does not change. Furthermore, Jesus said that Christians are called out from the world and that our citizenship is in heaven. "If you belonged to the world, it would love you as its own. As it is, you do not belong to the world, but I have chosen you out of the world. That is why the world hates you." John 15:19.

In fact, worldly ways are in opposition to God, "Do not love the world or anything in the world. If anyone loves the world, love for the Father is not in them. For everything in the world – the lust of the flesh, the lust of the eyes, and the pride of life – comes not from the Father but from the world. The world and its desires pass away, but whoever does the will of God lives forever." 1 John2:15-17.

In his appeal to world religious leaders, Pope Francis painted a rather bleak picture. "There is no alternative: We either build the future together or there will not be a future." He said these words at an international inter-religious meeting Feb 4, 2019 and added, "The time has come when religions should more actively exert themselves, with courage and audacity and without pretense, to help the human family deepen their capacity for reconciliation, the vision of hope and the concrete paths of peace." [87]

He recently met with Israeli President Shimon Peres and Palestinian Authority President Mahmoud Abbas in Vatican City and for the first time in history, Muslim prayers and readings from the Quran were heard in the Catholic holy place. "The pope said, too, that he hoped the interfaith prayers would foster peace specifically between Israelis and Palestinians." As quoted by The Washington Times.[88] The Catechism states regarding the church's relationship with Muslims, that the plan of salvation "also includes those who acknowledge the Creator, in the first place amongst who are the Muslims. These profess to hold the faith of Abraham and together with us they adore the one merciful God, mankind's judge on the last day."

While his passion for peace is a sincere and noble desire from a humanistic point of view, it does little to further the cause of Christ and the kingdom of God. Any one of a number of eloquent and knowledgeable speakers could have echoed the same words without any connectivity to Christianity. In secular linguistic connotations that focused on social equality and injustice, he failed to identify the root of all violence and inequity in the sinful nature of the human spirit. In what was a glorious opportunity to shine God's pure light into the darkness and glorify our heavenly Father, he delivered a message of human accomplishment and earthly perspective. When Jesus spoke, he cut right to the heart of individual human spiritual poverty.

Jesus said, "Blessed are the poor in spirit, for theirs is the kingdom of heaven.
Blessed are those who mourn, for they will be comforted.
Blessed are the meek, for they will inherit the earth.
Blessed are those who hunger and thirst for righteousness, for they will be filled.
Blessed are the merciful, for they will be shown mercy.

> Blessed are the pure at heart, for they will see God.
> Blessed are the peacemakers, for they will be called children of God.
> Blessed are those who are persecuted because of righteousness, for theirs is the kingdom of heaven. Mathew 5:3-10.

In the Sermon on the Mount, Jesus delivered the greatest oration of all time, that captivated his audience because he spoke as someone who had authority. He said, "You have heard it said to the people long ago, you shall not murder, and anyone who murders will be subject to judgement. But I tell you that anyone who is angry with a brother or sister will be subject to judgement. Again, anyone who says to a brother or sister, 'Raca,' is answerable to the court. And anyone who says, 'You fool!' will be in danger of the fire of hell." Mathew 5:21-22.

Later Jesus added, "You have heard that it was said, 'love your neighbor and hate your enemy.' But I tell you, love your enemies and pray for those who persecute you, that you may be children of your father in heaven." Mathew 5:43-44. "Therefore anyone who hears these words of mine and puts them into practice is like a wise man who built his house on the rock. The rain came down, the streams rose, and the winds blew and beat against that house; yet it did not fall, because it had its foundation on the rock." Mathew 7:24-25.

Pope Francis missed a tremendous moment to call all people to repentance. Paul wrote, "for all have sinned and fall short of the glory of God," Romans 3:23. With religious leaders from around the globe in his audience, he failed to glorify God. As an ambassador for Christ he never once mentioned Jesus! And herein lies the quandary of why religion can never solve the human riddle of sin. By placing his faith in religion, the pope summoned other leaders to join him in consolidating the collective institution of religious belief in a partnership of human effort.

Will this be a conglomeration of cherry-picked ideas and beliefs that in reality amounts to serving God with their lips while their hearts are far from him? In my second book (*Seeking Truth*) I illustrated how after Constantine legalized Christianity he used the church to expand the Roman Empire which resulted in the paganization of the church rather than the Christianization of pagans. If the religion lacks the truth of God, it is not of God. In the same way, the end time one world religion will not be built on the rock and will embrace all religions and contain the truth of none.

One other time in history, mankind began to collectively reach for heaven through a one world religion, and that was at a place called Babel, meaning "gate of God." They began building a tower by which they planned to reach the heavens by human effort. So the Lord confused their language and forced them to scatter over the face of the earth where they could no longer attempt solidarity through religion. Babel is equated to the city of Babylon in the Old Testament and is also referenced in the book of Revelation as symbolic of the perverted religion with which the rulers of the earth committed adultery with.

Without a solid foundation in the truth of God it will be possible to combine the world's religions into one all encompassing, all-inclusive fraternity that the pope believes will lead to global peace and brotherhood. In fact, the design is complete and the plans are in place to build the Abrahamic Family House which will be a huge complex housing a mosque, a church and a synagogue to be built on Saadiyat Island in Abu Dhabi, United Arab Emirates.[89] With a focus on the Old Testament scriptures as they relate to Abraham, the premise is that all of these groups worship the God of Abraham who created the world. The truth becomes lost when Jesus Christ enters the discussion since he claimed to be God and that no one could come to God except through him, therefore in order to reconcile these three belief systems, the resulting doctrine must become antichrist. And that is precisely what it will be. The religion of the antichrist.

In the spirit of compromise, the movement to combine the world's religions denies the Holy Spirit and the Holy Bible. The apostle John wrote, "This is how you can recognize the Spirit of God: Every spirit that acknowledges that Jesus Christ has come in the flesh is from God, but every spirit that does not acknowledge Jesus is not from God. This is the spirit of the antichrist, which you have heard is coming and even now is already in the world. 1 John 4:2-3. Rather than truth, the result is a haphazard combination of ideologies reduced to the lowest common denominator. Noticeably lacking is salvation and the forgiveness of sins which makes the entire effort impotent.

Jesus said, "Do not suppose that I have come to bring peace to the earth. I did not come to bring peace, but a sword. For I have come to turn 'a man against his father, a daughter against her mother, a daughter-in-law against her mother-in-law – a man's enemies will be the members of his own household.'" Mathew 10:34-36. The truth can be offensive to those who are in disagreement with what it reveals. The apostle Paul depicts the truth of scripture like this: "For the word of God is alive and active. Sharper than any double-edged sword, it penetrates even to dividing soul and spirit, joints and marrow; it judges the thoughts and attitudes of the heart." Hebrews 4:12.

Unholy prayers fall far below heaven. If there's one thing I've learned in my walk with the Lord, it's that communication is a two-way street. If we haven't listened to God, chances are he won't listen to us. It's been said many times that we have pushed him out of our schools, public spaces and homes and when disaster strikes, we ask "Where was God?" In the same way, if we dial Satan's number, why would we expect God to pick up? Jesus said, "I and the Father are one." Mathew 10:30. Being one with God, his thoughts were God's thoughts and his desires were God's desires. Even so, on the night he was betrayed, he prayed, "Father, if you are willing, take this cup from me; yet not my will, but yours be done." Luke 22:42. If we expect our prayers to be heard and answered by God, our will must match his will. It would be nonsensical to think we could ask God to contravene his own will since he is, after all, sovereign.

The oldest Christian Church has been undermined for nearly two thousand years as the institutional religious establishment adopted dogma contrary to scripture and this has resulted in a "less than credible" Christian religion (For an in-depth study please refer to my second book, *Seeking Truth*). Today, many "Christian" churches preach a social gospel or a prosperity gospel that has little resemblance to the practices of the first century Church. This lack of foundational truth leaves the followers of these institutions gullible and ripe for deception, just as Jesus warned, "Watch out that no one deceives you. For many will come in my name, claiming, 'I am the Messiah,' and will deceive many." Mathew 24:4-5. The apostasy of the last days will claim many victims who will not find the narrow gate. Jesus said, "Not everyone who says to me, 'Lord, Lord,' will enter the kingdom of heaven, but only the one who does the will of my Father in heaven. Many will say to me on that day, 'Lord, Lord, did we not prophesy in your name and in your name drive out demons and in your name perform many miracles?' Then I will tell them plainly, 'I never knew you. Away from me, you evildoers!" Mathew 7:21-23.

Apathy has crept into the Church in affluent congregations that have no need to look to God for their daily bread. Prayer requests don't include shelter and clothing, nor do the hearts of the materially satisfied seek spiritual water since they are no longer thirsty. This has incubated an apostasy that has enveloped the vast majority of western society and has been so slow and gradual that the spiritual hemorrhaging wasn't recognized until the church itself became spiritually bankrupt.

By wandering away from the Bible and embracing social issues these churches have lost touch with the truth of God's word. They've lost the discernment that comes with having God's laws written in their hearts and in their minds. They are easily led astray by secular ideologies and half-truths that distort the Bible and propose that it is allegorical or twist scripture to bolster their own desires as the prosperity gospel does. They know just enough to be gullible and fall for deception just as Eve did when the serpent said, "Did God really say, 'You must not eat from any tree in the garden?'" Genesis 3:1.

Books like the *Da Vinci Code* have planted the seeds of doubt about Jesus' life by depicting him as much less than he was. It sold more than 60.5 million copies illustrating how mankind desires to minimize the authority of God by hoping the Bible is somehow fallible, and therefore can be discarded. The theory of evolution has undermined the biblical version of our history to the extent that every high school graduate, questions or dismisses creation. The resulting ignorance of biblical truth is the ideal environment for the perfect storm to precipitate a global gospel of deception and obscurity.

Through complacency and undiscriminating acceptance of misinformation there is a great falling away from the body of Christ. It is no wonder that Jesus said, "Enter through the narrow gate. For wide is the gate and broad is the road that leads to destruction, and many enter through it. But small is the gate and narrow is the road that leads to life, and only a few find it." Mathew 7:13-14. Knowing the Bible is the key to discernment and Jesus emphasized this when he spoke, "It is written:

'Man shall not live on bread alone, but on every word that comes from the mouth of God.'" Mathew 4:4.

Groups like the Freemasons pray to the "Supreme Architect of the Universe" claiming that many paths wind up a mountain and all meet at the top. They believe that all religions can gather together around the same alter as brothers and unite in prayer. They seek divine illumination and oneness with all spiritual truth and claim to recognize the light, while the bearer is of less importance. Regardless of what your concept of God is, whether you are Christian, Jewish, Muslim, Hindu, or Buddhist, there is no differentiation, all are equal and the same to their worship.

In contemporary society being "spiritual" is a trendy way to distance oneself from any form of responsibility when it comes to righteousness. It is acceptable to discuss spirituality until you mention the name of Jesus. Then the red flags go up, warning lights flash and alarms sound, labeling you a Christian and therefore homophobic, racist, Islamophobic, chauvinistic, a bigot and a hypocrite. How many times have you heard, "I'm not religious, I'm spiritual?" The apostle Paul issued a stern warning to those who lack discernment when dealing with spirituality. "Dear friends, do not believe every spirit, but test the spirits see whether they are from God, because many false prophets have gone out into the world. This is how you can recognize the Spirit of God: Every spirit that acknowledges that Jesus Christ has come in the flesh is from God, but every spirit that does not acknowledge Jesus is not from God. This is the spirit of the antichrist, which you heard is coming and even now is already in the world." 1 John4:1-3.

The relativism that is prevalent in post-modern society has greatly influenced the notions of who or what God is and has even infiltrated the Church resulting in disunity and confusion. Unable to find footing in the rituals of religion and the platitudes of established institutions, those seeking spiritual experiences are at risk of being victimized by idolatry from the dubious choices they are presented with. Additionally, because of the emphasis on growing churches as opposed to growing faith, the truth of the Bible has been exchanged for a non-confrontational message of inclusivity that minimizes sin and magnifies social equity, and the platonic connection of a living and active relationship with Jesus has been lost. Without the objective standard of biblical truth that is foundational to Christianity, multitudes of church goers have been deceived by a counterfeit Christianity.

By compromising Christian doctrine so as not to offend Muslims, spiritualists or secular ideologies, the apostate church is ready to embrace the vision of the amalgamation of all religions into a single global religion. The concept of one global village has already taken root as humanity has been coerced into working together in combatting pandemics, climate change, poverty and inequality. As we band together and believe we can bring about world peace by setting aside our differences in what we believe regarding religion, the path leads directly to Jerusalem and the marriage of church and state with the consummation of human history.

In the thirteenth chapter of revelation we are introduced to the beast (antichrist) that comes out of the sea (human civilization) and was empowered by the dragon which is Satan. He is depicted as a beast because that is what he is in his heart. "The dragon stood on the shore of the sea. And I saw a beast coming out of the sea. It had ten horns and seven heads, with ten crowns on its horns, and on each head a blasphemous name. The beast I saw resembled a leopard, but had feet like those of a bear and a mouth like that of a lion. The dragon gave the beast his power and his throne and great authority. One of the heads of the beast seemed to have had a fatal wound, but the fatal wound had been healed. The whole world was filled with wonder and followed the beast. People worshipped the dragon because he had given authority to the beast, and they also worshipped the beast and asked, 'Who is like the beast? Who can wage war against it?'

The beast was given a mouth to utter proud words and blasphemies and to exercise its authority for forty-two months. It opened its mouth to blaspheme God, and to slander his name and his dwelling place and those who live in heaven. It was given power to wage war against God's holy people and to conquer them. And it was given authority over every tribe, people, language and nation. All inhabitants of the earth will worship the beast – all whose names have not been written in the Lamb's book of life, the Lamb who was slain from the creation of the world." Revelation 13:1-8.

Firstly, the dragon who is Satan was depicted in Revelation 12 as having seven heads and ten horns with seven crowns on its heads which is close to the description of the beast described above. This illustrates they are cut from the same cloth and by their very nature, they desire to rule the earth. The second noteworthy point is the mention of what seemed to be a mortal wound to one of the heads. There is a prophetic correlation here to Genesis 3:15 where God tells Satan, "I will put enmity between you and the woman, and between your offspring and hers; he will crush your head, and you will strike his heel." This prophecy was fulfilled when Jesus took back the land title for earth by becoming a sacrifice for all when he was crucified and rose again conquering death. If you recall, the apostle Paul mentioned that the spirit of the antichrist was already in the world at that time (1 John 4:3). God's comment in Genesis 3:15 also intimates that the antichrist is Satan's offspring, which illustrates the extent of how the antichrist is an imitation of Christ.

Thirdly, the beast is very similar to the beasts Daniel describes in Daniel 7:1-7. We must recognize that these beasts illustrate earthly powers and empires as God sees them and God sees them for what they truly are. The dragon (Satan) is the deceiver of the world and the beast (antichrist) will deceive the whole world so much so that all inhabitants of the earth will worship him.

Revelation 13 continues with the introduction of a second beast, but this one is from the earth. "Then I saw a second beast, coming out of the earth. It had two horns like a lamb, but it spoke like a dragon. It exercised all of the authority of the first beast on its behalf, and made the earth and its inhabitants worship the first beast, whose fatal wound had been healed. And it performed great signs, even causing fire to come down from heaven to the earth in full view of the people. Because of the signs it was given to perform on behalf of the first beast, it deceived the inhabitants of the earth. It ordered them to set up an image in honor of the beast who was wounded by the sword and yet lived. The second beast was given power to give breath to the image of the first beast, so that the image could speak and cause all who refused to worship the image to be killed. It also forced all people, great and small, rich and poor, free and slave, to receive a mark on their right hands or on their foreheads, so that they could not buy or sell unless they had the mark, which is the name of the beast or the number of its name.

This calls for wisdom. Let the person who has insight calculate the number of the beast, for it is the number of a man. That number is 666." Revelation 13:11-18

This second beast is the ultimate wolf in sheep's clothing. He is the accomplice of the antichrist and the false prophet. His appearance is peaceful, yet he speaks in the same deceptive tones as the antichrist. These are the two principals of the new world order. The one world government and the one world religion. Together they control everything from world faith, health, food supplies, banking, trade energy and politics. They control it all and they profit from it. All of the elements of evil are present in this partnership from coercion to mass killing prompting Jesus to say, "If those days had not been cut short, no one would survive, but for the sake of the elect those days will be shortened." Mathew 24:22.

The religious deception of the false profit leads to idolatry to the point where the antichrist is worshipped as a god by a subjected humanity. The significance of 666 has intrigued mankind ever since John wrote it down. Many have tried to infer the numbers into the alphabet in various languages with little or no luck but what we can glean from the text is that it is a man's number. The antichrist is a man. More than a spirit, essence or movement. Earlier we discussed the man of lawlessness and we can now reinforce that interpretation with this verse. In the same way that the number seven symbolizes perfection, and 777 the perfect holy trinity of the Father, Son and Holy Spirit, 666 falls short of perfection and symbolizes the unholy trinity of Satan, antichrist and false profit.

The fourteenth chapter of Revelation contains warnings against falling for the deception of the unholy trinity, "If anyone worships the beast and its image and receives its mark on their forehead or on their hand, they, too, will drink the wine of God's fury, which has been poured full strength into the cup of his wrath." Revelation 14:9-10. In verse 12 we find instructions for true believers in Christ, "This calls for patient endurance on the part of the people of God who keep his commands and are faithful to Jesus." Which echoes Revelation 13:10's call for, "patient endurance and faithfulness on the part of God's people."

Let's dive a little deeper into the 17th chapter of Revelation (touched on at the beginning of this chapter), where John is shown a woman sitting on a scarlet beast with seven heads and ten horns which is Satan. She sits by many waters and is "drunk with the blood of God's holy people, and the blood of those who bore testimony to Jesus." Revelation 17:6. An angel then explains the mystery to John of who the woman is and the beast she rides. "This calls for a mind with wisdom. The seven heads are seven hills on which the woman sits. They are also seven kings. Five have fallen, one is, the other has not yet come; but when he does come, he must remain for just a little while." Revelation 17:9-10.

The woman is none other than the corrupt institution of the global apostate church, whose conquest of wealth and power exceeded her love of the truth of God's word. The blood of martyrs from centuries of persecution of those she labeled as heretics has made her drunk with power and arrogance. The perversion of her dogma and clergy are the abominable things and the filth of her adulteries that fill her golden cup. She is dressed in purple and scarlet, glittering with gold, pearls and precious stones purchased with the wealth she coerced from her simple followers. She is also a city in the same way the Vatican is an independent city-state. The waters beside which the adulteress sits are peoples, multitudes, nations and languages.

The antichrist and his political affiliates then grow to hate the woman and do away with her as she is no longer needed to accomplish their agenda. Since he is already being worshipped as God, he has become religion himself and the new world order is his alone. "They will bring her to ruin and leave her naked; they will eat her flesh and burn her with fire. For God has put it into their hearts to accomplish his purpose by agreeing to hand over to the beast their royal authority, until God's words are fulfilled. The woman you saw is the great city that rules over the kings of the earth." Revelation 17:16-18.

The seven hills mentioned here direct our attention to Rome, a city notably built on seven hills. The kings who had fallen and the one who was, represent the great kingdoms of the past and present in John's time. They were Egypt, Assyria, Medo-Persia, Greece and the Roman Empire. The eighth king is eluded to by the prophet Daniel in his prophecy of the seventy weeks when he wrote, "After sixty-two sevens the Anointed One will be put to death and have nothing. The people of the ruler who will come will destroy the city and the sanctuary. The end will come like a flood: War will continue until the end, and desolations have been decreed. He will confirm a covenant with many for one 'seven.' In the middle of the 'seven' he will put an end to sacrifice and offering. And at the temple he will set up an abomination that causes desolation, until the end that is decreed is poured out on him." Daniel 9:26-27. The Romans sacked Jerusalem in AD 70 and destroyed the temple. The ruler Daniel is talking about here is the antichrist whose seven-year middle east peace treaty will be broken mid-way through it.

Furthermore, the statement that he must remain for a little while in Revelation 17:10 mirrors Jesus's words of those days being cut short and the forty-two months spoken of in Revelation 13:5 and is also substantiated by Daniel's seventieth week that is divided in two by the abomination that causes desolation. At this point the world will mourn over the loss of their worldly religion as the antichrist doubles down and the beast in him is allowed to run with reckless abandon. This will be the great tribulation that Jesus described in Mathew 24:21, "For then there will be great distress, unequaled from the beginning of the world until now – and never to be equaled again."

The violent nature of the Revelation narrative has produced a variety of responses from theologians and Christians in general. Some avoid it, some over analyze it and others embellish it. It is important to remember that the visions described by Daniel, John and Jesus are given from God's perspective. Compared to his perfect holiness, the worldly kingdoms are beasts. They are monsters that devour innocent people and discard them as trash. The deep state is also a beast that feasts on the flesh of society as it accumulates immeasurable fortunes at the expense of people like you and me. Together with the corrupt religion, the cabal is a component of mystery Babylon depicted in the Bible. The imagery in the book of Revelation paints a picture that show us the true heart of mankind. The events prophesied will come to pass, and they will be literally as evil as they are portrayed in scripture.

We are called to stand firm in the faith, with patience and perseverance, founded in the truth of the Bible and the rock that is Jesus Christ. "At that time many will turn away from the faith and will betray and hate each other. Because of the increase of wickedness, the love of most will grow cold, but the one who stands firm to the end will be saved. And this gospel of the kingdom will be preached in the whole world as a testimony to all nations, and then the end will come." Mathew 24:10-14.

GREAT TRIBULATION

Ever since Adam and Eve were evicted from the garden of Eden, the heart of civilization has steadily devolved and entropy has plagued the earth under the weight of sin. The apostle Paul wrote, "We know that the whole creation has been groaning as in the pains of childbirth right up to the present time. Not only so, but we ourselves, who have the firstfruits of the Spirit, groan inwardly as we wait eagerly for our adoption to sonship, the redemption of our bodies." Romans 8:22-23.

Humanity has shown that it is not capable of a sustainable existence due to the fallen nature of man and our propensity for violence to achieve our objectives. Satan continues to infiltrate society covertly, heinously and systematically, thereby undermining the good that God desires. As unrest grows, terrorism, crime, immorality, corruption, decadence and arrogance, along with poverty, famine, disease and the possibility of world war III, all threaten the survival of humanity. Man is certain to destroy himself and the world unless God intervenes. Our Creator knew this from the beginning and he has provided insight and prophecy to warn us in advance of our ultimate self-destruction.

As human history moves toward the end of the age, we are about to enter a period when the battle being fought between good and evil in the spiritual realms will spill over into our physical realm and encompass all of mankind as the conclusion of the confrontation nears. This period of global trouble will intensify to incredible proportions as civilization, the climate, the earth and all of creation become unstable in anticipation of the end that has been decreed. The cataclysmic culmination of the abuse and exploitation of our world and each other is about to rapidly accelerate toward the climax of history during the Great Tribulation and the return of Jesus Christ to make his victory complete.

Over half of the Bible is dedicated to the "last days," signifying the importance of this time in human history. As previously mentioned, the prophet Daniel wrote his book of prophecy around 600 BC and in it he speaks of a timeline which leads right up to our current generation. He prophesied that there would be seventy weeks of years, "to finish transgression, to put an end to sin, to atone for wickedness, to bring in everlasting righteousness, to seal up vision and prophecy and to anoint the most holy." Daniel 9:24.

This was written when Israel was under Babylonian rule and Daniel had been taken to Babylon to serve her king. Daniel was told in a vision while he was praying over the nation of Israel that the seventy weeks would commence when the decree was issued to rebuild Jerusalem. Here is that piece of scripture again: "Know and understand this: From the issuing of the decree to restore and rebuild Jerusalem until the Anointed One, the ruler, comes, there will be seven 'sevens' and sixty-two 'sevens.' It will be rebuilt with streets and a trench, but in times of trouble. After the sixty-two 'sevens,' the Anointed One will be cut off and will have nothing. The people of the ruler who will come will destroy the city and the sanctuary. The end will come like a flood. War will continue until the end and desolations have been decreed. He will confirm a covenant with many for one 'seven'. In the middle of the 'seven' he will put an end to sacrifice and offering. And on a wing of the temple he will set up an abomination that causes desolation, until the end that is decreed is poured out on him." Daniel 9: 25-27.

The final 'seven' will commence with the signing of a covenant with many, which will be a treaty between Israel and her middle east Arab neighbors. Today we are witnessing an aggressive agenda to accomplish this and provide a solution to the Palestinian problem. However, Daniel tells us that the facilitator of this accord will dishonor the agreement and set up the "abomination of desolation." Jesus highlights this in in his warnings about the last days (Mathew 24:15). He then elaborates to illustrate the severity of the tribulation that will come.

"For then there will be great distress, unequaled from the beginning of the world until now – and never to be equaled again. If those days had not been cut short, no one would survive, but for the sake of the elect those days will be shortened.'" Mathew 24:20-22. Thank God that time will be limited to 3 ½ years. Daniel's prophecy states in the middle of the 'seven' and in Revelation 13 we are told 42 months.

Let's reexamine what the signs that would precede the end of the world will be. We once again turn to Mathew 24 where, "Jesus answered, 'Watch out that no one deceives you. For many will come in my name, claiming, 'I am the Messiah,' and deceive many. You will hear of wars and rumors of wars, but see to it that you are not alarmed. Such things must happen, but the end is still to come. Nation will rise against nation, and kingdom against kingdom. There will be famines and earthquakes in various places. All these things are the beginning of birth pains.

Then you will be handed over to be persecuted and put to death, and you will be hated by all nations because of me. At that time many will turn away from the faith and will betray and hate each other, and many false prophets will appear and deceive many people. Because of the increase of wickedness, the love of most will grow cold, but the one who stands firm to the end will be saved. And this gospel of the kingdom will be preached in the whole world as a testimony to all nations, and then the end will come.'" Mathew 24:4-14.

Does our world resemble what is described in these verses of scripture? There have been false preachers claiming that they are the real Messiah. There have been wars and plenty of them. In fact, there was more deaths due to war in the 20th century than in the previous two thousand years since Christ, combined. The twentieth century has been called the century of war. We have had an increase in famines. Some say due to global warming however that has not been conclusively proven. It doesn't matter what is causing the famines and droughts though, what matters is that it is a sign that the earth is groaning. So ever since the fall in the garden, the birth pains have been happening. They have been getting more intense and closer together as we approach the advent of the second coming of Christ.

Jesus said the disciples would be persecuted and put to death, which indeed they were and in fact all Christians were persecuted and hated and in many countries they still are. Today there are more Christians being persecuted that an any time previously including the Roman times. He then added there would be a falling away from the faith and an increase in wickedness, which also has been happening on a worldwide scale. Jesus then concluded that the gospel would be preached to all nations and then the end shall come. Today for the first time in history, we are very near to this final sign that immediately precedes the end. Paul also wrote of the period just before the end, saying, "Don't let anyone deceive you in any way, for that day will not come until the rebellion occurs and the man of lawlessness is revealed, the man doomed to destruction." 2 Thessalonians 2:3.

In his second letter to Timothy, Paul wrote, "But mark this: There will be terrible times in the last days. People will be lovers of themselves, lovers of money, boastful, proud, abusive, disobedient to their parents, ungrateful, unholy, without love, unforgiving, slanderous, without self-control, brutal, not lovers of the good, treacherous, rash, conceited, lovers of pleasure rather than lovers of God – having a form of godliness but denying its power. Have nothing to do with them." 2 Timothy 3:1-5. Its as if Paul saw an hour of our current news, sports and entertainment on TV. Today's society is all these things.

When the man of lawlessness comes to power and installs his new world order the peace will be short lived and he will dishonor the Israel/Arab peace agreement, impose martial law and demand to be worshipped as God in the rebuilt temple in Jerusalem. He will regulate all financial transactions to those who pledge allegiance to him and deny those who don't. All who refuse to worship him will be killed (Revelation 13).

While the enigmatic language of Revelation causes many misinterpretations and even causes some to avoid it completely, if we are sincere in our desire to know the truth, we must dive into it without reserve. In John's vision, he sees Jesus in heaven and a scroll with seven seals that no one can open is given to him (Revelation 5). The fact that only Jesus is qualified to open the seals testifies to his position as higher than any other and his name being above every name (Philippians 2:9). These seals reveal events preceding Christ's return and even after. If you have ever heard of the four horses of the apocalypse, this is where they fit in.

The first seal releases a white horse, whose rider is bent on conquest. This represents a conqueror who subdues without bloodshed (Revelation 6:2) and is the covert power structure of the cabal. The deep state has been financing, manipulating and secretly exploiting the earth and civilization for centuries with the ultimate goal of ruling the world. They have been gaining in power and influence as time marches on and without getting their hands dirty they pull the strings of governments, corporations, and the military complex of the world and have accumulated the vast majority of the planet's wealth.

When the second seal is broken, a red horse is released whose rider is "given the power to take peace from the earth, and to make men slay each other. To him was given a large sword." Revelation 6:4. This seal corresponds with the wars and rumors of wars, and nation rising against nation that Jesus spoke of in Mathew 24. Although there have always been wars, the twentieth century marked a dramatic increase in frequency and intensity of man's battles, and global conflict will reach epic proportions during the Great Tribulation. Never before has man had the weapons of mass destruction at his disposal that he does in this present age. Mankind now has the capacity to destroy the world several times over so even a restrained release of that power has the potential of unleashing a nuclear winter that could result in a large percentage of the world's population dying.

The third seal is broken and it releases a black horse and its rider was holding a pair of scales. "Then I heard what sounded like a voice among the four living creatures, saying, 'A quart of wheat for a day's wages, and three quarts of barley for a day's wages, and do not damage the oil and the wine!'" Revelation 6:6. One quart of wheat would be enough food for one person. Three quarts of barley, although less nutritious would feed a small family. The interpretation here is of drought which makes food scarce and expensive. Vine crops and trees where olive oil and wine are derived are deeper rooted and less susceptible to drought unless it becomes very severe. Today Africa, Australia and South America continue to experience devastating droughts. These are the beginning of birth pains that Jesus spoke of in Mathew 24. This also represents a reversal to the cheap food policy currently in place while alcohol is taxed, making it expensive. This phenomenon was experienced in communist Russia when store shelves were empty, inflation was ludicrous and people drank copious amounts of vodka to cope. This will be amplified, multiplied and magnified when the antichrist comes to power. The elite will enjoy luxurious living while the working class will fall below the poverty line.

When Jesus opens the fourth seal, a pale horse was released and "Its rider was named death, and Hades was following close behind him. They were given power over a fourth of the earth to kill by sword, famine and plague, and by the wild beasts of the earth." Revelation 6:8. COVID 19 and civil unrest in response to the draconian control measures implemented to control it are just precursors of this rider's arsenal that will also be combined with wild animals preying on humans. I think it's important to recognize that none of these seals are the outpouring of God's wrath yet. These are the result of mankind's sin in a fallen world and the pinnacle of that sin is murder through abortion and a genetically modified virus that together kill millions. The third and fourth seals are the logical fallout to the wars and devastation of the second seal.

When the fifth seal is opened, John sees the souls of all those who were slain because of the word of God. These include all of the martyrs from the first century right up until the present day. There are currently more Christians being persecuted now than at any time previously including during the Roman Empire. These souls ask God, "How long, Sovereign Lord, holy and true, until you judge the inhabitants of the earth and avenge our blood?" Revelation 6:10. The gravity of their request is a sobering thought for those who believe in the goodness of man and deny our need for redemption. Someone has to take responsibility for the deaths of the martyrs. Someone has to be held accountable. Someone will be held accountable.

The sixth seal precipitates a great earthquake when it is opened, and the sun turns black, the moon turns red and the stars fall from the sky, which recedes like a scroll being rolled up and every mountain and island is removed from its place. Just as Jesus described in the twenty-first chapter of Luke, "There will be signs in the sun, moon and stars. On the earth, nations will be in anguish and perplexity at the roaring and the tossing of the sea. People will faint from terror, apprehensive of what is coming on the world, for the heavenly bodies will be shaken." Luke 21:25-26. The panic stricken people of the earth hide wherever they can and beg to escape and even be killed rather than face what is about to happen. This ominous vision is when God begins to pour out his wrath. "During those days men swill seek death, but will not find it; they will long to die, but death will elude them." Revelation 9:6.

At this point in the book of Revelation there are several things happening simultaneously and in rapid succession. What John sees in heaven and what is happening on the earth seem to overlap and do not necessarily represent chronological order in the way scripture lays them out. The seven-year tribulation reaches its mid-point and quickly proceeds to the culmination of world events in the second 42 months.

John then sees a great multitude that no one could count, wearing white robes and is told that they have come out of the great tribulation. These are the Church, the true believers in Christ who have been raptured. Let me explain why I believe these are not those who are killed for refusing to worship the antichrist. Their number is uncountable. After the rapture, those left on the earth will not have the discernment, the wisdom or the resolve to refuse to worship the antichrist in the face of death. Most will embrace him as the savior of the world as they willingly take his mark. There will of course be many Christians who are left behind after the rapture of the saints that come to their senses, but comparatively speaking, their number will be small.

One has to remember that the orthodox Jews are anticipating the arrival of their Messiah and will be proclaiming the antichrist as their man. Those not well grounded in scripture will lack the discernment to recognize who they are actually dealing with and will not know the difference between a false Messiah and the real thing. A great many will be deceived.

The seventh chapter of the book of Revelation introduces the divine protection of the remnant of Israel that will be saved. Twelve thousand people from each of the 12 original tribes of Israel, totaling 144,000 representing all of Israel. This is the same remnant that the apostle Paul wrote about in the eleventh chapter of Romans. "I do not want you to be ignorant of this mystery, brothers and sisters, so that you may not be conceited: Israel has experienced a hardening in part until the full number of Gentiles has come in, and in this way all Israel will be saved." Romans 11:25-26. What Paul is intimating here is not that every Israelis will be saved but all of Israel as represented by the 12 tribes equally. Additionally, when the full number of the Gentiles comes in is when the rapture of the Church happens. The dominoes fall quickly once the sixth seal is opened.

The true Church whose faith is credited to them as righteousness, stands as the pure bride of Christ before the throne of God. "These are they who have come out of the great tribulation; they have washed their robes and made them white as snow in the blood of the Lamb." Revelation 7:14. What a beautiful thing to be among that multitude! Paul wrote that the rapture of the Church would not occur until the man of lawlessness was revealed (2 Thessalonians 2:3), therefore the timing here is after Revelation 13 when the antichrist's true nature is revealed and he demands to be worshipped. Additionally, the one who holds the secret power of lawlessness back, will continue to do so until he is taken out of the way (2 Thessalonians 2:7). "And then the lawless one will be revealed, whom the Lord Jesus will overthrow with the breath of his mouth and destroy by the splendor of his coming." 2 Thessalonians 2:8. The Holy Spirit is withdrawn from the earth, the antichrist is revealed and the rapture all happen in rapid fire succession beginning with the seventh seal and proceeding to the seventh and final trumpet in a very short time. This concludes the Church age or the age of grace and ushers in the next age, the day of the Lord, the age of judgement.

Meanwhile, the seventh seal is opened and "there was silence in heaven for about half an hour." Revelation 8:1. Symbolic of the seventh day of creation when God rested, heaven rests for a short time after the seven seals have been opened. Then seven angels are given seven trumpets. The seventh seal is paralleled in other prophesies and its duration continues until the end of the book of Revelation. It is regarded as the "day of the Lord".

"For the day is near, the day of the Lord is near – a day of clouds, a time of doom for the nations." Ezekiel 30:3.

"Alas for that day! For the day of the Lord is near; it will come like destruction from the Almighty." Joel 1:15.

"Blow the trumpet in Zion, sound the alarm on my holy hill. Let all who live in the land tremble, for the day of the Lord is coming. It is close at hand –" Joel 2:1

"The sun will be turned to darkness and the moon to blood before the coming of the great and dreadful day of the Lord." Joel 2:31.

"'Therefore wait for me,' declares the Lord, 'for the day I will stand up to testify. I have decided to assemble the nations, to gather the kingdoms and to pour out my wrath upon them – all my fierce anger. The whole world will be consumed by the fire of my jealous anger.'" Zephaniah 3:8

"The sun will be turned to darkness and the moon to blood before the coming of the great and glorious day of the Lord." Acts 2:20.

"But the day of the Lord will come like a thief. The heavens will disappear with a roar; the elements will be destroyed by fire. And the earth and everything done in it will be laid bare." 2 Peter 3:10.

The seven trumpets are a series of plagues and wars as God delivers justice onto unrepentant man. This is very similar in theme to what he did to pharaoh when he would not let Israel leave Egypt. At the sound of the first trumpet, hail and fire mixed with blood fall upon the earth. This is serious stuff. A third of the earth is burned up including a third of all the trees and all the green grass. The fires of Australia, California, British Columbia and Siberia might look pale by comparison.

When the second trumpet sounds, "something like a huge mountain, all ablaze, was thrown into the sea." Revelation 8:8. This sounds to me like a gigantic asteroid that NASA will be awestruck by. Scientists estimate that there are several dozen close approaches by asteroids each year. These pass within one lunar distance of the earth which means they are closer than the moon to the earth. If a large enough asteroid were to pass this close, the gravitational pulls could very possibly result in a collision with disastrous consequences. An event of this magnitude would kill a large portion of sea creatures and create tsunamis that would destroy many coastal cities and kill millions of people.

The third trumpet could very well be a second asteroid since it is described as "a great star, blazing like a torch, fell from the sky." Revelation 8:10. A third of the earth's water will be poisoned by this asteroid resulting in the deaths of many more people. Perhaps it is a nuclear ICBM that makes it through the defensive safety net of a nation creating massive radioactive fallout that contaminates the water.

When the fourth trumpet sounds, the light of the sun, moon and stars is reduced by a third and a third of the day and a third of the night are without light. The smoke from fires and volcanic ash will block out the sun and moon by a third and result in crop failures and food shortages equivalent to a nuclear winter. However, mankind remains unrepentant just as pharaoh did when God struck him with the plagues in Egypt.

These first four trumpets are warnings. John then sees a giant eagle flying over the earth, calling, "Woe! Woe! Woe to the inhabitants of the earth, because of the trumpet blasts about to be sounded by the other three angels!" Revelation 8:13.

The fifth angel blows his trumpet and what seems to be a gigantic earthquake to the very core of the planet sends mountains of smoke into the atmosphere blocking out the sun. As if this isn't bad enough locusts with the power of scorpions descend upon the earth and torture the inhabitants of the earth for five months. The Church is still on earth at this point and will be divinely protected from this pestilence. In the same way that believers are called to understanding regarding the antichrist, "This calls for patient endurance on the part of the saints who obey God's commands and remain faithful to Jesus." Revelation 14:12, the Church must endure witnessing the chaos for a short period. Jesus also spoke of this time when he said, "Because of the increase of wickedness, the love of most will grow cold, but the one who stands firm to the end will be saved." Mathew 24:12. The end Jesus is speaking of here is the end of the age of the Church which occurs at the time of the rapture and not the end of the world at Armageddon.

When the sixth trumpet blows, there is a massive war involving two hundred million troops which will result in the death of one third of mankind. Those that remain afterward still do not repent and continue in their carnality. Two witnesses of Christ begin to prophesy in Jerusalem at this time, and they will continue to do so for 1260 days. They have the power to control the weather so that it does not rain while they are prophesying. They are eventually killed by the antichrist and their bodies lie in the street for three and a half days while the world gloats over them and celebrates by sending each other gifts (Revelation 11:10). Then just like Jesus, their bodies come alive after the three and a half days and they stand to their feet, terrifying the population. Then a loud voice comes from heaven and calls them up and they ascend on clouds just like Jesus did. Following this there is a huge earthquake and seven thousand people are killed in the city.

There are many students of scripture who view the two witnesses as allegoric and symbols of two witness movements, however, they are given human characteristics by John and could be interpreted literally as two prophets of God with God given supernatural powers. Some have postulated the witnesses as the prophet Elijah and Moses because Jesus visited with these two dignitaries at his transfiguration (Mathew 17). However, when we examine the language of Revelation 11:4 we are told they are two olive trees and two lampstands. The olive tree has always been symbolic of the nation of Israel and the apostle Paul elaborates in the eleventh chapter of Romans how the Gentiles who believe in Christ are grafted in as wild olive shoots on a cultivated olive root (Romans 11:11-31). The two olive trees are thus the Jewish believers and Christians.

Furthermore, lampstands are associated with churches in the first chapter of Revelation when the angel explains to John that, "The mystery of the seven stars that you saw in my right hand and the golden lampstands is this: The seven stars are the angels of the seven churches and, the seven lampstands are the churches." Revelation 1:20. This means that the two witnesses are two people groups, the Messianic Jews and the true Church, the body of believers with true faith in Jesus.

These two witnesses are blessed with great power to do supernatural things, meaning the true Church and converted Jews will be filled with the Holy Spirit in much the same way the disciples and the early Church believers were in the first century. "In the last days, God says, I will pour out my Spirit on all people. Your sons and daughters will prophesy, your young men will see visions, your old men will dream dreams." Acts 2:17. The narrative goes on to say this will happen just before the Lord returns (Acts 2:18-20).

"Now when they have finished their testimony, the beast that comes up from the abyss will attack them, and overpower and kill them." Revelation 11:7. Their bodies will lie in the streets and they will be refused burial but after three and a half days they are given the breath of life from God and they will rise, ready to be raptured.

The seventh trumpet is the last trumpet. This is the moment in time when the rapture takes place. Paul wrote, "Listen, I tell you a mystery: We will not all sleep, but we will all be changed – in a flash, in the twinkling of an eye, at the last trumpet. For the trumpet will sound, the dead will be raised imperishable, and we will be changed." 1 Corinthians 15:51-52.

Things are happening very quickly as I indicated to earlier, like dominoes falling, and even simultaneously with other events. Just as the angel says in Revelation 10:6, "There will be no more delay!" There will be mayhem and confusion as the sky tears apart, the stars fall, the earth shakes and death and destruction are everywhere.

The rapture will occur at a moment that will remain unknown however Jesus did provide signs that would precede it. He said it would be like the days of Noah, "For in the days before the flood, people were eating and drinking, marrying and giving in marriage, up to the day Noah entered the ark; and they knew nothing about what would happen until the flood came and took them all away." Mathew 24:38-39. The gospel of Luke records Jesus saying, "When these things begin to take place, stand up and lift your heads, because your redemption is drawing near." Luke 21:28. Even today our situational awareness should be on full alert as things can progress very quickly along the prophetic timeline. COVID 19 is a case in point where the world economy screeched to a halt in a matter of a few days.

In the twelfth chapter of Revelation John is given a vision of a pregnant woman with a crown of twelve stars. This is none other than the nation of Israel. The child she is about to give birth to is of course Jesus. However, "Then another sign appeared in heaven: an enormous red dragon with seven heads and ten horns and seven crowns on its heads." Revelation 12:3. The dragon is Satan and the scripture says he wanted to devour her baby boy as soon as he was born, which symbolizes the crucifixion of Christ, however, he was snatched up to heaven, referring to his resurrection and ascension.

Revelation 12 illustrates how heaven and God himself are outside of time and matter. This eternal nature is dovetailed into events that occurred 2000 years ago yet are still unfolding today and will continue to do so until the end of time, yet seems neatly instantaneous in scripture. Then there is a battle in heaven between Michael and his angels and Satan and his angels and Satan is hurled down to the earth. He then pursues the woman (Israel) until she is supernaturally delivered. What is so amazing about this is that it illustrates how God's ways are higher than our ways and what we see as a historical defeat for Jerusalem and the Jews, God uses to preserve their culture and identity. The Romans destroyed Jerusalem and the temple in

AD 70 and the Jews were dispersed among the nations in what amounts to divine protection from Roman annihilation.

We often ponder why God seems to let bad things happen to good people but we must always remember what Isaiah wrote, "'For my thoughts are not your thoughts, neither are your ways my ways,' declares the Lord. 'As the heavens are higher than the earth, so are my ways higher than your ways and my thoughts than your thoughts.'" Isaiah 55:8-9.

The dragon (Satan) then was enraged and went off to make war against those who obey God's commandments and hold to the testimony of Jesus. This signifies the persecution of Christians which was already occurring and continued right through the middle ages of the inquisition and the burning of martyrs at the stake by the institution of the church, continues today in parts of the world and will continue until the rapture. The chapter closes with the dragon standing on the shore of the sea.

Chapter thirteen begins with a beast with ten horns and seven heads and ten crowns on its horns, closely resembling the dragon, intimating their genetic and relational proximity. Anyone who has seen the movie Rosemarie's Baby will recall the scene where she copulates with a satanic looking being in a ritual like ceremony after which she conceives a child which turns out to be Satan's son. With the wealthy elite's penchant for strange perversions and alleged Satan worship, perhaps there is more fact than fiction to this movie which was released in 1968. That would make the antichrist 53 years old in 2021. The dragon (Satan) gives this beast (the antichrist) his power and authority. In the same way that Jesus was given the power and authority of his Father, God during his earthly ministry, the counterfeit Christ is given the power and authority of his father the devil. Just as Jesus's human ancestry traced back to King David, the antichrist's will include the lineage of the families in the cabal.

The identity of the horns and crowns is disclosed in the 17th chapter of Revelation, so let's jump ahead and find out just what John is writing about. "This calls for a mind of wisdom. The seven heads are seven hills on which the woman sits. They are also seven kings. Five have fallen, one is the other has not yet come; but when he does come, he must remain for a little while." Revelation 17:9-10. John goes on to say that the beast itself is the eighth king. The seven hills are Rome, since the city contains seven hills, namely, Palatine Hill, Capitoline Hill, Aventine Hill, Caelian

Hill, Esquiline Hill, Quirinal Hill and Viminal Hill. Also these seven heads represent seven kings, paralleling Daniel's vision of four beasts representing the kingdoms of Babylon, Medo-Persia, Greece and Rome. The scripture says however that there are seven kingdoms, five have which had fallen when John wrote Revelation. This discloses that Rome is the kingdom that "is" when John saw the vision. Therefore, Babylon, Medo-Persia and Greece must be kingdoms 3, 4 and 5, so the first two had to have fallen prior to the time that Daniel wrote in the sixth century before Christ. These are accepted as Egypt and Assyria since these kingdoms also oppressed the Israelites.

Daniel wrote about another vision, this time a dream by King Nebuchadnezzar of a statue which Daniel interpreted for him. The statue had a head of gold, its chest and arms were of silver, its belly and thighs were of bronze, its legs were iron and its feet were of iron mixed with clay. The statue also represented kingdoms. The head of gold was Nebuchadnezzar's kingdom of Babylon, the silver chest was the Medo-Persian empire that followed, the bronze belly and thighs were the Greek empire and Rome was the kingdom of Iron, however, its existence is two-fold. Daniel explained it as a divided kingdom (Daniel 2::41) since the feet are different from the legs. The ten toes correlate to the ten crowns the beast wears. The statue of Daniel 2 infers world kingdoms of influence as seen from man's perspective. The four beasts of Daniel 7 represent these same four kingdoms from God's perspective, that of beasts.

"One of the heads of the beast seemed to have had a fatal wound, but the fatal wound had been healed." Revelation 13:3. This is a mimicking of the death and resurrection of Jesus. In order to determine the meaning of this verse, we must go all the way back to the garden of Eden and the original sin. When God asked Adam if he had eaten of the tree, "The man said, 'The woman you put here with me – she gave me some fruit from the tree, and I ate it.' Then the Lord God said to the woman. 'What is this you have done?' The woman said, 'The serpent deceived me, and I ate.'

So the Lord God said to the serpent, 'Because you have done this, 'Cursed are you above all livestock and all wild animals! You will crawl on your belly and you will eat the dust all the days of your life. And I will put enmity between you and the woman, between your offspring and hers; he will crush your head, and you will strike his heel.'" Genesis 3:12-15.

The reason Jesus came to earth was to defeat Satan (1 John 3:8). Satan bruised Christ's heel by taking ahold of Judas Iscariot, causing him to betray Jesus, ultimately leading to his crucifixion. Jesus delivered a mortal wound to the devil by resurrecting and conquering death. "Therefore God exalted him to the highest place and gave him the name that is above every name." Philippians 2:9. This biblical truth will be brought into question when the antichrist comes to power and demands to be worshipped as God.

The antichrist will seem insurmountable as a leader and compel the whole world to follow him. He will also be arrogant and blaspheme and slander the name of God. The only people who will not worship him will be true believers. "This calls for patient endurance and faithfulness on the part of the saints." Revelation 13:10. That the antichrist is an individual person and not a system or symbol is reinforced by the number of the beast, "This calls for wisdom. If anyone has insight, let him calculate the number of the beast, for it is a man's number. His number is 666." Revelation 13:18.

The person of the antichrist and what he represents will not be revealed until the time when he can no longer be stopped from a human perspective. In this same way, the cabal that operates covertly to run the world will one day come out into the open once their power and control are beyond any points of resistance in the world. Paul wrote, "And now you know what is holding him back, so that he may be revealed at the proper time. For the secret power of lawlessness is already at work; but the one who holds it back will continue to do so until he is taken out of the way. And then the lawless one will be revealed, whom the Lord Jesus will overthrow with the breath of his mouth and destroy by the splendor of his coming." 2 Thessalonians 2:6-8.

The antichrist will emerge from an oligarchy that includes royalty, wealth, power and influence. He will also be a descendant of the Roman Empire in fulfillment of Daniel 9:26. As he rises above the covert history of his predecessors, he will revel in the limelight as his brand of plutocracy has the completely deluded populations of the post-truth generation eating out of the palm of his hand. In the same way that celebrities and sports stars are envied and emulated, he will capture the imaginations of the materialistic, liberal "woke" and "progressive" opponents of God who call evil good and good evil, with charisma and stature, and his wealth will provide instant credibility to his message.

He will make the UN his platform to preach of a better way to solve the world's increasing problems of poverty, starvation, climate change, civil unrest, wealth inequality and the middle east problem, all while turning a blind eye to the sexual perversion, drug and alcohol abuse and the corruption rampant among his elite class. The deep state will rally behind him and the masses will adore him. He will be quick to provide solutions and his influence will garner the admiration of Pope Francis who will become his trusted ally. Together they will claim to right the wrongs of the past and endeavor to issue in a utopian age with a new world order consisting of a one world government and one world religion to the applause of everyone without the Holy Spirit.

In John's next vision, he sees another beast, this time it comes up out of the earth. "He had two horns like a lamb, but he spoke like a dragon." Revelation 13:11 The implication here is a gentle demeanor implying religious connotations combined with deceitful words. I believe it is important to resist the temptation to correlate this figure with an institution or a movement since the attributes given to it are personal. This beast is the false prophet, the leader of the apostate church that will teach that all people worship God in their own way, that there are several paths to salvation and that church doctrine is more authoritative than the Bible. He is later described in chapter 19:20 and again in chapter 20:10, which states, "And the devil, who deceived them, was thrown into the lake of burning sulfur, where the beast and the false prophet were thrown." Two beasts and the dragon depicting the antichrist, the false prophet and Satan. Together, the constitute the unholy trinity.

The false prophet is given power to do miraculous signs and wonders, even causing fire to come down from heaven (Revelation 13:13). The coming tribulation will be a spiritual time and even though the Holy Spirit will be filling believers and empowering them (as it is already) to heal and see visions, Satan will diminish those accomplishments with supernatural power of his own. It is at this point, in the middle of a world stage filled with mayhem and chaos that the antichrist will set up the abomination that causes desolation, spoken of by the prophet Daniel (Daniel 12:11) in the rebuilt temple in Jerusalem. Jesus also prophesied about it saying, "So when you see standing in the holy place 'the abomination that causes desolation,' spoken of through the prophet Daniel – let the reader understand – then let those who are in Judea flee to the mountains." Mathew 24:15-16.

Preterists will have you believe that these events were all fulfilled in AD 70 when the temple was destroyed by the Romans, even to the point of suggesting the book of Revelation was written in the 60's rather than the accepted date of around 95 AD. One of the strongest pieces of evidence countering this view is the fact that in the 60's, there was not yet any church in Laodicea (Revelation 3:14) therefore how could John write to one? Additionally, the evidence is overwhelming that we are surrounded by the signs preceding the return of Christ in this present age. There are others who hold the book of Revelation strictly to allegory however that view is counterintuitive since every old testament prophecy that was fulfilled regarding Jesus was fulfilled literally. When Jesus foretold the destruction of the temple in Mathew 24:2, "'Do you see all these things?' he asked. 'Truly I tell you, not one stone will here will be left on another, every one will be thrown down.'" When the Romans destroyed the temple, the fire was so hot that all the gold melted and ran down between the rocks of the foundation. The Roman soldiers literally pried every stone apart to get at the gold.

At this point in the earthly timeline, the antichrist will impose the "mark of the beast, "He also forced everyone, small and great, rich and poor, free and slave, to receive a mark on his right hand or on his forehead, so that no one could buy or sell unless he had the mark, which is the name of the beast or the number of its name." Revelation 13:16-17. For the first time in history, the technology now exists with quantum dot tattoos, micro-chip implants, digital banking and e-transfers of funds along with one central digital clearing house capable of monitoring all transactions in the world. What was incomprehensible only a few short decades ago is now reality and it illustrates just how literal the book of Revelation can and will be fulfilled.

Why has God waited so long to judge the evil and destroy Satan? Why has he allowed evil to flourish and corruption to grow, for violence to become so prevalent among mankind? What is the point of permitting humanity to carry on through so many wars that destroyed millions of lives? Why has he allowed so much heartache and pain? It has been 2000 years since Jesus ascended to heaven to prepare a place for believers. The apostle Peter wrote, "Above all you must understand that in the last days scoffers will come, scoffing and following their own evil desires. They will say, 'Where is this 'coming' he promised? Ever since our ancestors died, everything goes on as it has since the beginning of creation.' But they deliberately forget that long ago by God's word the heavens came into being and the earth was formed out of water and by water. By these waters also the world of that time was deluged and destroyed. By the same word the present heavens and earth are reserved for fire, being kept for the day of judgement and destruction of the ungodly.

But do not forget this one thing, dear friends: With the Lord a day is like a thousand years, and a thousand years are like a day. The Lord is not slow in keeping his promise, as some understand slowness. Instead he is patient with you, not wanting anyone to perish, but everyone to come to repentance." 2 Peter 3:3-9.

God is patient, waiting on the full number of Gentiles destined to repent and be saved to come into his family. In the same way that he was willing to spare Sodom and Gomorah if Lot could find anyone righteous, he is providing humanity today with the opportunity to repent. He has extended the olive branch, put in place the pardon and offered the gift of salvation to anyone who believes in Jesus Christ and his resurrection.

In my first book, *Truth Cries Out,* I wrote about the harvest that Jesus spoke of and how humanity was like a growing crop. There comes a time when the crop is mature, that it must be harvested or it will go to waste. That crop is now mature and is ready to yield its bounty. There are currently more people alive than have lived in all of human history combined. Jesus said, "Very truly I tell you, unless a kernel of wheat falls to the ground and dies, it remains only one seed. But if it dies, it produces many seeds." John 12:24. Humanity has grown for many generations. People have reproduced and then died in the cycle of life for thousands of years. The gospel has been shared throughout the world and now more than at any time previously, there are more souls to save and fill heaven with and The Lord is ready to harvest the earth.

However, God is also just and he will judge the world and evil will not go unpunished. Pre-tribulation rapture proponents point out that Paul wrote, "For God did not appoint us to suffer wrath but to receive salvation through our Lord Jesus Christ." 1 Thessalonians 5:9. However, everything up until this point has been the result of humanity's sin and acceptance of evil living in their midst. The first half of the Great Tribulation is a warning period in response to mankind's decadence, unrestrained evil and hardness of heart.

It is tribulation and hardship, and while it will be horrible considering the pain and suffering it will inflict upon civilization, the wrath of God has not even begun to be poured out yet. It is this wrath that Paul was speaking of in 1 Thessalonians 5:9. This will be examined fully in the next chapter.

THE WRATH OF GOD

"The secret things belong to the Lord, but the things revealed belong to us and to our children forever, that we may follow all the words of the law." Deuteronomy 29:29. When the Prophet Daniel was given insight into the last days, he was told, "Go your way, Daniel, because the words are rolled up and sealed until the time of the end. Many will be purified, made spotless and refined, but the wicked will continue to be wicked. None of the wicked will understand, but those who are wise will understand." Daniel 12:9-10.

There is a great deal of overlap between the Book of Revelation, the seventieth week of Daniel's prophecy (specifically Daniel 9:27) and Jesus's words in Mathew 24, which help to navigate through the symbolism and signs of the book. Throughout the Bible, prophecy is always fulfilled literally and those that attempt to interpret Revelation without that same degree of literalness, will find it confusing and abstract in nature. Applying this principle of literal interpretation yields a much clearer revelation that maintains remarkable cohesiveness with other prophetic scriptures within the Bible.

There is no doubt that God will punish the nations of the earth for their idolatries and disobedience as is foretold in the Bible. Understanding that God's wrath is a response to sin is fundamental to recognizing that he loves us and has extended an olive branch to humanity through Jesus Christ. Despite all that the inhabitants of the earth will experience in the coming tribulation, we must acknowledge that God is sovereign and seek the attributes of who he is. The Bible says God is love, "Whoever does not love does not know God, because God is love. 1 John 4:8. In fact the entire 4th chapter of 1 John makes a very sound apology of God's love for us. God's wrath within the context of Revelation is not necessarily anger but judgement expressed as wrath.

God is slow to anger, and he is patient. He tolerates evil so through it all, the door is always open to repent and be saved. The apostle Peter wrote, "The Lord is not slow in keeping his promise, as some understand slowness. He is patient with you, not wanting anyone to perish, but everyone to come to repentance." 2 Peter 3:9. As we witness the moral fabric of humanity disintegrating and signs that God's wrath is about to be poured out onto the world, we must take notice that the time is short and when the full number of Gentiles has come in, the door will be closed and it will be too late. Throughout the Bible we are told how God's wrath has been stored up from the beginning when sin first entered the world. Because God is just, he cannot allow sin to go unpunished so the time will come when he will reimburse the wages of every sin and bring judgement to every evil. "For the great day of their wrath has come, and who can withstand it?" Revelation 6:17

God's wrath is not disproportionate to sin and while we see enormous pain and suffering, we must view it from the perspective of the holiness of God. He is so pure that sin cannot enter his presence and even our best deeds are like filthy rags when compared to his holiness. God hates the sin but loves the sinner, so when we repent and turn from our sin, we receive the full measure of his love. When we don't, we deserve the full measure of his wrath. We must never forget that while we were still sinners, God sent his only Son to die for us. Christ died for us because of God's love for us.

The twelfth chapter of Daniel contains a parallel prophecy of the end times to what we find in the New Testament. "At that time Michael, the great prince who protects your people, will arise. There will be a time of distress such as has not happened from the beginning of nations until then. But at that time your people – everyone whose name is found written in the book – will be delivered. Multitudes who sleep in the earth will awake: some to everlasting life, others to shame and contempt. Those who are wise will shine like the brightness of the heavens, and those who lead many to righteousness, like the stars for ever and ever. But you, Daniel, close up and seal the words of the scroll until the time of the end. Many will go here and there to increase knowledge." Daniel 9:1-4

In Daniel's vision the angel tells him the length of time it will take to accomplish this time of distress and fulfill the prophesy. "The man clothed in linen, who was above the waters of the river, lifted his right hand and his left hand toward heaven, and I heard him swear by him who lives forever, saying, 'It will be for a time, times and a half time. When the power of the holy people has been finally broken, all these things will be accomplished.'" Daniel 12:7. Daniel is talking about the same three and a half years that the beast is given to rule in Revelation 13:5, "The beast was given a mouth to utter proud words and blasphemies and to exercise his authority for forty-two months."

It is these three and one half years that God pours his wrath out onto the earth to punish the nations for their transgressions against him. There will be a lot of things happening simultaneously and I believe the chaos and mayhem will be absolutely terrifying. John wrote, "Then I saw another angel flying in mid-air, and he had the eternal gospel to proclaim to those who live on the earth – to every nation, tribe, language and people. He said in a loud voice, 'Fear God and give him glory, because the hour of his judgement has come. Worship him who made the heavens, the earth, the sea and the springs of water.'" Revelation 14:6-7.

God will call his people home before he pours his wrath out on the world. Paul wrote, "For God din not appoint us to suffer wrath but to receive salvation through our Lord Jesus Christ." 1 Thessalonians 5:9. I don't see anywhere in scripture that the rapture will occur before the tribulation, however, once the man of lawlessness is revealed and sets up the abomination of desolation (Daniel 11:31, Daniel 12:11, Mathew 24:15, Revelation 13:14-15, 2 Thessalonians 2:3-4), the seventh and final trumpet will sound and Jesus will fetch his bride (the Church).

It is at this point when the age of grace ends and the age of judgement begins. Before I go any further I just want to make a quick commentary on hermeneutics and dispensationalism. Understanding that scripture does not contradict itself and that the New Testament in no way, shape or form supersedes the Old Testament is essential to interpreting the Bible. God's promises to the nation of Israel in the Old Testament will all be literally fulfilled in the future, just as Christ's promises to believers will.

The Gentile nations all benefit from Israel's rejection of their Messiah, however, the time will come when Israel itself will accept him. The Apostle Paul wrote, "I do not want you to be ignorant of this mystery, brothers and sisters, so that you may not be conceited: Israel has experienced a hardening in part until the full number of Gentiles has come in, and in this way all Israel will be saved." Romans 11:25-26.

Dispensationalism divides biblical history into time periods or dispensations, that align with God's treatment of humanity and distinguishes between Israel and the Church. The Old Testament and the four gospels of the New Testament consists primarily of God's interactions with the nation of Israel, while the Church age begins on the day of Pentecost in the second chapter of the book of Acts. The Church age will end with the rapture of believers and will be followed by a period of judgement, followed by Christ's return and millennial reign on earth, after which God will destroy the heavens and earth and replace them with the eternal heavens and earth. Some theologians will further divide the Old Testament into pre-flood and post-flood, or other dispensations.

Additionally, just as the Holy Spirit came into the world on the Day of Pentecost at the beginning of the Church age, He will be withdrawn from the world at the end of the Church age at the rapture. Paul tells us how the Holy Spirit is what holds the antichrist back from being revealed until the time is right. "For the secret power of lawlessness is already at work; but the one who holds it back will continue to do so till he is taken out of the way." 2 Thessalonians 2:7. Like dominoes falling, the events at the midpoint of the Great Tribulation will occur in rapid fire sequence, one triggering the next and many simultaneously as the world will transition into the age of judgement.

Also of significance is the Day of Atonement (Leviticus 16) as it marked the annual close of Israel's judgement for the year. There are many parallels and dual implications throughout scripture and as I stated earlier regarding dispensationalism, new revelations must harmonize with older revelations in scripture and do not change, alter or modify previous scriptures. In the same way that Moses was appointed by God to lead Israel out of Egypt and their enslavement, Jesus was appointed to lead all people out of our bondage to sin. And just as the Israelites were tested in the desert, we are also tested in our lives and only those who remain faithful can enter the promised land.

Moses was the mediator between God and Israel and Jesus became our mediator when the curtain of the temple was torn in two at his crucifixion. "For this reason Christ is the mediator of a new covenant, that those who are called may receive the promised eternal inheritance" Hebrews 9:15. When Moses went up to meet God on Mt. Sinai and receive the ten commandments, he was gone for forty days. The people grew tired of waiting for him to return and rather than remaining faithful, they conjured up excuses to justify pressuring Aaron to make a golden calf. "So the next day the people rose early and sacrificed burnt offerings. Afterwards they sat down to eat and drink and got up to indulge in revelry." Exodus 32:6.

Before Jesus ascended to heaven, he promised he would return. Just as Moses did not immediately return, Jesus also has been away a long time. Humanity's response is much the same as that of the Israelites, including falling away from the faith, mocking God and indulging in debauchery. Peter wrote about the last days in his second epistle, "First of all you must understand that in the last days scoffers will come, scoffing and following their own evil desires. They will say, 'Where is this 'coming' he promised? 2 Peter 3:3-4. And Just as Moses drew a line in the sand and commanded the people to make a choice to be with God or be punished, Jesus offers that same choice. When Christ returns for his Church, those who remain afterwards will meet with God's wrath, and he will not hold back.

When Jesus appeared to the disciples after his resurrection, "He said to them, 'This is what I told you when I was with you: Everything must be fulfilled that is written about me in the Law of Moses, the Prophets and the Psalms. Then he opened their minds so they could understand the Scriptures." Luke 24:44 -45. He showed them the profound beauty and completeness of God's eternal plan by tying everything together for them. We now must endeavor to understand the prophecies written for the last generation of the age. To seek the will of God through discernment provided historically in the pages of the Bible and by the Holy Spirit as our guide.

Despite the twisted messages of the prosperity gospel and progressive Christianity, the Bible is clear that God will judge humanity for its ongoing sin. This sin and rejection of God will reach its pinnacle in the second half of the tribulation when all of the world will serve the antichrist and do so gladly. Evil in the world will become so prolific and perverted that humans will revel in the lies of liberalism, materialism and sexuality. We are already seeing the precursor to this where good is called evil and evil is called good by society. Just imagine it without a conservative and Godly opposition with no Christians remaining.

Through a one world government combined with a one world religion, without resistance the antichrist's control will be total and complete. The world will believe it has finally produced a utopian society and celebrate mankind as the creator of his own destiny. When the antichrist demands to be worshipped as god, society will gladly comply, believing he has rescued them from the evils of the past, including Christianity and morality. However, the party will be short-lived as God sends seven plagues and pours out seven bowls of judgement on the earth.

Signs of the insidious nature of the antichrist begin to surface when anyone not willing to worship him as a god are sentenced to death. This combined with the rapture of the true Church will awaken some to the peril of the moment and will begin a migration of truth seekers who realize the Bible is true. They will become obstinate to the antichrist and will be martyred for their newfound faith. The two witnesses mentioned earlier will have no doubt planted the seeds that grow into dissension from the false prophet and his counterfeit religion. "Then I heard a voice from heaven say, 'Write: Blessed are the dead who die in the Lord from now on.'" Revelation 14:13.

At this time, John saw three angels and heard three proclamations. First, he saw an angel with the eternal gospel who proclaimed it to every nation, tribe, language and people. Second, an angel proclaimed that Babylon the Great had fallen. This is the apostate church that adulterated the gospel and became a one world religion. The third angel proclaimed that anyone who worshipped the antichrist and accepted his mark was condemned to everlasting torment and they would drink full strength the wine of God's wrath.

John then sees God's temple in heaven and angels emerge and proclaim that the time to harvest the earth has arrived and the grapes of the earth would be gathered and cast into the winepress of God's wrath. Blood flowed on the earth as high as a horse's bridle. At this point the seven bowls of God's wrath commence to be poured out.

John sees seven angels with the seven last plagues in the fifteenth chapter of Revelation. They are called the last because they represent the last of God's wrath and the conclusion of judgement of the inhabitants of the world. These angels are instructed to pour seven bowls of God's wrath on the earth. These bowl judgements are very similar to the seven trumpets insofar as the first is directed at the land, the second at the sea, the third with rivers and fountains of water, the fourth the sun, the fifth darkness, the sixth the Euphrates River and the seventh at lightning, thunder and a great earthquake. They are not however, the same judgements since there are differences in magnitude and chronological timing.

"The first angel went and poured out his bowl on the land, and ugly sores broke out on the people who had the mark of the beast and worshipped his image." Revelation 16:2. More than unsightly, these sores will no doubt include pain and suffering through infection and irritation. "The second angel poured out his bowl on the sea, and it turned into blood like that of a dead man, and every living thing in the sea died." When you consider that 71% of the earth is covered by water and how much mankind relies on the earth's oceans for food, starvation will become widespread very quickly and it quickly becomes apparent that "If those days had not been cut short, no flesh would survive, but for the sake of the elect those days will be shortened." Mathew 24:22.

"The third angel poured out his bowl on the rivers and springs of water, and they became blood." Revelation 16:4. The angel justifies God's judgement by proclaiming that humanity has shed the blood of the saints and prophets therefore they deserve to drink blood. In the 23rd chapter of Mathew, Jesus issues seven warnings to the Teachers of the Law and the Pharisees. In the first he chastises them for impeding the relationship between God and his people. "Woe to you, teachers of the law and Pharisees, you hypocrites! You shut the door of the kingdom of heaven in people's faces. You yourselves do not enter, nor will you let those enter who are trying to." Mathew 23:13.

He goes on to reprimand them saying, "You travel over land and sea to win a single convert, and when you have succeeded, you make them twice as much a child of hell as you are." Mathew 23:15. Just as many, many

Christian denominations throughout the last two thousand years, through unforced errors in interpretation of scripture, have resulted in hypocrisy and heresies expressed as church dogmas, the Jewish religious leaders built a system of religion, not a fellowship of faith with the Lord. My second book *Seeking Truth* explores this in depth. Jesus calls these religious leaders blind guides, leading the people astray because of their lack of discernment and unwillingness to submit themselves completely to God therefore they taught from a human perspective and deviated from God's purposes.

"Woe to you, teachers of the law and Pharisees, you hypocrites! You give a tenth of your spices – mint, dill and cumin. But you have neglected the more important matters of the law – justice, mercy and faithfulness. You should have practiced the latter, without neglecting the former. You blind guides! You strain out a gnat but swallow a camel. Woe to you, teachers of the law and Pharisees, you hypocrites! You clean the outside of the cup and dish, but inside they are full of greed and self-indulgence. Blind Pharisees! First clean the inside of the cup and dish, and then the outside also will be clean. Woe to you, teachers of the law and Pharisees, you hypocrites! You are like whitewashed tombs, which look beautiful on the outside but on the inside are full of the bones of the dead and everything unclean. In the same way, on the outside you appear to people as righteous but on the inside you are full of hypocrisy and wickedness.

Woe to you, teachers of the law and Pharisees, you hypocrites! You build tombs for the prophets and decorate the graves of the righteous. And you say, 'If we had lived in the days of our ancestors, we would not have taken part with them in shedding the blood of the prophets. Go ahead and complete what your ancestors started! You snakes! You brood of vipers! How will you escape being condemned to hell? Therefore I am sending you prophets and sages and teachers. Some of them you will kill and crucify; others you will flog in your synagogues and pursue from town to town. And so upon you will come all the righteous blood that has been shed on earth, from the blood of righteous Abel to the blood of Zechariah son of Berekiah, whom you murdered between the temple and the altar. Truly I tell you, all this will come on this generation." Mathew 23:23-36.

The history of the Christian church under the papacy remarkably resembles the transgressions Jesus highlights in these passages of scripture. How many times throughout history has God sought correct the actions of his people only to be rejected over and over again. God's desire for us to be faithful and his immense love for his people was evident when Jesus made his triumphal entry into Jerusalem at the culmination of his earthly ministry. "As he approached Jerusalem and saw the city, he wept over it and said, 'If you, even you, had only known on this day what would bring you peace – but now it is hidden from your eyes." Luke 19:41. The gospel of Mathew narrates the same scene adding, "Jerusalem, Jerusalem, you who kill the prophets and stone those sent to you, how often I have longed to gather your children together, as a hen gathers her chicks under her wings, but you were not willing." Mathew 23:37. This intense love of the Father demonstrates why the following week is called the Passion that climaxed with the ultimate expression of God's love for humanity with the sacrifice of Jesus on the cross.

The Jewish religious leaders brought condemnation on themselves and all of Israel for murdering the prophets which resulted in the siege of Jerusalem in AD 70 and the destruction of the temple and the Jewish diaspora. The papacy and the corruption of the apostate church are guilty of the deaths of the Christian martyrs over the last two thousand years and they too will see justice for their treachery.

"The fourth angel poured out his bowl on the sun, and the sun was given power to scorch people with fire. They were seared by the intense heat and they cursed the name of God, who had control over these plagues, but they refused to repent and glorify him." Revelation 16:8-9. The true nature of the human heart is revealed here, as they refuse to accept God despite what are obviously divine judgements. Man's response in this theatre exemplifies how it is folly to believe that people will repent if they could only just witness God's supernatural power firsthand. Man didn't believe in Jesus rising from the dead and they won't believe God's display of divine judgement in the tribulation either.

"The fifth angel poured out his bowl on the throne of the beast, and his kingdom was plunged into darkness. Men gnawed their tongues in agony and cursed the God of heaven because of their pains and their sores, but they refused to repent of what they had done." Revelation 16:10-11. The tragedy of humanity's belligerence towards the Creator is truly a sad testimony to the fallen state of man. We see it in society even today when people are confronted with overwhelming evidence for the existence of

God yet they choose to deny him and mock those who preach the truth. If only humanity would see the error of their ways and repent before God is left with no choice but to pass judgement on civilization before it destroys itself.

"The sixth angel poured out his bowl on the great river Euphrates, and its water was dried up to prepare the way for the kings from the East." Revelation 16:12. The reason for this is to provide access for the invasion of Israel. The antichrist and the false prophet then summon the world's leaders to gather their armies for the battle of Armageddon. With his kingdom crumbling around him, the antichrist will focus his anger upon Israel, the only remnant of God's kingdom upon the earth. He will be so blinded in rage that he will settle for nothing less than every army in the world assembled together to annihilate the Jews. This is to be more than just a battle, it will be an all-out war and when the sign of Jesus's return appears in the heavens, all of the military might in the world will redirect their assault towards Christ and his armies approaching on the clouds of heaven.

Armageddon is Greek translated from the Hebrew Megiddo, which related to Mount Megiddo that is located adjacent to the plain of Megiddo in the middle east. This area witnessed many battles in the Old Testament, including Barak and the Canaanites (Judges 4) and Gideon and the Midianites (Judges 7) and also saw the deaths of Saul and Josiah.

"Look, I come like a thief! Blessed is the one who stays awake and remains clothed, so as not to go naked and be shamefully exposed." Revelation 16:15.

The proclamation in verse 15 is the fulfillment of predictions given by Jesus in Mathew 24:43 and Luke 12:39, comparing Christ's second coming to a thief. Paul uses this same comparison in 1Thessalonians 5:2 and Peter in 2 Peter 3:10. The apostle Paul states however, "But you, brothers and sisters, are not in darkness so that this day should surprise you like a thief. You are all children of the light and children of the day. We do not belong to the night or the darkness. So then, let us not be like others, who are asleep, but let us be awake and sober. For those who sleep, sleep at night, and those who get drunk, get drunk at night. But since we belong to the day, let us be sober, putting on faith and love as a breastplate, and the hope of salvation as a helmet. For God did not appoint us to suffer wrath but to receive salvation through our Lord Jesus Christ." 1 Thessalonians 5:4-9.

"The seventh angel poured out his bowl into the air, and out of the temple came a loud voice from the throne, saying 'It is done!' Then there came flashes of lightning, rumblings, peals of thunder and a severe earthquake. No earthquake like it has ever occurred since mankind has been on the earth, so tremendous was the quake." Revelation 16:17-18. This results in worldwide destruction that levels every mountain, destroys every island, every city and is punctuated by one hundred pound hailstones crushing men. The armies of the world are destroyed and Christ arrives as King of Kings and Lord of Lords.

Chapters 17 and 18 of revelation illustrate the destiny of Babylon the Great whom we touched on earlier. Depicted by a woman that John describes as "dressed in purple and scarlet, and was glittering with gold, precious stones and pearls. She held a golden cup in her hand, filled with abominable things and the filth from her adulteries. This title was written on her forehead: MYSTERY BABYLON THE GREAT THE MOTHER OF PROSTITUTES AND THE ABOMINATIONS OF THE EARTH.

I saw that the woman was drunk with the blood of the saints, the blood of those who bore the testimony of Jesus." Revelation 17:4-6. There is no doubt that the woman represents the ecclesiastical body of the institutional church of Rome. John also writes that she sits on many waters that, "are peoples, multitudes, nations and languages." Revelation 17:15. The final piece of the puzzle of who this woman represents comes in the final verse of the chapter, "The woman you saw is the great city that rules over the kings of the earth." Revelation 17:18.

When you contemplate the wealth, history, geography and political influence of Vatican City and the heresies of the papacy there is little room left for doubt about the identity of this adulterous woman, Mystery Babylon. In her cup is the blood of the saints that have been martyred throughout the history of the church at the hands of organized religion. The false prophet who claims to be God's highest representative on earth can be none other than the pope himself. As he propagates the notion of one God for all religions, a one world religion and supports a one world government he will be instrumental in building and sanctioning the new world order envisioned by the UN and the secret cabal that funds it.

The unholy alliance between the apostate church and government debauches the spiritual nature of the church and completely compromises her integrity in light of scripture. Believers have been called out of the world and are not part of the world. The apostle Paul wrote, "Do not conform to the pattern of this world, but be transformed by the renewing of your mind. Then you will be able to test and approve what God's will is – his good, pleasing and perfect will." Romans 12:2. Again in 2 Corinthians 6:17, he wrote, "Therefore come out from them and be separate, says the Lord. Touch no unclean thing, and I will receive you."

This is not a new concept to belief in God. The nation of Israel was set apart from all other nations as a distinct society founded on its relationship with the Lord. "for you are a people holy to the Lord your God. Out of all peoples on the face of the earth, the Lord has chosen you to be his treasured possession." Deuteronomy 14:2. In the same way that Israel forgot her covenant with God, assimilated other nations into themselves and worshipped idols, this Christian religious institution has forgotten that she is betrothed to Christ as his bride and has committed adultery with the rulers of the world and become Mystery Babylon.

As far back as aligning with emperor Constantine, there has always been an element of political interest and the pursuit of power, influence and wealth underlying the dealings of the most established church of Christianity. What began as a fellowship of faith quickly became and enterprise of corruption and it continues right up until today with the papacy's pursuit of world peace through political means. Mystery Babylon's adulteries include the despicable sexual abuse of nuns and youth throughout the age of the church and abusing her power and authority by running the Vatican as a business intent on accumulating wealth. For further insight and a deep dive into this historic record, please refer to my second book *Seeking Truth* and the chapter *The Enemy Within*.

This unholy marriage between the apostate church and the antichrist mimics the New Covenant that Christ established with the true Church as his betrothed bride. John's words in the seventeenth and eighteenth chapters of Revelation demonstrate the utter contempt that God has for the blatant filthiness of this adulterous relationship. For a short period of time it will seem that the false church will actually hold power and sway over the antichrist in deceiving the world to worship him.

However, there will come a time when the antichrist no longer needs this religious establishment and he will grow tired of the politically correct narrative of the UN to appease the masses. The antichrist will destroy the apostate church who only serves to slow him down and he break away from the oligarchy of his past as he brings forward his autocratic agenda, and begins his tyrannical rule of terror. He will despise all that is good and even the cabal will reel at his violent evil nature. All the government leaders that have grown wealthy from the corruption of this religious power structure will realize that the power, influence and wealth they sought for so long has been usurped by one of their own who has subjugated even them beneath him.

Scripture says that all of the merchants of the earth will mourn over the fall of Mystery Babylon and that all of her wealth will brought to ruin in one hour. All of the riches she accumulated through her corruption and exploitation of her congregants will be taken from her and she will be brought down to nothing in an hour. The fortunes that the wealthy elite have pursued and use to own governments, bribe lawmakers and buy votes will also evaporate overnight and even the new world order of the antichrist will suddenly seem shaken and vulnerable. His single minded hatred for Israel will overcome his ambition for middle east peace. The man of lawlessness will then show his true colors and renounce the seven year accord he facilitated with Israel and he will demand that she be wiped from the face of every map. He will summon the nations to bring forth their armies to destroy this tiny country that simply will not be beaten down.

In the thirty eighth chapter of the book of Ezekiel, there is a prophecy about an end time war where it is written, "This is what the Sovereign Lord says: I am against you, Gog, chief prince of Meshek and Tubal. I will turn you around, put hooks in your jaws and bring you out with your whole army – your horses, your horsemen fully armed, and a great horde with large and small shields, all of them brandishing their swords. Persia, Cush and Put will be with them, all with shields and helmets, also Gomer with all its troops, and Beth Togarmah from the far north with all its troops – the many nations with you.

Get ready; be prepared, you and all the hordes gathered with you, and take command of them. After many days you will be called to arms.

In future years you will invade a land that has recovered from war, whose people were gathered from many nations to the mountains of Israel, which had long been desolate. They had been brought out from the nations, and now all of them live in safety. You and all your troops and the many nations with you will go up, advancing like a storm; you will be like a cloud covering the land." Ezekiel 38:3-10.

In verse 14 the prophesy continues, "This is what the Sovereign Lord says: In that day, when my people Israel are living in safety, will you not take notice of it? You will come from your place in the far north, you and many nations with you, all of you riding upon horses, a great horde, a mighty army. You will advance against my people Israel like a cloud that covers the land, so that the nations may know me when I am proved holy through you before their eyes."

The apocalyptic scene is further elaborated upon in verse 18, "This is what will happen in that day: When Gog attacks the land of Israel, my hot anger will be aroused, declares the Sovereign Lord. In my zeal and fiery wrath I declare that at that time there will be a great earthquake in the land of Israel. The fish in the sea, the birds in the sky, the beasts of the field, every creature that moves along the ground, and all the people on the face of the earth will tremble at my presence. The mountains will be overturned, the cliffs will crumble and every wall will fall to the ground." Ezekiel 38:18-20.

This coalition of nations is evident in our generation and have aligned themselves against Israel today. They include Russia (Magog), Iran (Persia), some of the smaller former Soviet states (Meshek and Tubal), Turkey (Togarmah), Ethiopia and Libya (Cush). Noticeably absent is Syria which the Bible predicts will be destroyed in Isaiah 17:3, "Damascus will no longer rule. And those who live in Syria who are left alive will be like the shining-greatness of the sons of Israel." Today Syria is incapacitated after several years of civil war and the ISIS invasion and unable to mount any sort of attack upon Israel even if it wanted to.

When you contemplate the destruction of civilization at the end of the age, recognizing that man will destroy himself if left to his own devices, it is apparent that God's judgments are merciful acts rather than prolonging the painful self-inflicted demise of humanity. If God were not to intervene, it would not change the outcome, just the length of time to complete the destruction of the earth. Without God's intervention there is absolutely no hope for man whatsoever. Through his intervention we receive the hope of salvation through Jesus Christ.

Forget about putting hope in the ingenuity of man. Forget about believing in yourself, having faith in the human spirit, following your heart and the power of positive thinking. There is only one place where hope can be found and that is at the foot of the cross. It is counterintuitive to be angry with God for pouring his wrath out on an unrepentant humanity when complete and total blame for the human condition and predicament lies with man himself. Man's unrepentance through all of these bowls of God's wrath demonstrates the truth of the preceding statements. Even eternal punishment in the lake of fire will not compel man to have remorse because of his heart of stone.

In the fourth chapter of Genesis, when Cain and Abel made offerings to God from their produce, God saw the sincerity in their hearts and God found favor with Abel but not Cain. Cain was angry at God for his own sinful heart. Rather than seeking to draw near to the Lord, Cain refuses to confront his own lack of love for God and takes his anger out on his brother and kills him. This sin then leads to another when God asks Cain where his brother is and he lies in an attempt to conceal the truth from God, as if that were even possible.

Throughout the Bible, from Genesis to Revelation, the deficiencies in the human condition are demonstrated and exemplify how man is caught in a perpetual cycle of sin until he seeks God and repents. This is evident in the history of the nation of Israel and the cycle of being blessed by the Lord then falling away, losing the blessings, repenting and being blessed once again. Why was the nation of Israel so quick to chase after other religions and worship idols, after experiencing the profound miracles and power of God first hand? Why does humanity refuse to follow the Lord and instead choose to indulge itself in worldly temptations, such as greed, the pursuit of money and power and sexual immorality? Why do people continue to deny the existence of God despite overwhelming evidence for the historicity of Jesus Christ?

Simply put, man was created in the image of God (he has a spirit) unlike other animals. He was given dominion over all the earth and everything in it and on it (Genesis 1:26). When Satan deceived Adam and Eve, they capitulated their position of sovereignty over the earth to him and the sinful nature of man is the result. Jesus won that sovereignty back and believers merely have to claim it. The vast majority of the world remains deceived, believing they can fix the mess they have created and will ultimately accept Satan's solutions for society. Even more tragic, much of civilization fails to even see their predicament and lives their lives recklessly, denying God's existence and the knowledge of the truth.

True believers are called to a much higher standard. We are called to focus our lives on Jesus and bear fruit for him. We are called to be humble and patient, enduring until he returns. When we do so, Jesus, who is faithful and true, will take us home to be with him forever. "Since you have kept my command to endure patiently, I will also keep you from the hour of trial that is going to come on the whole world to test the inhabitants of the earth." Revelation 3:10.

End of the Age

"Surely the Sovereign Lord does nothing without revealing his plan to his servants the prophets." Amos 3:7. The end of the age has been predicted in the pages of the Bible in amazing detail therefore it is requisite to study prophecies about the last days to gain understanding of what must take place and where we stand right now in a contextual significance to God's plan.

Israel is critical in unlocking end times prophecy and will be center stage when all is fulfilled. Jesus said, "Now learn this lesson from the fig tree: As soon as its twigs get tender and its leaves come out, you know that summer is near. Even so, when you see all these things, you know that it is near, right at the door." Mathew 24:32-33.

Three days is an important time period in the Bible. When God asked Abraham to, "Take your son, your only son Isaac, whom you love, and go to the region of Moriah. Sacrifice him there as a burnt offering on one of the mountains I will tell you about." Genesis 22:2, the anguish in his heart must have been overwhelming. His son Isaac was promised by God to him many years before and it wasn't until Abraham was one hundred years old and his wife Sarah was ninety that she became pregnant and Isaac was born. Being asked now to sacrifice him and end his life must have been devastating.

"Early the next morning Abraham got up and saddled his donkey. He took with him two servants and his son Isaac. When he had cut enough wood for the burnt offering, he set out for the place God had told him about. On the third day Abraham looked up and saw the place in the distance. How much uncertainty filled Abraham's heart it doesn't say, but it does record that he believed that God would somehow save Isaac. "Isaac spoke up and said to his father Abraham, 'Father?'

'Yes my son?' Abraham replied. 'The fire and the wood are here,' Isaac said, 'but where is the lamb for the burnt offering?' Abraham answered, 'God himself will provide the lamb for the burnt offering, my son.' And the two of them went on together." Genesis 22:7-8.

They travelled for three days before Isaac was to be offered as a sacrifice. In a parallel event, God offered his one and only Son, Jesus Christ as a sacrifice for the atonement of sin for all people. And just as Abraham's faith in God was credited to him as righteousness, our faith in Christ is credited to us as righteousness. God took three days to accomplish the crucifixion and resurrection of Jesus as well, in the same way as the foreshadowing scripture of Genesis 22.

Putting the pieces of the prophetic puzzle together is paramount in recognizing how late the hour is and how little time we have left. When Peter wrote about the delay in the Lord's return he said, "But do not forget this one thing, dear friends: With the Lord a day is like a thousand years, and a thousand years are like a day.

The prophet Hosea wrote about judgement for Israel because of its great sins against God and warned them that God would uproot them from their land and scatter them abroad. "For I will be like a lion to Ephraim, like a great lion to Judah. I will carry them off with no one to rescue them." Hosea 5:14. He goes on to say that God will restore Israel, "Come, let us return to the Lord. He has torn us to pieces but he will heal us, he has injured us but he will bind up our wounds. After two days he will revive us, on the third day he will restore us, that we may live in his presence." Hosea 6:1-2.

This is another foreshadowing of the nation of Israel rejecting her Messiah and subsequently being punished by the destruction of Jerusalem and the temple in AD 70 and being dispersed throughout the nations of the world. Using the logic of a thousand years for a day, Israel was revived as a nation after two thousand years and the millennial reign of Christ will happen on the third day when Israel will live in his presence.

After God led the Israelites across the Red Sea on dry land, he told Moses, "Go to the people and consecrate them today and tomorrow. Have them wash their clothes and be ready by the third day, because on that day the Lord will come down on Mount Sinai in the sight of all the people." Exodus 19:10-11.

Israel's existence today is miraculous evidence of prophetic fulfillment. How the Jewish people could remain an identifiable ethnic group and be restored to their homeland after 1900 years is nothing less than the power of God. "Who has ever heard of such things? Who has ever seen things like this? Can a country be born in a day or a nation be brought forth in a moment? Yet no sooner is Zion in labor than she gives birth to her children." Isaiah 66:8. The fact that Israel is thriving as a nation again should be a wake-up call to every believer on earth. The Christian Church should seriously contemplate the sheer improbability of the Jews being back in Israel due to man's orchestrated efforts alone.

In 1267, Rabbi Moses ben Nachman (Nachmanides 1194-1270), viewed the desolate land and commented, "Many are Israel's forsaken places, and great is the desecration. The more sacred the place, the greater the devastation it has suffered. Jerusalem is the most desolate place of all." He did however, make a statement that was profoundly hopeful, in that the desolation signifies and, "constitutes a good tiding, proclaiming that during all our exiles, our land will not accept our enemies..... Since the time we left it (the land) has not accepted any nation or people, and they all try to settle it.... That is a great proof and assurance for us." As quoted in the Jerusalem Post, Tuly Weisz, Sept. 23, 2017.

Four hundred years later, Mark twain visited the Holy Land in 1867 and agreed with Nachmanides' observations but went beyond just hope with what has proven to be a prophetic prediction, "that Israel will remain desolate until the Jewish people assume control. But when the people of Israel finally return to the land pf Israel, the region will once again flourish thanks to Divine providence." Jerusalem Post, Tuly Weisz, Sept. 23, 2017.

Not only is it amazing that Israel is a nation again, but the fact that Jerusalem is her capital is more proof of the hand of God orchestrating her affairs. Jerusalem was chosen as Israel's capital in ancient times as recorded in the sixth chapter of 2 Chronicles where God speaks, "Since the day I brought my people out of Egypt, I have not chosen a city in any tribe in Israel to have a temple built so that my name might be there, nor have I chosen anyone to be ruler over my people Israel. But now I have chosen

Jerusalem for my name to be there, and I have chosen David to rule my people Israel." 2 Chronicles 6:5-6.

Today Israel flourishes with the tender care of farmers who have irrigated the desert and created a vibrant agriculture industry consisting of fresh fruits, flowers, fine wines, preserved goods and organic food. The country also excels in electronics, agrotechnology, telecommunications, computer equipment and alternative energy. "But you, mountains of Israel, will produce branches and fruit for my people Israel, for they will soon come home. I am concerned for you and will look on you with favor; you will be plowed and sown, and I will cause many people to live on you – yes, all of Israel. The towns will be inhabited and the ruins rebuilt. I will increase the number of people and animals living on you, and they will be fruitful and become numerous. I will settle people on you as in the past and will make you prosper more than before. Then you will know that I am the Lord. I will cause people, my people Israel to live on you. They will possess you, and you will be their inheritance; you will never again deprive them of their children." Ezekiel 36:8-12.

After seventy-five years of shaky treaties and elusive peace, today Israel is on the cusp of signing historic agreements that will secure peace in the middle east. With Jared Kushner as his point man, Donald Trump has succeeded where so many before him failed in producing any outcomes in the middle east. By brokering deals between Israel and The United Arab Emirates, Bahrain, Sudan and Morocco, Kushner has effectively reduced Iran's influence in the region and laid the foundation for more middle east states to follow suit. What began as the deal of the century will be completed as something of far greater significance in the future.

Peace in Israel is paramount to the fulfillment of prophecy concerning the end of the age. The antichrist will have the honor of bringing to fruition what will appear to be the deal of the millennium. The Prophet Daniel wrote, "He will confirm a covenant with many for one 'seven.' In the middle of the 'seven' he will put an end to sacrifice and offering. And at the temple he will set up an abomination that causes desolation, until the end that is decreed is poured out on him." Daniel 9:27. The significance of this peace accord is that it will mark the beginning of the countdown to the end. Seven final years, culminating in the destruction of the ungodly, unrepentant world, Satan and his unholy trinity with him.

Daniel gives us insight into the antichrist by describing him as being a little horn that rises up out of ten horns that are part of one of four beasts that he saw in a vision. An angel interpreted his vision for him. The four beasts represented four kingdoms that rule the world. The fourth beast was different from the first three who proved to be the Medo-Persian empire, the Greek empire and the Roman empire. The fourth beast had ten kings or rulers and was made up of a coalition of former Roman Empire countries of which the deep state is implicitly imbedded because of its covert nature, making it very different from the previous kingdoms. The little horn rises up after the other horns and proceeds to subdue three of the other horns.

"He will speak against the Most High and oppress his saints and try to change the set times and the laws. The saints will be handed over to him for a time, times and a half time." Daniel 7:25. In the eleventh chapter of Daniel, the angel goes on to explain what this arrogant and blasphemous king will be like. "The king will do as he pleases. He will exalt and magnify himself above every god and will say unheard-of things against the God of gods. He will be successful until the time of wrath is completed, for what has been determined must take place." Daniel 11: 36. Daniel elaborates further in chapter 12 saying, "From the time the daily sacrifice is abolished and the abomination that causes desolation is set up, there will be 1290 days." Daniel 12:11.

This is almost identical to the beast John describes in the thirteenth chapter of Revelation that also has ten horns with ten crowns on its horns, each with a blasphemous name. This is indicative of the evil intrinsic nature of the power coalition the antichrist will emerge from. This beast opened its mouth, "to blaspheme God, and to slander his name and his dwelling place and those who live in heaven. He was given power to wage war against God's holy people and to conquer them. And he was given authority over every tribe, people, language and nation." Revelation 13:6-7.

At the mid-point of the treaty, the antichrist will erect a statue of himself and demand to be worshipped as God. John wrote in Revelation, "The beast was given a mouth to utter proud words and blasphemies and to exercise his authority for forty-two months." Revelation 13:5.

In addition to these timelines, the Gentiles are prophesied to trample the holy city of Jerusalem for forty-two months (Revelation 11:2) and the two witnesses that John describes will prophecy for one thousand two hundred and sixty days before they are killed and lie in the streets for three and one half days (Revelation 11:8). "The inhabitants of the earth will gloat over them and will celebrate by sending each other gifts...." Revelation 11:10. Then they are resurrected and ascend into heaven.

Jesus also mentions this time as part of the signs of the end of the age. "So when you see standing in the holy place, 'the abomination that causes desolation,' spoken through the prophet Daniel – let the reader understand – then let those who are in Judea flee to the mountains. Let no one on the housetop go down to take anything out of the house. Let no one in the field go back to get their cloak. How dreadful it will be in those days for pregnant women and nursing mothers! Pray that your flight will not take place in winter or on the Sabbath. For then there will be great distress, unequalled from the beginning of the world until now – and never to be equaled again." Mathew 24:15-21.

Finally, Paul's description in his second letter to the church at Thessalonica completes the portrait of the antichrist. "Don't let anyone deceive you in any way, for that day will not come until the rebellion occurs and the man of lawlessness is revealed, the man doomed to destruction. He will oppose and will exalt himself over everything that is called God or is worshipped, so that he sets himself up in God's temple, proclaiming himself to be God." 2 Thessalonians 2:3-4.

The rebuilt temple in Jerusalem is essential for the antichrist to fulfill these prophecies, yet many have interpreted the temple described in these scriptures as symbolic or spiritual. Up until the last few decades this may have rational but today the Temple Institute's endeavors to promote building a third temple are very real. What Orthodox Jews are hoping for is that the Messiah will rebuild the temple which perfectly fits the puzzle. The man they desire may ultimately turn out to be none other than the antichrist himself.

In addition to the pandemonium surrounding the antichrist's rule of terror, World War III will thrust civilization into even more chaos. Here is a refresher for you from an earlier chapter: Russia, (Magog), Iran (Persia), Turkey (Rosh, Meshech and Tubal), Sudan (Cush), Germany (Gomer), Egypt and Libya (Put) and their allies will all be drawn into conflict with Israel. "Son of Man, set your face against Gog, of the land of Magog, the chief prince of Meshech and Tubal; prophesy against him and say: 'This is what the Sovereign Lord says: I am against you, Gog, chief prince of Meshech and Tubal. I will turn you around, put hooks in your jaws and bring you out with your whole army – your horses, your horsemen fully armed, and a great horde with large and small shields, all of them brandishing their swords. Persia, Cush and Put will be with them, all with shields and helmets, also Gomer with all its troops, and Beth Togarmah from the far north with all its troops – the many nations with you.

Get ready; be prepared, you and all the hordes gathered about you, and take command of them. After many days you will be called to arms. In future years you will invade a land that has recovered from war, whose people were gathered from many nations to the mountains of Israel. Which had long been desolate. They had been brought out from the nations, and now all of them live in safety. You and all your troops and the many nations with you will go up, advancing like a storm; you will be like a cloud covering the land." Ezekiel 38:2-9.

From the language in this prophecy it seems clear that this will take place during the time that Israel is living under the protection of the seven-year peace accord facilitated by the antichrist. Today we can see the alignment that has formed between these nations against Israel positions them in a coalition that could be ready to advance on short notice. Syria is absent as illustrated earlier, after several years of civil war, and has been reduced to rubble and without Russia's aid is completely helpless. "A prophesy against Damascus: 'See, Damascus will no longer be a city but will become a heap of ruins.'" Isaiah 17:1.

The purpose of this war is to bring glory to God. "You will advance against my people Israel like a cloud that covers the land. In days to come, Gog, I will bring you against my land, so that the nations may know me when I am proved holy through you before their eyes." Ezekiel 38:16. Despite the overwhelming odds in the coalition's favor, the Lord will bring them to ruin. "This is what will happen in that day: When Gog attacks the land of Israel, my hot anger will be aroused, declares the Sovereign Lord. In my zeal and fiery wrath I declare that at that time there shall be a great earthquake in the land of Israel. The fish in the sea, the birds in the sky, the beasts of the field, every creature that moves along the ground and all the people on the face of the earth will tremble at my presence. The mountains will be overturned, the cliffs will crumble and every wall will fall to the ground. I will summon a sword against Gog on all my mountains, declares the Sovereign Lord. Every man's sword will be against his brother. I will execute judgement on him with plague and bloodshed; I will pour down torrents of rain, hailstones and burning sulfur on him. And so I will show my greatness and holiness, and I will make myself known in the sight of many nations. Then they will know that I am the Lord." Ezekiel 38:18-23.

The prophet Zechariah wrote, "I am going to make Jerusalem a cup that sends all the surrounding peoples reeling. Judah will be besieged as well as Jerusalem. On that day, when all the nations of the earth are gathered against her, I will make Jerusalem an immovable rock for all the nations. All who try to move it will injure themselves." Zechariah 12:2-3.

How a tiny country like Israel effects political decisions all over the world, impacts which countries are allies and which are enemies, and will ultimately determine the stage of the war to end all wars is truly amazing. God will defeat the armies of the nations who attack Israel in the last days with supernatural phenomenon the likes of which the world has never seen before. The devastation will make the destruction of Pharaoh's warriors in the Red Sea look like an act of compassion and mercy.

Earlier in our examination of the Great Tribulation we saw how events would unfold in rapid succession like dominoes falling. The battle of Gog and Magog and their allies against Israel will take place smack in the middle of the outpouring of God's wrath on an unrepentant world. In the midst of plagues and widespread death, the antichrist demanding everyone receive his mark in order to buy and sell, and the new world order, right on the heels of World War III, just when it seems things could not possibly get worse..... they get worse.

The battle of Armageddon will be the last great battle of the last days, after which there will be no more war. The prophet Zechariah wrote, "A day of the Lord is coming, Jerusalem, when your possessions will be plundered and divided up within your very walls.

I will gather all the nations to Jerusalem to fight against it; the city will be captured, the houses ransacked and the women raped. Half of the city will go into exile, but the rest of the people will not be taken from the city. Then the Lord will go out and fight against those nations, as he fights on a day of battle. On that day his feet will stand on the Mount of Olives, east of Jerusalem, and the Mount of Olives will be split in two from east to west, forming a great valley, with half of the mountain moving north and half moving south. You will flee by my mountain valley, for it will extend to Azel. You will flee as you fled from the earthquake in the days of Uzziah king of Judah. Then the Lord my God will come, and all the holy ones with him.

The Prophet Joel conveyed a similar prophecy, "I will gather all nations and bring them down to the valley of Jehoshaphat. There I will put them on trial for what they did to my inheritance, my people Israel, because they scattered my people among the nations and divided up my land." Joel 3:2.

On that day there will be neither sunlight nor cold, frosty darkness. It will be a unique day – a day known only to the Lord – with no distinction between day and night." Zechariah 14:1-7. Jesus spoke of this time as well in the twenty fourth chapter of Mathew, "Immediately after the distress of those days 'the sun will be darkened, and the moon will not give its light; the stars will fall from the sky, and the heavenly bodies will be shaken.'" Mathew 24:29.

John portrays the same event in the nineteenth chapter of Revelation. "I saw heaven standing open and there before me was a white horse, whose rider is called Faithful and True. With justice he judges and wages war. His eyes are like blazing fire, and on his head are many crowns. He has a name written on him that no one knows but he himself. He is dressed in a robe dipped in blood, and his name is the Word of God. The armies of heaven were following him, riding on white horses and dressed in fine linen, white and clean. Coming out of his mouth is a sharp sword with which to strike down the nations. 'He will rule them with an iron scepter.' He treads the winepress of the fury of the wrath of God Almighty. On his robe and on his thigh he has this name written:

KING OF KINGS AND LORD OF LORDS

And I saw an angel standing in the sun, who cried in a loud voice to all the birds flying in midair, 'Come, gather together for the great supper of God, so that you may eat the flesh of kings, generals, and the mighty, of horses and their riders, and the flesh of all people, free and slave, great and small.'

Then I saw the beast and the kings of the earth and their armies gathered together to make war against the rider on the horse and his army. But the beast was captured and with it the false prophet who had performed the signs on its behalf. With these signs he had deluded those who had received the mark of the beast and worshipped its image. The two of them were thrown alive into the fiery lake of burning sulfur. The rest were killed with the sword coming out of the mouth of the rider on the horse, and all the birds gorged themselves on their flesh." Revelation 19:11-21.

The armies of the world will be defeated supernaturally for the second time within the three and one half years of the rule of the antichrist, only this time Jesus Christ himself will stand on the Mount of Olives as leader of a multitude of heavenly host. His victory will be swift, total and complete. He will bind up the antichrist and the false prophet and send them to their eternal destiny to be tormented forever in the fiery lake of sulfur.

The devil will then be chained up and tossed into the abyss for a thousand years. "And I saw an angel coming down out of heaven, having the key to the Abyss and holding in his hand a great chain. He seized the dragon, that ancient serpent, who is the devil, or Satan, and bound him for a thousand years. He threw him into the Abyss, and locked and sealed it over him, to keep him from deceiving the nations anymore until the thousand years were ended. After that, he must be set free for a short time." Revelation 20:1-3.

I don't know about you but when I read these words of scripture I want to cheer out loud for the triumph of good over evil! After all the storms we go through in life, after all the obstacles Satan has put in front of us trying to divert our attention and focus off of the Lord, I want to celebrate his capture and imprisonment. Every part of me wants to rejoice in the revenge the Lord imparts on those who killed the martyrs and persecuted the people of God. I want to proclaim the goodness of Christ from the rooftops and worship the Lord forever!

There is more to the narrative though and John shares more of this scene as he sees the souls of the people who were killed by the antichrist. "I saw thrones on which were seated those who had been given authority to judge. And I saw the souls of those who had been beheaded because of their testimony about Jesus and because of the word of God. They had not worshipped the beast or its image and had not received its mark on their foreheads or their hands. They came to life and reigned with Christ a thousand years. (The rest of the dead did not come to life until the thousand years were ended.) This is the first resurrection. Blessed and holy are those who share in the first resurrection. The second death has no power over them, but they will be priests of God and of Christ and will reign with him for a thousand years." Revelation 20:4-6.

What a beautiful scene this will be. The great faithfulness of those who stood strong until the end of their earthly lives. Those who hung onto the words of Jesus when he said, "Whoever wants to be my disciple must deny themselves and take up their cross and follow me. For whoever wants to save their life will lose it, but whoever loses their life for me and for the gospel will save it. What good is it for someone to gain the whole world, yet forfeit their soul? Or what can anyone give in exchange for their soul?" Mark 8:34-37. These who had conviction on par with the martyrs from throughout the ages who have died for their faith ever since Jesus ascended to heaven. I pray we can all have this level of discipline and obedience in our lives. For those that do, there is a great reward waiting in heaven.

"Then I saw a great white throne and him who was seated on it. The earth and the heavens fled from his presence, and there was no place for them. And I saw the dead, great and small, standing before the throne, and books were opened. Another book was opened, which is the book of life. The dead were judged according to what they had done as recorded in the books. The sea gave up the dead that were in it, and death and Hades gave up the dead that were in them, and each person was judged according to what they had done. Then death and Hades were thrown into the lake of fire. The lake of fire is the second death. Anyone whose name was not found written in the book of life was thrown into the lake of fire." Revelation 20:11-15.

When we discipline our children we often feel a sense of poignancy but it must pale compared to the heartbreak God must feel when he condemns people for their sins. But even that could never constitute a juxtaposition of Christ's death on the cross. The depth of love that God has for us is immeasurable and the heaviness in his heart when he sees our sin must be overwhelming. However, with great power comes great responsibility and in order to be just God must both exalt and condemn. We can only kneel in reverence.

At the end of the age Christ will set up his millennial kingdom and rule the earth from Jerusalem. There are differing views in eschatology regarding whether this will be an actual one thousand years or if it simply means a long time however, based on the precision of and the importance of timing in the prophecies we have examined thus far, it is counterintuitive that it would be anything but a literal one thousand years.

Students of eschatology have posited three different interpretations of the millennium. Premillennial, the position I hold, is that when Christ returns he will reign in person on earth for one thousand years after which a new heaven and new earth will be formed.

The A-Millennial view is that the entire period from the ascension of Christ in the first century up until his return is considered the millennium and that Jesus currently rules over a spiritual kingdom that will be consummated upon his return and a new heaven and new earth will be created at that time. A concept of St. Augustine in AD 400, it was adopted by the Roman Catholic Church in AD 431 at the Council of Ephesus.[90] This view however, is nonsensical since Satan has not been bound up and incarcerated in the Abyss for one thousand years and is free to tempt people and deceive them at will.

The Post-Millennial school of thought believes the same as A-Millennialism, with the added opinion that there will be widespread peace and prosperity before the return of Christ because of the gospel being preached to all of the world. This rationale originated with Daniel Whitby (1638-1726), a Unitarian in England.[91] I find this view is also irrational as long as Satan is allowed to influence humanity's behavior. This is also a counter view to the prophecies of the last days which we have examined.

Based on the narrative of the twentieth chapter of Revelation, the culmination of the current age is the return of Jesus to defeat the antichrist and bind up and imprison Satan for one thousand years and him setting up his millennial kingdom which will precipitate the peace and prosperity foretold in prophecy. In this way every promise made by God to the nation of Israel will be kept and fulfilled.

"In the Last days
The mountain of the Lord's temple will be established

As the highest of the mountains;
It will be exalted above the hills,
And peoples will stream to it.
Many nations will come and say,
'Come, let us go up to the mountain of the Lord,
To the temple of the God of Jacob.
He will teach us his ways,
So that we may walk in his paths.'
The law will go out from Zion,
The word of the Lord from Jerusalem.
He will judge between many peoples
And will settle disputes for strong nations far and wide.
They will beat their swords into plowshares
And their spears into pruning hooks.
Nation will not take up sword against nation,
Nor will they train for war anymore.
Everyone will sit under their own vine
And under their own fig tree,
And no one will make them afraid,
For the Lord Almighty has spoken."
Micah 4:1-4

In the same way that spiritual battles are manifested in the physical realm, Christ's millennial reign will be a manifestation on earth of his spiritual position as King of Kings and Lord of Lords and the name above all names. He will encapsulate the epitome of "Emmanuel," God with us, in a second fulfillment of his virgin birth and the "government will be on his shoulders. And he will be called Wonderful Counsellor, Mighty God, Everlasting Father, Prince of Peace." Isaiah 9:6.

Israel will finally accept him as their Messiah and so they will be saved (Romans 11:25-26). In the same way, the prophet Zechariah's prediction that Jesus would arrive in Jerusalem as a lowly King riding on a donkey (Zechariah 9:9) and later be Lord over all the earth (Zechariah 14:9). The entire culmination of prophecy precipitated through God's methodology of making the first last and the last first. "But God chose the foolish things of the world to shame the wise; God chose the weak things of the world to shame the strong." 1 Corinthians 1:27.

The beauty, complexity and completeness of scripture are interwoven into the millennial reign of Jesus Christ on the earth as a physical, tangible ruler and counsellor of all mankind. In this way, all of the word of God will be fulfilled before heaven and earth pass away, fulfilling Jesus's words, "For truly I tell you, until heaven and earth disappear, not the smallest letter, not the least stroke of a pen, will by any means disappear from the Law until everything is accomplished." Mathew 5:18.

"Remember the former things of long ago;
I am God, and there is no other;
I am God, and there is none like me.
I make known the end from the beginning,
From ancient times, what is still to come.
I say, 'My purpose will stand,
And I will do all that I please.'"
Isaiah 46:9-10.

Spiritual Warfare

We all go through challenges and periods when it seems the universe has aligned against us. Ever since the lockdowns precipitated by the COVID 19 pandemic, many have struggled with isolation and statistics show that depression, domestic violence and suicide have increased. Social media can bring out the worst in people as many lash out at others under the cloak of impunity, mocking and belittling those who don't agree with their opinion. It is critical to maintain our composure and treat each other with the respect and love we all deserve always, and times when we are forced into restrictions and lockdowns are especially crucial.

Often when the going gets tough we blame God for our hardship. I'm sure you've heard it said that a loving God would not allow bad things to happen to good people. Nothing could be further than the truth. Not many lay blame at the foot of Satan for their sufferings. We were all created with the freedom of choice. That freedom facilitates not only the flexibility to make choices that have positive outcomes but also ones that produce failure. We must also realize there are constant spiritual battles taking place all around us that influence our experiences, choices and infiltrate our very thoughts and perceptions.

If mankind never acknowledges that we are spiritual beings, we will never realize the battles we fight are of a much greater significance and are of a much deeper imputation than is apparent on the surface. In our naivety the decisions we make will be based upon incomplete information and are therefore limited in their potential. We will remain unequipped to solve our problems and be at the mercy of the dark forces at work all around us and by viewing our struggles as non-spiritual we will seek non-spiritual solutions. With all of our technological advances and our increase in knowledge, society embraces and celebrates the human spirit yet seems oblivious to the spirituality of man.

Furthermore, unless we acknowledge that we are in a war, we will never fully appreciate just how real the battles being fought are and how much impact they carry into our lives. In turn, our worldview is much more holistic when we realize that the physical realm is just one component of a much larger existence and what we say and do on earth influences our eternal destiny. Without this important ingredient, our lives are spiritually dead. Without awakening to this reality, we cannot comprehend that there are hidden forces battling to influence the outcome of our lives and of civilization. Without this fundamental understanding, we render ourselves impotent in struggles that involve our welfare and that of our friends and family. Without this realization, we will never see the blindfolds that have been in place both personally and on society collectively. Without discernment that only comes from the Lord we are fair game for our adversaries. "For the Lord gives wisdom; from his mouth come knowledge and understanding." Proverbs 2:6.

Our struggles with low self-esteem, depression, failure and temptation are all assaults by the devil so we are called to be vigilant. "Be alert and of sober mind. Your enemy the devil prowls around like a roaring lion looking for someone to devour." 1 Peter 5:8. We must remember what we have in Christ when we face spiritual battles. There is no name under heaven greater than the name of Jesus, therefore, we must claim his victory as our own. Spiritual battles require spiritual armor, so in the same way that we wouldn't go onto a physical battlefield unarmed and without armor, we must equip ourselves for the unseen.

"For our struggle is not against flesh and blood, but against the rulers, against the authorities, against the powers of this dark world and against the spiritual forces in the heavenly realms. Therefore, put on the full armor of God, so that when the day of evil comes, you may be able to stand your ground, and after you have done everything, to stand. Stand firm then, with the belt of truth buckled around your waist, with the breastplate of righteousness in place, and with your feet fitted with the readiness that comes from the gospel of peace. In addition to all this, take up the shield of faith, with which you can extinguish all the flaming arrows of the evil one. Take the helmet of salvation and the sword of the Spirit, which is the word of God." Ephesians 6:12-17.

Priscilla Shirer in her Bible study entitled *The Armor of God,* wrote, "Everything that occurs in the visible, physical world is directly connected to the wrestling match being waged in the invisible, spiritual world." Additionally, "The effects of the war going on in the unseen world reveal themselves in our strained and damaged relationships, emotional instability, mental fatigue, physical exhaustion and many other areas of life. Many of us feel pinned down by anger, unforgiveness, pride, comparisons, insecurity, discord, fear.... The list goes on. But the overarching, primary nemesis behind all these outcomes is the Devil himself." [92]

Understanding our adversary is paramount to our ability to overcome him and his unholy cortege. His fundamental weapon is deception and he will even have you believe he doesn't exist so he can go about his business undetected. He is the master of treachery and even masquerades as an angel of light (2 Corinthians 11:14). It is no coincidence that the cabal uses the very same tactics as Satan. They have the same arsenal of weaponry and appeal to the same personal triggers that perpetuate the greatest response.

Demonic forces often present themselves as harmless phenomenon such as palm reading, psychic fortune telling, horoscopes, trot cards and Ouija boards. There is even danger in yoga through emptying yourself in order to relax, however, there is danger that the void can be filled by demonic spirits. What many see as nothing more than home décor can be intrinsically demonic because of the spirit associated with a particular item such as divination tools, books, music, statues of Buddha or objects of the occult. These items can act as a bridge between spiritual realms and the natural world through which evil spirits can manifest themselves and influence the lens we see things through. They can hinder our relationship with Christ, keep us in bondage to sin and interfere with our spiritual discernment.

All these things open your spirit up to bondage, to being yoked to demonic spirits, spiritual oppression and separate you from God. They have no legal authority over you unless you invite them in and you may very well have extended an open invitation simply through different items in your home. The nineteenth chapter of the book of Acts tells us of the dangers associated with demonic spirits, when a man who was demon possessed handed a severe beating to those who were trying to drive it out of him. In response to this event and, "a number who had practiced sorcery brought their scrolls together and burned them publicly." Acts 19:19.

The dangers are very real that we can live in a state that positions us as enemies of God and the Bible is clear that certain people cannot inherit the kingdom of heaven. "He who overcomes will inherit all this, and I will be his God and he will be my son. But the cowardly, the unbelieving, the vile, the murderers, the sexually immoral, those who practice magic arts, the idolaters and all liars – their place will be in the fiery lake of burning sulfur. This is the second death." Revelation 21:7-8.

Also in Deuteronomy we read, "Let no one be found among you who sacrifices his son or daughter in the fire, who practices divination or sorcery, interprets omens, engages in witchcraft, or casts spells, or who is a medium or spiritist or who consults the dead. Anyone who does these things is detestable to the Lord…" Deuteronomy 18:10-12.

The Bible gives ample evidence of spiritual interactions with man. Perhaps one of the most recognizable is the life of Job. Despite Satan's attempt to cause Job to curse God by ruining his physical life through destroying his family, home and finances, he remained faithful to God in his words and actions.

When we find ourselves embroiled in spiritual battles we may find that like Job, our friends may fail us in the midst of our hardships, we often feel abandoned by God and are compelled to blame God for our suffering, or we fall into sin because of our frailty, which brings about a perception of even further isolation from the Lord and we ultimately blame ourselves for being unworthy. In reality, blame lies at Satan's feet because of his spiritual accomplices doing their best to cause us to curse God.

Like Job, we can garner spiritual strength by recognizing that God is in control, he is right beside us in the middle of the storm and he permits bad things to happen to good people in order to develop perseverance and wisdom through reaching out to him. "But he knows the way that I take; when he has tested me, I will come forth as gold. My feet have closely followed his steps; I have kept to his way without turning aside. I have not departed from the commands of his lips; I have treasured the words of his mouth more than my daily bread." Job 23:10-12.

As I look back at my own life I can see exactly where Satan took me out at the knees and caused the destruction of my first marriage through depression that led to seeking affirmation from worldly values. Just as I began to draw near to the Lord, the devil attacked in a way that severed the bond I was developing with God and sent me down a trajectory of hardship that lasted over twenty years. After my second divorce, and a deep spiritual encounter with Jesus, I was redeemed and welcomed to the family of God as the prodigal son (Luke 15:11-32). Hindsight is 20/20 and it is clear to me now how Satan works and how it is crucial to place God first and foremost in our lives. "But seek first his kingdom and his righteousness, and all these things will be given to you as well." Mathew 6:33.

By retaining a posture of humility one can avoid the trap that follows the prideful in their pursuit of success. "Where does wisdom come from? Where does understanding dwell? It is hidden from the eyes of every living thing, concealed even from the birds of the sky. Destruction and Death say, 'Only a rumor of it has reached our ears.' God understands the way to it and he alone knows where it dwells, for he views the ends of the earth and sees everything under the heavens. When he established the force of the wind and measured out the waters, when he made a decree for the rain and a path for the thunderstorm, then he looked at wisdom and appraised it; he confirmed it and tested it. And he said to the human race, 'The fear of the Lord – that is wisdom, and to shun evil is understanding." Job 28:20-28.

We have absolutely nothing to fear from Satan or his demons. We have absolutely nothing to fear from the spirit realm. "'No weapon forged against you will prevail and you will refute every tongue that accuses you. This is the heritage of the servants of the Lord, and this is their vindication from me.' Declares the Lord." Isaiah 54:17.

However, when we don't keep ourselves armed with the full armor of God we leave ourselves vulnerable to spiritual attack. You must have your house in order or it will fall. A house divided cannot stand. Jesus said, "If a house is divided is against itself, that house cannot stand." Mark 3:25. Additionally James instructs, "the one who doubts is like a wave of the sea, blown and tossed by the wind. That person should not receive anything from the Lord. Such a person is double-minded and unstable in all they do." James 1:6-8.

Society has allowed Satan to divide the Church, to divide families, to divide cities and to divide nations. Today the United States is divided and polarized more than at any time in history. Canada is deeply divided as well. The political left has driven a wedge between what used to be mainstream values and its liberal agenda that is the product of the devil. Mainstream isn't mainstream, its blatant sexual immorality, anti-family, accepting of sin and it disguises itself as progressive. There's absolutely nothing progressive about it! Progressive is defined as relating to or characterized by progress. Today's progressive is regressive and it is a social devolution from a higher state to the lowest common denominator. It is repulsive and offensive.

Secular society lives in denial of God and the spiritual realms. This folly leaves people at the mercy of Satan who thrives in the deception that he doesn't exist. By living in such blindness, humanity is vulnerable to spiritual hijacking without even realizing it. By refusing to believe in God, civilization is at a perpetual disadvantage to spiritual forces. There are many church goers today who don't believe in the demonic realms and are ineffectual because of it. James wrote, "You believe there is one God. Good! Even the demons believe that – and shudder." James 2:19.

Other than true believers in Jesus Christ, civilization today has conceded to the dark side! In an effort to be tolerant and inclusive it has allowed Satan to walk right in and take over. Not only has society given Satan the keys to the house, it has handed over the mortgage! Society has become enslaved to the devil. Sodom and Gomorrah were sister cities to many cities today. What was once only heard about from Las Vegas, Amsterdam or San Francisco is now commonplace in nearly every city on the planet.

Battles fought in the spiritual realms become manifested in the physical realm. By embracing sin society has handed over control to the demonic who revel in sin. By permitting the agenda of special interest groups, governments today have not only allowed demons to spread their sinful agendas, they have taken up their plight and elevated them to the point of impinging their values on the silent majority. Transgender, homosexuality, pedophilia, or gender as a social construct. These are not wholesome spiritual values! These are promoted and propagated by demonic spiritual forces in our midst and are applauded by our governments as woke expressions of individuality.

In the same way that the difference between a healthy man and a drug addict or an alcoholic are the decisions they made, and the difference between a person condemned to hell and a person destined for heaven are the decisions they made, and the difference between our society today that is heading toward the gutter and the society of our forefathers is the decisions that were made. Even the Christian church today is buying in with Progressive Christianity, the prosperity Gospel and others, feeding out of the very hand of the devil. They live to satisfy the flesh! They aren't concerned with the eternal wellbeing of their congregants. Jesus said, "Whoever is not with me is against me, and whoever does not gather with me scatters." Mathew 12:30. What has happened to the concept of storing up treasures in heaven?

We see the Christian churches in China, North Korea, Iran and Africa spreading like wild fire while they are being persecuted and people are being killed and imprisoned for their faith and we pray for them and wish they could be like us. They are not the ones in poverty, we are. We have become the lukewarm church of the third chapter of Revelation in verse 16. We need to be more on fire for Jesus than society is for the demonic forces that control the fleshly desires of man! Many churches today cannot tell the difference between the wolf and the sheep!

The Roman Catholic Church openly recognizes Mary as a deity, prays to her and even validates visions of Mary seen by people, including the 1917 vision near Fatima, Portugal, the 1531 visions near Guadalupe, Mexico and more recently at Medjugorje, Bosnia and Herzegovina in 1981. These are real spiritual deceptions engineered to mislead believers and the oldest established church through a complete lack of discernment has fallen for them. "And no wonder, for Satan himself masquerades as an angel of light." 2 Corinthians 11:14.

Millions of people who call themselves Christians are deceived about what it means to be a Christian. Many believe that you simply have to align with Christian social values, be raised in a Christian home or come from a Christian country. Even Hitler believed in God and proclaimed Jesus as Lord and Savior in a speech more than once. Society is guilty of redefining what it is to be a Christian. The Jehovah's Witnesses, Mormons, Christian Scientology, Progressive Christianity and the Prosperity Gospel use the term Christian loosely and incorrectly. They constitute false teachings and

Jesus spoke of this type of spiritual deception when he said, "Not everyone who says to me, Lord, Lord will enter the kingdom of heaven, but only the one who does the will of my Father who is in heaven." Mathew 7:21.

No one can claim to be a Christian unless they have proclaimed their belief in Jesus as the Christ and have repented of their sins. This means turning from their past life of sin and following Jesus and being obedient to him. This includes bearing good fruit such as being baptized, loving others as Christ did and testifying that Jesus alone has the power to save. Anything less than an "all in" attitude will not be an enduring faith. Christianity is a relationship with Jesus as opposed to a religious enterprise.

Complacency can become the enemy of salvation and there are many, many people who identify as Christians who are at risk of not receiving eternal life on the coming day of the Lord. The Bible refers to them as the lukewarm Church. "I know your deeds, that you are neither hot nor cold. I wish that you were either one or the other! So, because you are lukewarm – neither hot nor cold – I am about to spit you out of my mouth. You say, 'I am rich; I have acquired wealth and do not need a thing.' But you do not realize that you are wretched, pitiful, poor, blind and naked." Revelation 3:15-17.

If the Christian Church is no match for spiritual forces, then civilization as a whole is without hope. If believers don't have fire and passion for Jesus how can they expect to engage in a battle with foes on fire for Satan? Foes that are seasoned warriors from millennia of battles. Foes that are part of a larger army of hidden operatives in an orchestrated, systemic war on humanity. The very same spiritual forces that guide the cabal to covertly pull the strings of governments and rulers that control the world.

The narrative of political correctness and inclusivity is another deception designed to neuter opposition to the erosion of personal rights and freedoms and to silence the church and biblical morality. When the message from the pulpit cannot speak about condemnation, repentance, or judgement for fear of being labeled as hate speech, that church has already lost the battle. If pastors are not willing to offend people with the gospel of Christ, they have succumbed to the enemy. If the truth of the gospel is offensive, good! Because the truth is what sets you free! The truth of Jesus is what changes people.

Today society doesn't want to be judged. People put their hand in your face and say "don't judge me" and they label you as a hypocrite. They like to blame God for everything and say a loving God would never send people to hell. Yet they almost never blame Satan for misfortune. You don't hear people blaming Satan for their lot in life.

Much of society is acutely naïve to the evil in the spiritual realms and as many seek "spiritual awakening" they venture into uncharted waters without supervision or understanding. Medium.com states, "A Spiritual Awakening, simply put, is a series of events that occur in order to align you with your highest purpose in your lifetime. The idea of the Spiritual Awakening doesn't belong to any one religion, but certain practices do. Regardless of religious alignment, you can experience an Awakening – however through the process, you'll naturally start to identify less with the rules and strict practices of structured religion and instead, turn to yourself and begin practices that align with your truest nature." [93]

In order to achieve enlightenment seekers must shed their "ego" which is defined as everything "you" and includes everything you associate with your self-worth. Your ego is considered corrupted by your life experiences and therefore doesn't reflect the true you. Your ego is who you wish you could be instead of who you are. As your ego grows, your spirit suffers. According to the website, you end up with a distorted perception of the world and only by shedding our ego can we progress to our true selves.

However, in order to shed the ego, you must go through what they call the "Dark Night of the Soul." This is a period of time that precedes the actual awakening. It is the "cosmic clearing of energies, structures, and beliefs that do not align with your highest good. The writer, Mikaila Simone, in this case lost everything when she shed her ego. She went from living in a house to living in her car in the matter of months. In her own words, "I have never felt a fear so thick and deeply permeating in my entire life."[94]

She now feels the chakras are aligned and her psychic gifts are flourishing. She claims she remembers who she was before she came into this life and she is learning to navigate this life in a way that is more authentic to her spirit. Tragically, this is a classic example of demon possession. By emptying herself of who she was, she left a vacant space for a demonic spirit to move in and call home. It isn't herself she remembers in a previous life it is the spirit's inhabitance of someone else.

Jesus talked about how spirits need to inhabit people as recorded in Mathew 12:43-45. "When an impure spirit comes out of a person, it goes through arid places seeking rest and does not find it. Then it says, 'I will return to the house I left.' When it arrives, it finds the house unoccupied, swept clean and put in order. Then it goes and takes with it seven other spirits more wicked than itself, and they go and live there. And the final condition of that person is worse than the first."

There is a dark spirituality surrounding the martial arts. They were originally designed as a combination of meditation involving physical techniques to strengthen the body and awaken the spiritual dimension in life. Robert Buratti writes, "The true value in studying Martial Arts lies not in learning the technique or system itself, but in the acquisition of internal qualities that are developed through the learning process. The physical exercises are the concrete examples of abstract philosophical principles. Footwork systems teach the student about the qualities of energy, ebb and flow, and both creative and destructive potential. Handwork patterns teach the student about balance, dynamics and the intuition of natural spirit." [95]

"In Martial Arts, death is a constant presence." Buratti adds, "All spiritual systems confront death, for confronting death is perhaps the most important element of spirituality." He goes on to say that overcoming the fear of death releases great powers. The mastery of energy or "Chi" is both the artist's connection to his enemy and his strongest weapon against them. Energy manifests itself as spirit.

Thai Chi Chuan also incorporates cosmology and the Yin Yang symbol represents equal amounts of Yin and Yang, yet the Yin portion contains small amounts of Yang and vice versa. It is an endless cycle of unity and interaction of energy much like Zen which cannot be rationalized, only experienced. Therefore, it is difficult to tell where spirituality ends and martial practice begins. The mind is free to flow, unconscious of itself, an empty minded-ness, much like Buddhism.

One cannot have a cavalier attitude about spirituality. The darkness of the spiritual world is both heinous and insidious. With naïve curiosity, people are often drawn to explore spirituality or into the occult only to find themselves incrementally progressing deeper into exceedingly egregious territory. Many find themselves addicted to drugs and for others, suicide is the only way out.

Even UFO's and alien encounters are spiritual deceptions that have many believing lies that are contrary to Biblical truth. In my book *Truth Cries Out*, I shared the story of Joe Jordan, an investigator of UFO sightings and alien abductions, who learned through his experiences that these phenomenon, that aliens are spiritual beings. In one case a brand new Christian, during an alleged alien abduction cried out, "Jesus help me!" and the encounter immediately stopped. Joe has documented over four hundred cases of people who have had their alien abduction episodes halted in the name of Christ.

The alien deception is so profound that many people attribute the miracles recorded in the Bible to aliens and even believe we were created by aliens. Christianity is under attack and we must draw on the Holy Spirit to navigate these muddy waters. "The person without the Spirit does not accept the things that come from the Spirit of God but considers them foolishness, and cannot understand them because they are discerned only through the Spirit." 1 Corinthians 2:14.

The Bible says we are to test all spirits we encounter. "Dear friends, do not believe every spirit, but test the spirits to see whether they are from God, because many false prophets have gone out into the world. This is how you can recognize the Spirit of God: Every spirit that acknowledges that Jesus Christ has come in the flesh is from God, but every spirit that does not acknowledge Jesus is not from God. This is the spirit of the antichrist which you have heard is coming and even now is already in the world.

You, dear children, are from God and have overcome them, because the one who is in you is greater than the one who is in the world. They are from the world and therefore speak from the viewpoint of the world, and the world listens to them. We are from God, and whoever knows God listens to us; but whoever is not from God does not listen to us. This is how we recognize the Spirit of truth and the spirit of falsehood." 1 John 4:1-6.

Spiritual battles play themselves out in our physical world and individual lives. Our response creates a ripple effect that resonates out to others and ultimately has a profound effect on world events. It is no wonder that we live in a world that has forsaken God. It is because of our collective denial of God and rebellion against God's precepts that has placed humanity in the position it is in regarding our capitulation to the cabal and ultimately to Satan. So when you contemplate the magnitude of these spiritual battles it becomes apparent that the sheer size of the spiritual realms dwarfs out planet and the human population on it by a large factor and in turn, reveals the magnitude of God since his infinite nature surpasses it all collectively.

Civilization as a whole has been misled by the lies of Satan, and we should not be surprised since he is the father of lies. He was cast out of heaven and is the ruler of the earth. When Jesus was tempted in the wilderness by Satan, the devil offered him the world. "The devil led him up to a high place and showed him in an instant all the kingdoms of the world. And he said to him, 'I will give you all their authority and splendor; it has been given to me, and I can give it to anyone I want to. If you worship me, it will all be yours.'" Luke 4:5-7

Knowing your enemy is imperative to defeating him. Knowing the magnitude of the spiritual forces that influence the world is requisite to comprehending the totality of the delusion Satan has orchestrated in civilization. Understanding the darkness that has mastery over the cabal elucidates why society is the hostage of the deep state. When we examine the world from a global perspective we can see how Satan has his fingers in every pie, manifested through the covert power of the elite plutocracy that coerces governments and world leaders into activating their will. When we look at things from a four hundred thousand-foot level we can appreciate how the spiritual battles being waged have an endgame of world control.

Knowing the power we have in Christ Jesus, liberates us from the deception of the devil, and frees us from the mendacity that we are insignificant pawns in a greater more meaningful theatre. John wrote that we should not fear spiritual attacks, "You, dear children, are from God and have overcome them, because the one who is in you is greater than the one who is in the world." 1 John 4:4. Furthermore, Jesus confirmed this with his proclamation that, "All authority in heaven and on earth has been given to me." Mathew 28:18.

With the knowledge that there is no name under heaven greater than the name of Jesus, Christians are equipped with the one weapon that compels all demonic forces to stand down. In Christ's name every true believer has the authority to prevail against Satan. The dominion over the earth that Adam and Eve lost to Satan was won back by Christ when he triumphed over death and resurrected. That victory is ours to claim and Satan and his legions must yield to its authority.

We are called to be strong in the Lord and in his mighty power. "Put on the full armor of God, so you can take a stand against the devil's schemes." Ephesians 6:11. The full armor of God includes all of God's promises which are truth, righteousness, the gospel, faith, salvation, the word of God and prayer. Christians are not purposed for weakness but for strength. We are called to resist Satan and draw strength from the Lord. "Submit yourselves, then, to God. Resist the devil, and he will flee from you." James 4:7.

The Prophet Elisha warned the King of Israel of impending attacks by the King of Syria on several occasions prompting the Syrian leader to suspect a traitor within his ranks. When he was informed that Elisha received divine warnings which he passed onto his king, he became determined to kill the prophet. "Then he sent horses and chariots and a strong force there. They went at night and surrounded the city.

When the servant of the man of God got up and went out early the next morning, an army with chariots and horses had surrounded the city. 'Oh no, my lord! What shall we do?' the servant asked.

'Don't be afraid, the prophet answered. 'Those who are with us are more than those who are with them.'

And Elisha prayed, 'Open his eyes, Lord, so that he may see.' Then the Lord opened the servant's eyes, and he looked, and he saw the hills full of horses and chariots of fire all around Elisha." 2 Kings 6:14-17.

Elisha's servant lacked the spiritual awareness that God was protecting them. This didn't negate the fact that the army of flaming horses and chariots were there. In the same way, our lack of spiritual awareness doesn't make spiritual battles any less real. Charles Spurgeon used the analogy that if a person committed a murder which was witnessed by four people, he could not disprove evidence with non-evidence. If he produced forty people who did not see him do it, their testimony is worthless. By comparison, if forty people declare that there is no Holy Spirit, it only proves that forty people don't know what others do know. (Charles Spurgeon, Three Sights Worth Seeing).

Matt and Lora Higgens, missionaries in Kenya, reported in 1960, how their vehicle stopped seventeen miles short of Nairobi and they were forced to spend the night in their land rover. This was during the Mau Mau uprising that had already resulted in people being killed and dismembered. They claimed Psalm 4:8, "In peace I will lie down and sleep, for you alone, Lord, make me dwell in safety." and went to sleep. The next day they got the vehicle running and completed the trip. Before they left Nairobi, they were visited by a local pastor who relayed how a member of the Mau Mau had confessed to him how he and three others had crept up on the land rover to murder the missionaries, but when they saw the sixteen men surrounding the vehicle, they reconsidered and retreated.

Higgens responded that they were alone. A few weeks later they learned from a friend in the U.S. that God had placed a heavy prayer burden upon his heart so he got together with sixteen men from the church to pray for him and his wife on their journey.

A similar story of Reverend John G. Paton, a missionary in the New Hebrides Islands relayed how hostile natives surrounded his mission one night, intent on burning them out and killing them. He and his wife prayed during the night for God's protection and in the morning were amazed that the attackers had left at some point before dawn. A year later, when the chief accepted Jesus as his savior and became a Christian, Mr. Paton asked him why he and his men had spared him and his wife that night. The Chief replied, "Who were all those men you had with you there?" He went on to describe seeing hundreds of big men in shining garments with drawn swords guarding the mission.

Spiritual realms exist in a dimension adjacent to our physical realm and are just as real as the things we see, hear, feel, smell and touch. Heaven and hell are real. Heaven as a place betrays our ability to conceive something beyond our scope of conception. Heaven is a dimension which humanity has no way of describing based on our three dimensional, physical experience. In the same way that we cannot conceptualize God's omnipresence, the reality of heaven is equal to the reality of God. The omnipresence of God transcends all of our comprehension since he is beyond our ability to comprehend.

Furthrmore, the spirit world does not occupy time, space and matter, therefore, it may be even more real than our physical existence as we know it. Physicists are searching for six more dimensions in addition to the physical one we inhabit. They believe there are other universes which are either parallel or are explained using the Calabi-Yau manifold and exist with ours.

Paul, in his second letter to the church at Corinth wrote, "I know a man who fourteen years ago was caught up to the third heaven. Whether it was in the body or out of the body I do not know – God knows. And I know that this man – whether in the body or apart from the body I do not know, but God knows – was caught up to paradise and heard inexpressible things, things that no one is permitted to tell." 2 Corinthians 12:2-4.

In quantum mechanics, the tiniest particles are studied and the profound discoveries have been both complex and often hard to accept by researchers since they don't always obey the laws of nature. For example, experiments have detected a single beryllium atom in two slightly different locations at once and found that certain pairs of particles can somehow influence each other even if they are miles apart. Rather than leading to conclusions that attempt to deny the existence of the spiritual realm, quantum mechanics "offers an intriguing look at the deeper details of God's creation." [96]

Scientists have tried to bridge the gap between quantum mechanics and Einstein's theory of relativity mathematically with a factor they call the cosmological constant. Problems surface when the calculations don't match observable factors in the universe such as the fact that the universe seems to be expanding at an accelerating rate. Because the force driving the galaxies apart is a mystery to scientists, they have labeled it "dark energy." I would call it the power of God.

Lucas Lombriser, an assistant professor of theoretical physics at the University of Geneva in Switzerland explains that, "The cosmological constant (dark energy) currently constitutes about seventy percent of the energy content in our universe, which is what we can infer from the observed accelerated expansion that our universe is presently undergoing. Yet the constant is not understood. Attempts to explain it have failed, and there seems to be something fundamental that we are missing in how we understand the cosmos. Unraveling the puzzle is one of the major research areas in modern physics. It is generally anticipated that resolving the issue may lead us to a more fundamental understanding of physics." [97]

The universe is the expression of God's creativity and imagination manifested in the physical dimension. The Spiritual realms preceded the physical realm and therefore are superior to the physical. Satan was cast out of heaven to the earth thereby restricting the physical world from achieving the perfection of God's realm. Our earthly parents are physically unable to provide perfect nurturing and upbringing and therefore bring forth incomplete and flawed children in a fallen state in need of redemption. Therefore, it is only through the sacrifice and atonement of Jesus on the cross that we can be reconciled to our true Father in heaven and rescued from our physical affliction. Our physical lives are simply a manifestation of our true selves that must be left behind before we can stand in the presence of the Almighty face to face.

Satanic spiritual forces wreak havoc on everything about our physical lives, all day, every day in a concealed theatre of warfare. The success of their battle plan depends on an unsuspecting mankind, that is in denial that there even is a war and attributes warnings about its existence as nothing more than conspiracy theories. For those with an innate sense that there is more than meets the eye, there is a victory to be claimed through our faith in the Son of God.

"Be alert and of sober mind. Your enemy the devil prowls around like a roaring lion looking for someone to devour. Resist him, standing firm in the faith, because you know the family of believers throughout the world is undergoing the same kind of sufferings. And the God of grace, who called you to his eternal glory in Christ, after you have suffered a little while, will himself restore you and make you strong, firm and steadfast." 1 Peter 5:8-10.

Believers in Christ are called to emulate him in the way that we live and that means having love and compassion for each other. Resisting the temptation to kick someone when they are down and instead help them get back up. Its the little things that add up to making a huge difference so we must be kind and empathetic when we see our fellow man in turmoil and suffering. Fight back at the devil and his schemes that would have us believe we are all nothing more than animals, competing for space and food.

Comprehending the nature of how our adversary the devil endeavors to drive us away from God helps to rationalize the spiritual war going on, and focusing on our Creator and his love for us provides the strength to win the battles. Love is more powerful than anything, because God is love.

Only love can break down the devil's strongholds and the evil running rampant in our world. Only love can feed the hungry and clothe the poor. Only love can make us whole and complete and it all begins with one act of kindness to someone who is struggling.

THE DEMOLITION OF DEMOCRACY

In 2020 the battle being fought in the spiritual realms played itself out on the world stage as the covert forces of evil boiled to the surface and became visible for all of the world to see. Nowhere was this more obvious than in the U.S.A. where one man stood between personal rights, power and freedom and a rapid progression to a new world order propagated by the dark forces of the cabal. In fact, from the moment Donald J. Trump became a candidate in the 2016 presidential election he was viewed by the deep state and the entrenched political bureaucracy as an illegitimate politician and he has been the victim of attack in the form of monstrous lies and blatant misconduct by the left wing political establishment ever since.

Declassified Obamagate documents have revealed that in the months leading up to the 2016 presidential election and afterward, the democratic party endorsed and participated in the ongoing spying and wiretapping of the Trump campaign. Their allegations of Russian collusion based on the bogus information supplied by Christopher Steel who admitted to leaking the information to help Hillary Clinton (who hatched the scheme in April 2016) cover up her email scandal. Her blatant disregard for ethics and integrity amounted to a premeditated plan to dishonor her opponent and overthrow the president of the United States and was known to the FBI, the DOJ, and the intelligence chiefs, yet nothing was ever done.[98]

Their conspiracy of silence combined with the biased narrative of the mainstream news networks enabled the deep state to effectively neuter the United States government as they wasted valuable time and resources maliciously impeaching a president (not only once but twice) rather than carry on the business of running the country.

The FISA court was misled and essentially countermanded despite warnings by a supervisory special agent that the operation was politically motivated and he subsequently walked away from the task force because of the corruption. The FBI deliberately impeded the release of the declassified documents in an effort to delay the public from knowing the truth before Biden was sworn in as president on January 20, 2021. This constituted more evidence of the deep state's influence and grip on power in the United States and their desperation to remain hidden.

After unsuccessfully trying to remove president Trump after nearly four years of scheming, back room dealing, alleged collusion with Russia and attempted impeachment, through an obsessive, compulsive, coup d'etat attempt, all stops were pulled, in a ramped up assault during the presidential election of 2020. Through unprecedented deception, lies and omissions of truth, society was intentionally gas lighted to accept the pre-emptive undermining of the democratic process.

In an orchestrated effort, fraudulent activity and irregularities in the electoral process were witnessed on an unparalleled level, in a systematic, relentless abuse of the law and the constitution of the United States. Mail in ballots were sent to absentee voters, deceased people, people who had moved out of the voting state and even non-citizens. Many people received more than one ballot and some received ballots already filled out. Some people who showed up to vote were turned away and told they had already voted. Eyewitnesses reported seeing boxes of ballots all with the same signature. In a partisan political agenda, ineligible votes were even counted several times, mass vote dumps occurred in the middle of the night and there was unexplainable vote switching from one candidate to another and never in favor of Trump.

Hundreds of thousands of votes were illegally tallied for Joe Biden after polls closed and without the scrutiny of observers. In counties that were trending solidly throughout election day, vote dumps that were blatantly and overwhelmingly pro Biden stood out as statistical anomalies and red flags that these were not organic votes. In the state of Michigan, the lawsuit brought forward by the Amistad Project claimed "officials illegally counted or threw out no fewer than 508,016 ballots."[99]

Furthermore, the lawsuit alleged the Detroit City Council approved a $1 million contract to the firm P.I.E. Management to hire 2000 workers to man the polls and ballot counting machines at the TCF Center. These workers were paid $50/hour and Facebook CEO Mark Zuckerberg has been implicated in funding this expense to the tune of $400 million which was paid through the group CTCL to Democrat favoring election officials and municipalities.

The mainstream media was complicit in controlling what information voters had, in order to determine which candidate would receive their vote. Trump was continually attacked by the media from the minute he won the 2016 election and the official narrative painted him as a corrupt buffoon and Russian puppet. On the other side of the floor, investigations into the Biden family's foreign business dealings and corruption were never covered by the mainstream media and even suppressed. The major news networks have become so blatantly left wing and obviously an extension of the establishment, that they can no longer be considered mainstream. Rather than reporting the news, today's major news broadcasts promote a narrative intended to influence public opinion and coerce social values to align with the cabal's agenda.

The voting trends exhibited in the senate and house of representatives races were counter to the presidential voter trends which statistically is nonsensical and indicative of the meddling and rigging of votes. It is counterintuitive that a presidential candidate that was clearly not the strongest candidate in history would receive the record number of votes ever, as the official narrative claimed.

The voting machines themselves were shown to be capable of being programmed to switch votes, discard votes and duplicate votes in a manner illustrating corruption in their design. This was learned to be a design that originated in Venezuela so Hugo Chavez could hold elections and never lose. The Dominion voting machines that were used were connected to servers in Germany so that they could be remotely manipulated to steal the election for the dark forces of the deep state.

The deep state wanted so badly to eliminate Trump, they were willing to come out from their dark corners and risk being identified, in order to have him lose. They used multiple intelligence agencies including MI6, the CIA, FBI and NSA in attempt to impose Biden on the American people. In 1967 they assassinated JFK, in 1981 they attempted to assassinate Ronald Reagan and in 2020 they were so sure they would get away with mass election fraud that they didn't go to that extreme measure with Trump.

In the months leading up to the election, riots broke out across America as Black Lives Matter and ANTIFA staged protests, looted stores and burned buildings in an attempt to convince voters that Trump's America was a violent and racist one. These riots and protests were funded by members of the cabal whose financial aid bused participants in from other states and delivered pallet loads of bricks conveniently to areas where the riots happened.

In a desperate attempt to hold onto their fabricated Biden victory, democratic DOJ attorney generals dismissed the legal actions of Trump's campaign and the suits brought forward by Sidney Powell and the SCOTUS resisted getting involved with what it considered "state" legal issues or dismissed cases on procedural grounds without ever hearing the evidence. Even when the State of Texas sued the swing states of Michigan, Wisconsin, Pennsylvania and Georgia for rendering the votes of Texans impotent by their tolerance of election fraud and were joined by seventeen other states, the supreme court refused to engage.

It became obvious the SCOTUS feared retribution by the deep state and it is very possible that lives were threatened and/or bribes were made. The power wielded by the cabal proved to be greater than the will of the highest court in the land and justice itself succumbed to the dark evil that has been growing unchecked and is now greater than any resistance mounted against it. When the entire system of law and order in a democratic country reach this level of corruption, the country is doomed to fall into authoritarian hands.

The riots and demonstrations leading up to the 2020 U.S. presidential election and the 2021 assault on the capitol ahead of the inauguration are prime examples of how the cabal implements their strategy. Known ANTIFA operatives and rioters infiltrated the legitimate pro Trump crowd on January 6, 2021, instigated the move to storm the capitol building and led the charge, breaching security, breaking windows and occupying the offices of government.

In what appeared to be a planned draw down of capitol police, many officers were reportedly sent home that morning and a very insignificant police presence remained to monitor the permitted occupation of more than five hundred thousand people for the planned demonstration. That is illogical and suspiciously insinuates a pre-planned agenda by the deep state to sabotage the moment and effectively seize the narrative from the Trump supporters, thereby framing them, which was immediately amplified by House Democrats and the mainstream media.

Hypocrisy was on full display as Trump was once again vilified by the establishment as they stood guilty of the very things they accused him of. Nancy Pelosi's own words from the aftermath of the 2016 election that "the election was hijacked," returned to haunt her and signaled the deeply imbedded pretense in the political arena. In a rushed and baseless charge of enticing violence, the House Democrats voted to impeach Trump an unprecedented second time, without following due process. No discussion or debate was allowed (Trump was once again acquitted by the senate). With only two weeks left until the inauguration date, it amounted to a knee jerk reaction of desperation as Trump refused to concede and promised to keep fighting to bring down the house of cards.

The establishment's sense of entitlement and insatiable desire to rule combined with their allegiance to the deep state was a revelation of just how corrupt the swamp had become and the double standards it applied to those who opposed them. For most of 2020, the Democrat party endorsed and encouraged the violent and illegal riots of BLM and ANTIFA yet subsequently cried foul when the capitol was assaulted after a Trump speech in which he called for a "peaceful and patriotic demonstration at the capitol." They were hardly in any position to claim the moral high ground yet in their hypocrisy they labeled the riots as insurrection.

Blatant media bias was once again evident in the coverage of the U.S. capitol riots and shut down, with news outlets calling the protests "treason and rebellion," in sharp contrast to the weeks of insurgency during the BLM protests that were hailed as peaceful demonstrations despite collateral damage estimated at hundreds of millions of dollars and many deaths. The police were celebrated heroes for quelling the January 6th uprising, while throughout the BLM protests police brutality was the featured narrative with calls for defunding of the police echoing around the world. While unfortunate, the storming of the Capitol served as justification for the installation of over 25,000 military personnel in Washington D.C. in order to protect the corrupt establishment in the transition leading up to the inauguration.

After four years of lies about Russian collusion by the democratic party, suppression of the truth, the propagation of the left's agenda by mainstream media and the blatant disregard for Republican legal challenges by a biased and corrupt department of justice, it is no wonder that half of American voters became disenfranchised and were ready to revolt. For four years the justice system entertained Democrat lawsuits over the 2016 presidential election yet slammed the door when Republicans questioned the 2020 electoral outcome despite the sworn affidavits of hundreds of eyewitnesses to fraud at the risk of the penalty of perjury. At no point was evidence allowed to be presented by the courts while the news networks worked overtime to remind viewers of Trump's baseless claims of voter fraud without evidence.

Authoritarianism has become standard operating procedure by bureaucrats, judges, corporations, and all branches of government. Political correctness and the "woke" movement are expressions of authoritarianism by a "don't judge me" culture. When a democratic system refuses to allow opposing viewpoints to be debated it is no longer democratic. When government representatives cease to represent their constituents and delegitimize opposition and half the country's voters, the system is no longer democratic. By single mindedly pursuing the destruction of Trump's presidency and everything he stood for, including the citizens who voted for him, the governing bodies demonstrated their love for power at the expense of the citizens and the nation.

In a deplorable response to the official narrative, corporate America fell in line with the deep state by proclaiming they would no longer donate monies to the Republican party. Big tech exercised their marketplace muscle when Twitter banned Donald Trump indefinitely and Google and Amazon took Parler out at the knees in an egregious infringement on freedom of speech and the right to competition in the marketplace. America has become a battleground between a much deeper fight than left vs right and democracy vs communism. It is the theater of the ultimate battle for truth, the war between good and evil. America has been played by the cabal. By accepting wealth through donations and outright bribery the bureaucratic creatures of the swamp have been blindfolded to the truth. Jesus said, "If the blind lead the blind, both will fall into a pit." Mathew 15:14.

With Joe Biden in the Whitehouse the door has been opened for globalism to overpower the final bastion of nationalism in the world and the deep state will accelerate the agenda of a new world order. On his first day in office, he re-entered the Paris Accord, the Iran deal, re-joined the WHO, cancelled the construction of the Keystone XL pipeline and the border wall. The Biden administration's connections with Black Rock Investments (the world's largest investment firm) are disturbing as the company's size, influence and business partners are red flags to U.S. sovereignty as three of its executives are in Biden's government. Several Blackrock board directors serve in key roles in the Biden administration. In addition, several high profile players from the Obama administration who have been active in businesses involved in the middle east, now serve in Biden's government.

Many of the same faces that were involved in Hillary Clinton's foreign affairs fiascos and email scandal are now back in the limelight. Additionally, the Biden team includes many former executives from big tech, including Facebook, Twitter, Amazon, Google and Apple. This informal partnership yokes government with the big tech machinery to control and spread propaganda as well as influence policy making. On top of all of this, there is also widespread speculation that Biden will be short lived as president and will be replaced by Vice President Kamala Harris to allow her even more extreme left agenda to be implemented.

The "business" of climate change is back to front and center as radical climate guru John Kerry has been appointed to the position of Special Envoy for Climate. Expect a systematic dismantling of America's natural resources sector much like the decimation under Trudeau's Canada. The Biden administration will embrace the great reset and has positioned itself and its private enterprise partners to receive a windfall of wealth at the expense of the middle class.

There will be no recovery for capitalism and free enterprise. The sovereignty of the USA has now been compromised and the end of the republic is within the realm of possibility. Foreign interests from China,

Russia, Iran, Italy and even Cuba are suspected to have contributed to the undermining of the electoral process in the 2020 U.S. election, illustrating the extent the cabal went to in order to remove Trump from office.

Trump's proclamation that the U.S.A. would choose independence over global governance, control, and domination in front of the UN was an intentional demonstration of his nationalist agenda. It infuriated the deep state and proponents of a new world order and prompted George Soros to strike back at Davos in 2018. "Clearly I consider the Trump administration a danger to the world. But regardless it is a purely temporary phenomenon that will disappear in 2020." [100]

Ultimately, the cancel culture that endorsed the toppling of statues, and the renaming of sports teams, singing groups and pancake syrup has decided that in order to achieve unity in the USA, voters who voted against the left must be silenced and cancelled as well. In doing so the travesty by a culture that painted all blacks with a broad brush augmented as hypocrisy when it painted all Trump supporters with a broad brush. Unity does not mean consensus to these deluded crusaders of the cabal but rather subjugation through censorship and the confiscation of hunting rifles from law abiding citizens. Democracy has been blamed for the political polarization in North America as socialist ideologies have taken root in the younger generations of the population.

The causes for discontent, meanwhile are anything but the product of democracy and are in truth antidemocratic in the very nature of their beliefs. Groups like Black Lives Matter and ANTIFA are socialist to the core and even boast of Marxist training for members within their organizations. In the aftermath of the 2020 US presidential election Joe Biden called for healing as if his political allies and the Democrats had nothing to do with the sowing of dissention for the previous four years.

It is truly mind boggling how truth has been exchanged for lies and how the official narrative designed by the cabal has permeated and shaped society through the corruption of politics, social media censorship and the blatant bias of the mainstream news networks. It is additionally shocking when you realize the depths that the plutocracy has gone to satisfy their greed for power and money, and what is even more surprising is how society has accepted it.

In the larger picture, the dark agenda of the deep state promoting more government control, decreased parental rights, abortion on demand, the sexualization of children, LGBTQ and pedophilia acceptance, the erosion of the traditional family, rubber stamp divorces and the greatest anti-Christian ideologies in American history has been complicit in the demise of the social fabric that built North America.

The education system has been overwhelmed by socialist and communist indoctrination, the media has been bought and subjugated to the extreme left's propaganda. Furthermore, the normalization of pornography and promiscuous lifestyles, that only a generation ago were considered obscene, and the break-down of cultural standards and morality can be attributed to covert influences of the cabal.

In Canada the Trudeau government has introduced legislation in the form of Bill C-6, that restricts parents, counsellors and faith leaders from expressing opinions or giving advice regarding gender or sexual behavior. The bill criminalizes any form of conversion therapy regarding transgender counselling, and teaching children biology or social studies (even through home schooling) concepts contrary to liberal ideology. Canadians can be sentenced with up to five years in prison under this bill.

Furthermore, the bill will give police surveillance powers to investigate and enforce this law. This includes surveillance of the offices of counsellors, churches, and private homes, since parents' conversations and actions are key components of the bill. The Trudeau government relishes in the unprecedented latitude offered to it through the tolerance of draconian government interventions facilitated by the coronavirus.

When John F. Kennedy learned that the CIA were out to stop him from exposing everything, he set up the organization of "Q" which was the highest level of military intelligence designed to alert the president of deep state interference in power. Unfortunately, Q wasn't prepared for the events of November 22, 1963 in Dallas Texas. Since then, Q has continued to exist and has remained invisible for the most part until the internet which saw it evolve to include an anonymous grass roots faction which has become known as Q Anon.

Perhaps no other group has been associated with conspiracy theories more than Q Anon. What should be far more alarming is that some of their claims may be true. Because much of what they proclaim sounds pretty farfetched, they release information in small doses and encourage people to research things for themselves. Tragically, overzealous patriots can take up the cause independently and carry out acts of protest which was in all likelihood a contributing factor in the takeover of the congress on Jan.6th 2020 in the U.S. capitol, which Q Anon predicted in advance.

They also predicted that there will be many arrests of child traffickers and pedophiles, some in very high places. Even the Queen of England was not beyond the reach of their secret justice prophecies. They aspire to dismantle the deep state and restore equity in society. How successful they will be remains to be seen. Regardless of how things turn out, the U.S. is headed for a civil war and martial law. Q Anon knows the cabal will not go down without a fight, therefore, this is will be and already has become a very diametrically opposed theatre.

Q Anon's most infamous claim is that JFK Jr. is alive and is in fact Q. He was to be revealed to the world when Trump remained in office and the cabal was taken down and would be instrumental in running the new world order instituted by Trump's reclamation of control of the world by the forces of good. It was speculated that since JFK was assassinated and died from a mortal head wound, that JFK Jr. could be construed as his reincarnate. Since he has been presumed dead ever since his plane went down in the Atlantic Ocean on July 16, 1999, JFK Jr. alive and working behind the scenes to avenge his father's death, would indeed be shocking. This would be a fulfillment of Revelation 13:3, "One of the heads of the beast seemed to have had a fatal wound, but the fatal wound had been healed. The whole world was filled with wonder and followed the beast."

No matter what your perception of Q Anon's predictions of subduing the cabal, delivering the type of justice necessary to expose the deep state, and bringing about a utopian new world order, the entire narrative counters biblical prophecy. It is the product of a human solution to a spiritual problem therefore it is flawed and no matter how many elements of truth are put forward it is not the truth of Jesus Christ. Furthermore, the end result would be a new world order made up primarily of a one world government much like the deep state is planning, only it will be run by the military.

When the Lord opens a door, no one can close it and when he closes a door, no one can open it. There is no doubt that despite the inherent human flaws of Donald Trump, the Lord was using him to further his purposes upon the earth. So many people sincerely hoped that Trump would retain the presidency however, without America's complete repentance and return to God, it could not happen. When the prophet Jonah warned the city of Nineveh that it was about to be destroyed because of its sin, the king ordered that all the people and even the animals fast and petition God to relent. They were spared (Jonah 3:10). Even though thousands of people prayed, the United States collectively did not plead with the Lord for restoration. Half of the country's population continued reveling in sin, denying God and supporting the left's agenda of LGBTQ rights, abortion and general rebellion against the Most High.

The signs are everywhere that we are living in the last days. This isn't simply some feeble attempt to counter an ideology or movement with rhetorical arguments. This is destiny. This is biblical. The same deep state that has allowed Hillary to get away with deleting thousands of emails, that covers up the sex trafficking of children by the wealthy and powerful and secretly funds riots and destruction of private property and sows the seeds of discord in society has its sights set on total population control.

There has only been one wrinkle in the plan that threatened to unravel the scheme and set it back by a decade. One man pushed back against the establishment and singlehandedly put the brakes on globalism. Donald Trump stood between the plutocratic ambitions of the UN, the WHO, the WEF and the socialist and corporate agenda of the cabal and personal rights and freedoms. This is why the U.S. election was such a hotly contested event. It was ultimately a power struggle between good and evil and Trump was the final obstacle in the path toward a one world government that hinges on the collapse of democracy. His defeat is a defeat of democracy and we all are defeated with him. With Biden in the Whitehouse, the world is now on a fast track to a totalitarian global government that will subjugate civilization and culminate with the advent of the Great Tribulation and the revealing of the antichrist.

With the foundations for peace laid in the middle east, the precedence has been set that peace agreements with Israel are achievable and the door is now open for a world leader to pick up the momentum generated by the Trump administration. This will be an all-encompassing peace accord that facilitates the rebuilding of the Jewish Temple in Jerusalem and re-establishes the daily sacrifices.

There is growing sentiment in Israel to build the third temple and the Temple Institute has already made the sacred vessels to be used in the temple. They are made to the exact specifications written in the Bible, and have been constructed from the original source materials. Included are the musical instruments to be played by the Levites, the golden crown of the High Priest, the sacred robe of the Kohen Gadol (High Priest), the High Priest's Choshen (breastplate), Ephod and the tzitz and the gold and silver vessels use in the incense and sacrificial services. The Menorah (seven branched candelabra), made of pure gold, the golden Incense Altar, and the golden Table of the Showbread, are all complete. [101]

The building of the third temple is requisite for the fulfillment of the end time prophecies of Ezekiel (Ezekiel 42), Daniel (Daniel 9:27) and Jesus (Mathew 24:15-16). The Temple Institute's School is training certified, DNA tested Cohen (descendants of the High Priest Aaron) to perform the temple duties. Even the red heifer is being bred in Israel to be sacrificed in the ritual purification of the priests and the vessels so they can formally enter the holiest of holies.

The Muslim claim to the temple mount and the Dome of the Rock are all that remain to impede the temple construction. Once the impending peace accord is struck and the Palestinian Authority inevitably concedes their claims of exclusivity to the mount, the temple will be erected quickly. It has only been in the last 30 years that the efforts to rebuild the Jewish temple have been pursued earnestly and they testify that we are indeed living in the last days before the return of Yeshua HaMashiach to Jerusalem. [102]

The Church in the United States of America has been warned that they have been examined and have been found wanting. The Lord has just fired a warning shot over the bow of the Christian ship and it is time to change course. It is time for Christians to get right with God.

Many so called "prophets" spoke presumptuously of God's favor and plans for continued blessings for the USA, forgetting Jesus's own words for the last days regarding the appearance of false prophets (Mathew 24:11). While America is the home of many sincere Christian believers, it is also a place where false doctrine and deceived Christians abound. "Not everyone who says to me, 'Lord, Lord' will enter the kingdom of heaven, but only the one who does the will of my Father who is in Heaven. Many will say to me on that day, Lord, Lord, did we not prophesy in your name and in your name drive out demons and in your name perform many miracles?' Then I will tell them plainly, 'I never knew you, away from me, you evildoers!'" Mathew 7: 21-23.

It is human nature to perceive world events from your personal vantage point, and Americans have inadvertently attempted to reverse engineer scripture in order to place the United States in end times prophecy. In reality North and South America are not global factors in the last days, as prophecy is focused on the middle east and the nation of Israel during end times.

Sadly, rather than blessings, the USA is heading for collapse because her transgressions and iniquities have not ceased. By subverting the 2020 election, the cabal through the combined forces of the left wing political establishment, the mainstream media and corporate titans, sealed America's fate as a nation that has forsaken God. The moral minority cannot atone for the immorality of Las Vegas, San Francisco, New York, New Orleans and Hollywood. In the same way that Israel's failure to keep her covenant with God resulted in her punishment and the dispersing of the Jews among the nations, the United States (and Canada) will be punished for turning away from the Lord. After removing God from schools, courthouses, governments and most of society, America has turned her back on the precepts that made her great. America's idolatry of materialism and liberal values that celebrate sexual promiscuity, pornography and promote LGBTQ lifestyles have become so blatant and offensive that God has removed his favor from the nation and the land can no longer be healed. The deep divisions within her borders will cause her demise and she will fall from her position of prominence on the world stage.

The words of the apostle Paul resonate as I contemplate North America's fate. "For although they knew God, they neither glorified him as God nor gave thanks to him, but their thinking became futile and their foolish hearts were darkened. Although they claimed to be wise, they became fools and exchanged the glory of the immortal God for images made to look like mortal man and birds and animals and reptiles.

Therefore God gave them over in the sinful desires of their hearts to sexual impurity for the degrading of their bodies with one another. They exchanged the truth of God for a lie, and worshipped and served created things rather than the Creator – who is forever praised. Amen" Romans 1:21-25.

It is thought provoking to contemplate why North America doesn't factor into end time biblical prophecies. When the U.S.A. has dominated the world scene for the last 200 years, it's hard to imagine the most powerful country in the world and a close ally of Israel not involved in the middle east end times wars. Perhaps it will be torn apart by civil war as its deeply divided population turns on itself with the continued subliminal antagonizing influence of the deep state. One thing seems certain though. The U.S. is noticeably absent in the conflicts of the last days. America will be removed from its role of Israel's big brother, leaving Israel alone and seemingly at the mercy of the Arab states. This will be what opens the door for the antichrist to negotiate peace with Israel and her adversaries and also succeed in setting up a new world order.

The power vacuum left by America's destruction will be filled by the new world order and the cabal's agenda 21. The deep state's demolition of democracy has been systematic and absolute. The world is about to erupt into a full blown era of evil in which the very nature of goodness will be subverted, and there will be a significant shift in world affairs. We are about to witness the rapid progression towards a new world order and ultimately the one world government of the final global dictator, the son of perdition, the man of lawlessness, the antichrist. We are about to enter the seventieth week of the prophecy of Daniel.

CONNECTING THE DOTS

With the COVID 19 pandemic altering world economies, changing societal behavior and dominating the news media, the cabal has seized the opportunity to further their agenda for a new world order on a global scale. World governments have been coerced into lockdowns, mandatory mask wearing and cash has been vilified as a legitimate form of currency. As the narrative evolves, leaders have begun to promote "The Great Reset," in an effort to stimulate buy in from a skeptical public. Visions of a post COVID world include: the end of home ownership, the end of car ownership, the end of single family dwellings, the end of paper currency, the end of jobs, and who knows what else, and all by the year 2030. The plan calls for forgiveness of mortgage, credit card and personal loan debts in exchange for title and relinquishing all ownership.

This conveniently corresponds with the UN's agenda 2030 and the two share common denominators. Climate change is the fulcrum that justifies all other measures to arrive at a sustainable existence for what will be left of the human race. It is a plan for the wealthy elite that reduces the carbon footprint of humanity (through population reduction) to a level that can only be enjoyed by the precious few. Their fear of extinction has propagated a sinister solution that they must eliminate the majority of the population before it's too late to save the planet. So scared of death are the plutocracy, that they are willing to euthanize most of the people on earth for the greater good and so save themselves.

Underlying the social inequalities that the agenda plans to resolve is the concept that "Private land ownership is a principal instrument of accumulation and concentration of wealth and therefore contributes to social injustice." [103]

Canada has become a textbook example of how the deep state uses weak political leaders as "puppets" to enact their agenda in countries. Prime Minister Justin Trudeau's lack of empathy for his own country and the voters that propelled him to power is just the personality trait required to buy into the globalist dream of a new world order. Early in his tenure as Prime Minister his comments that Canada was the first post national state, and that there was no core identity and no mainstream in Canada made headlines as third and fourth generation Canadians were snubbed in favor of immigration.

Trudeau has been used by the cabal to implement the UN's playbook on a regional level, thereby decimating Canada's oil and gas industries in the response to a fabricated climate emergency and exploiting the COVID 19 "pandemic" to expedite their agenda. With a minority government, by instilling fear through misinformation and manipulation of the coronavirus, Trudeau was able to manipulate the New Democrat Party to support his Liberals in implementing draconian measures that coerced Canadians to voluntarily relinquish many of their rights and freedoms and had many begging for more restrictions. The Prime Minister's admiration for communist regimes like Cuba and China is no secret.

Justin Trudeau's allegiance to the UN and cooperation with the deep state has left Canada vulnerable to the undermining of its sovereignty. It has been demonstrated that foreign interference in Canada through the clandestine targeting of resource industries like the "tar sands" through environmental groups, which has landlocked Alberta oil, decimated B.C.'s forestry industry, and even coordinated First Nations protests such as the 'Wet'suwet'en blockades of the Coastal GasLink pipeline, have cumulatively resulted in the loss of over a hundred thousand jobs (including the service sectors). Foreign actors have been exposed by the likes of Ottawa MP David McGuinty, chair of the National Security and Intelligence Committee of Parliamentarians, Rennie Marcoux, executive director of the committee's secretariat and attorney Vivian Krause in her ongoing battle to uncover the espionage conducted by foreign interests within Canada's borders.

Trudeau uses the same terminology as the UN and the WEF to

convey the concepts of a new world order. On September 29, 2020 in his speech to the UN the language Trudeau used, portrayed his allegiance to the global elite and their vision for the future. "This pandemic has provided an opportunity for a reset. This is our chance to accelerate our pre-pandemic efforts, to reimagine economic systems that actually address global challenges like extreme poverty, inequality, and climate change."[104]

Canada is now in the precarious position of the global leader in growing its debt more than any other country in 2020 and is now poised to exceed a trillion dollars, recording the biggest jump in non-financial sector debt, ahead of Japan, the U.S. and the U.K. "Canada also saw the largest increases in household and non-financial corporate debt."[105] In an insane race to the bottom, Trudeau's offer of a reset by forgiving people's debts, the country could then be forced into receivership if it cannot service its debt and find itself at the mercy of the IMF and ultimately under the UN's control. This possibility looms large for a country of less than forty million people and an intentionally crippled natural resources sector, which hindsight will prove was part of the plan all along.

WEF founder and executive chairman Klaus Schwab has stated, "now is the historical moment, the time, not only to fight the virus but to shape the system for the post corona era." On the WEF's website you will find 8 predictions for the world in 2030:

1) All products will have become services.
2) There is a global price on carbon.
3) US dominance is over. We have a handful of global powers.
4) Farewell hospital, hello home-spital.
5) We are eating much less meat.
6) Today's Syrian refugees, 2030's CEO's.
7) The values that built the West will have been tested to the breaking point.
8) By the 2030's we'll be ready to move humans toward the Red Planet. [106]

The WEF produced and released a video, that has since been taken down, that envisioned life in 2030 and began with the statement, "In 2030 you will own nothing and you will be happy." When you contemplate this statement you immediately realize it is speaking about communism. The terrifying thing about this is that the elite ruling class will own everything. The video also claimed whatever you want you will rent. Obviously if there are things to rent, they are owned by "someone" and "someone" will profit from that ownership but it won't be small business or the middle class.

Projections in the video asserted that due to climate change, a billion people would be displaced from their homes because of rising sea levels and that will mean an increase of refugees into developed countries. These preposterous claims have no basis in truth and if you examine the claims of catastrophic climate change proponents over the past few decades they have amounted to nothing but conjecture. Not one thing has come to pass that these climate "experts" have predicted.

The UN warned in 1989 that unless sea level rise was not stopped, entire nations would be wiped out by the year 2000. In 2006 Al Gore's "An Inconvenient Truth" warned that unless we took drastic measures to curb greenhouse gases, the world would reach a point of no return in ten years. In 2008 he claimed the north polar ice cap would be ice free by 2014. Alexandria Ocasio-Cortez warned in 2019 that the world would end in 12 years if we don't address climate change immediately. Greta Thunberg's crusade over climate change amounted to the blatant flogging of a tired ideology that was financed by the wealthy elite in a desperate attempt to revive a narrative that was clearly losing traction.

In Bible prophecy concerning the last days there is a lot of detail but little is written about weather patterns. Jesus did say there would be earthquakes and famine in various places but that we should not be alarmed. He warned, "There will be signs in the sun, moon and stars. On the earth, nations will be in anguish and perplexity over the roaring and tossing of the sea." Luke 21:25. Indeed, today the catastrophic climate change narrative certainly has most nations very concerned over sea level rise and the potential loss of millions of homes.

During the final judgements, the fourth angel poured out his bowl on the sun and the sun was given the power to scorch people with fire (Revelation 16:8-9). By the time this happens, climate change will be the least of society's worries as death and destruction will be everywhere. The book of Genesis is clear that, "As long as the earth endures, seedtime and harvest, cold and heat, summer and winter, day and night will never cease." Genesis 8:22.

The WEF claims western values such as freedom, and Judeo Christian principles will be tested to the breaking point, meaning the cultural values of refugees will challenge and displace western values. It is already evident that the traditional western family is not reproducing at a sustainable rate and that without immigration western populations will decline. The WEF sees this as an open door to fill this void and transform western society from within. The greatest value targeted by this ideology is the belief that Jesus is the salvation and hope for humanity. Since communism recognizes the state as the ultimate authority over the lives of citizens, there is no room for God therefore Christianity will become public enemy number one.

The utopian society depicted by the WEF has hidden caveats that include tracking your every move, totalitarian government control, and no private ownership, meaning people will rely on the government for everything. Even Prince Charles has gotten in on the action and produced a video outlining the agenda. When what has happened in Canada is duplicated in every country, sovereignty will succumb to the new world order and pave the way for a one world government led by a one world dictator introducing a one world currency.

5G will be instrumental with its increased capabilities and speed, and is being touted as the fourth industrial revolution. It is estimated that it will add thirteen trillion dollars to the global economy by 2035 and add 22 million jobs.[107] With potential to facilitate digital desires for the greater good, such as digital identification for the world's population and worldwide use of digital currencies, 5G is also a Trojan horse with its capabilities of increased surveillance. Because the millimeter waves 5G uses can only travel short distances (about 1000 feet), cellular relays will have to be installed on every city block. 5G towers are already visible everywhere. In China, this advanced geolocation ability has already been paired with an expansive network of surveillance cameras equipped with facial recognition technology, in its social credit program.

5G technology will facilitate our smart phones, smart homes and smart automobiles to act as surveillance systems and ultimately to control what we can and cannot do and to incriminate us when we fall outside the established parameters of authority. It will be a component of an all-encompassing subjugation of humanity to artificial intelligence controlled by the deep state and extend to limiting our ability to buy and sell.

Huawei and Deloitte published a white paper entitled, Combatting COVID 19 with 5G: Opportunities to improve public health systems. The paper includes, "key features of 5G can synergise with other technologies to enhance the effectiveness of pandemic prevention and treatment, as well as drive the digital transformation of healthcare systems in response to major public emergencies." It is an analysis of China's control and treatment of COVID 19 and highlights its application in data transfer, contagion monitoring, patient monitoring and surveillance and its potential worldwide.

The rise of China as a global power has raised alarm in the U.S. with the Director of National Intelligence warning that China poses "the greatest threat to democracy and freedom world-wide since World War II."[108] Despite its human rights record, China is becoming more influential in the UN and is assimilating its Belt and Road Initiative into the UN's SDG's (Sustainable Development Goals) through monetary incentives to secure the support of other member states.[109] China's geopolitical ambitions are additionally leveraged through appealing to other authoritarian regimes in order to rally support. China views the UN as a tool to advance its own national interests and amplify its ideologies globally. They will play a significant role in the last days. "The sixth angel poured out his bowl on the great river Euphrates, and its water was dried up to prepare the way for the kings from the East." Revelation 16:12.

As global leaders obtrude their ideologies through more forceful methods it becomes evident that Marxism is the very foundation driving their aspirations and they blame capitalism and democracy for everything from climate change to human inequality. Through venues like the WEF, the UN, and the WHO, these leaders exert tremendous influence over governments and heads of state around the globe and thereby are able to produce shifts in paradigms and realities of civilization. Additionally, these ideologies impact business leaders as they participate in the dialog and mold a new framework for the future. This was clearly demonstrated with the shutdown of small businesses as part of the pandemic response while large corporate outlets remained open.

The clever wording from the WEF's Great Reset calls for reimagining economies and governance models which is a covert message that imagines the end of free enterprise and market driven economies in favor of communism. Democracy is blamed for societal discontent while it is the very same plutocratic leaders who financed and organized the rioting and racial discord in the first place. The same gas lighting techniques that were employed to create a pandemic narrative in order to supply a lucrative solution are being used to undermine any confidence in democracy and capitalism.

The massive government spending due to COVID response strategies that has resulted in enormous government debt is now being exploited to promote the illusion that democratic systems have failed and the world is now presented with a unique opportunity to "reset" or reinvent democracy, or do away with it altogether. This has created the perception that democracy is broken and doesn't work and that market driven economies are the cause of inequality and poverty in the world. Nothing could be further from the truth. The democratic and capitalistic systems of the last 100 years have precipitated in the highest standard of living the world has ever known and elevated more people into the middle class than at any time prior in history.

"Building Back Better," has become the catch phrase along with SDG's such as ending global poverty and hunger, combating inequalities, and protecting the planet. Of course these discussions deny the existence of any dark forces manipulating world events in order to subjugate populations, just as they deny the existence of God and believe man can create the solution to his own problems. Whether they admit it or not, whether they are aware of it or not and whether they intend to or not is irrelevant though, because the spiritual forces of evil in the heavenly realms are what is currently orchestrating the realities of the physical world.

The plutocracy that wants to convince us that humanity is doomed due to catastrophic climate change and are quite willing to sacrifice the majority of the 7.5 billion lives on the planet, sees the earth as their exclusive playground. They want us to believe that our only hope is to eliminate carbon emissions completely at all costs and they will stop at nothing to achieve it. Carbon will be taxed to such an extent that driving will exceed the budgets of most people, thereby dramatically limiting individual freedom. By enslaving and restricting the poor to cities where they can be monitored, the globe will be open only to those who can afford the steep price of admission.

The same dark power structure that has exploited a virus and coerced the world to buy into their scheme of draconian control through a massive global propaganda campaign, offers the solution in rushed vaccines that have little to no testing and only serve to line their pockets with gold. Through their controlling of the official narrative through the media, censoring any counter narratives, dictating the therapies doctors prescribe and silencing doctors who successfully use alternatives, society has become subjugated to the cabal whether we believe it or not.

COVID tests that incorporate collecting biometric data such as heart rate combined with video surveillance in real time and facial recognition technology from smartphones, allowing for third party monitoring from a regulatory or health insurance perspective were patented in 2015 and 2017 by Richard A. Rothschild. The functionality of the system also permits the data to be analyzed to determine whether a person is suffering from a viral infection such as COVID 19 using a pulse oximeter to acquire pulse and blood oxygen saturation percentage which it transmitted wirelessly. An accelerometer within the smart phone is used to ensure the data is accurate and measure the movement of the user. This information is available from both the United States and Netherlands patent registries. [110]

Today we are being conditioned to accept increased government control over our lives because of a virus with a 99.75% survival rate and to believe a vaccine is required before our lives can return to normal. Will a vaccine raise the survival rate to 99.8%? Society shames its own for not wearing masks while the WHO warns that variants of the virus will soon mean the vaccine could quickly become ineffective against the new varieties. Shutting down the world economy in the name of safety has resulted in enormous losses for the middle class and monumental gains for the wealthy who own big pharma and big tech.

COVID 19 is not going away and there are more pandemics on the horizon. Whether you believe this was all planned or not, this is the new normal. The COVID 19 pandemic serves as the prototype to assess society's willingness to submit to draconian controls and measures including global vaccination initiatives. Civilization is now at the mercy of the Rothchilds banks, the IMF, the WHO, big pharma and the handful of families that run them. Will the new normal include your child having to take violin lessons virtually because it will be illegal to leave your house?

Is COVID 19 biblical? I believe it is just one of many pestilences humanity must live with during the Great Tribulation. The WHO says that the COVID 19 case fatality rate is reasonably low compared to other emerging diseases and that "the existence of a vaccine is no guarantee of eliminating or eradicating an infectious disease." [111]

The John Hopkins Center for Health Security has published a futuristic pandemic scenario (on their website) much like the Event 201 planning exercise that preceded COVID 19 by a few short weeks. The SPARS Pandemic 2025-2028 is depicted as a fictional emergency event that will feature a more severe virus precipitating an even more totalitarian response from authorities. It projects a SPARS fatality rate of fourteen to fifteen percent and over fifty percent for people over the age of sixty-four. Once again, vaccinations play a critical role in controlling the pandemic in an ongoing proliferation of big pharma's shadow over the global population.

The rush to vaccinate the population for a virus with such a low case fatality rate is a sham. The side effects including anaphylactic shock, neurological reactions and cardio vascular disease, reflect the absence of sufficient testing and we are only at the beginning. If the COVID 19 vaccines were held to the same standards that other products are, they would be immediately pulled from the marketplace. Yet the medical community maintains the narrative of how vaccination is essential to combat the pandemic.

By relying on messenger RNA through the component of a spike protein to elicit an immune response, a non-neutralizing antibody is created which allows antibody dependent enhancement which allows the messenger RNA to replicate thereby stimulating the production of antibodies to fight it. Complications arise from the fact that the spike protein, while permitting the production of the hyperactive white blood cells that attack the invader, also inhibits the effect of the secondary white blood cells responsible for the repairs and clean-up of the battle scene, or the healing process. [112]

What this means is that when the vaccinated person eventually is exposed to an actual coronavirus (of which there are seven that effect humans), the result is antibody dependent enhancement and an autoimmune response causing widespread deaths. These deaths will then be attributed to new variants of the coronavirus which we will be told require new vaccines and therefore increased pressure to vaccinate the entire population with the new vaccines. The side effects of these untested vaccines of which death is the focal point, also include side effects severe enough to impact people's ability to function in their daily lives. Debilitating side effects chronic implications requiring further drug therapies thus enslaving humanity to big pharma in a multi trillion-dollar play.

Bill Gates has said that vaccines have provided him with a twenty to one return on investment, explaining his sudden rebranding from Microsoft tech magnate into a philanthropist on a mission to improve the health of the third world through vaccinations. Doesn't it seem odd that he suddenly became a concerned citizen after a career of ruthless business practices and establishing a business monopoly that crushed competitors? Is it any wonder he is at the forefront of the pandemic response team without any medical training whatsoever?

Is this a script designed to create a global demand for vaccines through an intentionally introduced series of pandemics that subjugate humanity to those who will profit handsomely from them? At what point did doctors cease to be experts in anatomy, physiology and biochemistry and become proponents of pharmacology? Why has hydroxychloroquine been vilified and the vaccine de jour been glorified? Does this constitute a sinister plan to cull the global population through eugenics and big pharma's impunity to malpractice and subsequent experimentation on society through rushed research and production of vaccines? Is this a plan to incrementally enslave civilization through fear and terrorism tactics so that personal rights and freedoms will be voluntarily conceded to authority? Will you one day require a permit to transport your child's violin across town for their violin lesson? How much are you willing to relinquish to the government in the name of safety?

Vaccinations have become the leverage point the cabal has been waiting for to subject humanity to total control. You want a student loan, mortgage relief, or life insurance? Provide proof of vaccination. You want to renew your driver's license, your passport, or purchase food? Simply scan your quantum dot tattoo with its digital record of vaccination. Vaccinations are now a control weapon. A big stick held over the heads of humanity to oppress society and create a dependency on authority through fear of a pandemic and the resulting economic collapse, which has forever changed our lives. We are being brainwashed into believing that our lives are endangered unless we accept draconian control measures.

At the same time, COVID deaths are overestimated and intentionally increased by the way patients are handled. In nursing homes and hospitals, the vulnerable are placed in jeopardy by moving COVID patients into their proximity without proper precautions and Meanwhile, suicide rates are skyrocketing as job losses and bankruptcies soar in the face of lockdowns. Eroding equity in the middle class is being gobbled up by huge gains in wealth by the elite. This is all part of a greater plan.

Authorities today have created fear through intimidation that if you articulate something that is contrary to the official narrative in universities, government, research, etc. that you will be blacklisted or fired. This was the case with Susan Crockford, a world renowned zoologist with the University of Victoria British Columbia, when she published research showing the Polar Bear population has grown substantially in recent years which is opposite to the claims of climate change proponents. In similar fashion, America's Frontline Doctors, Canadian Dr. Roger Hodkinson and others, have experienced pushback and even death threats for their position opposing the agenda of fear. Any opinions that disagree with the "official narrative" are censored on social media and suppressed by the mainstream news.

The media has grossly sensationalized the arbitrarily predicted pandemic death numbers and inaccurate reporting of causes of deaths which has resulted in an over-exaggerated response. The seasonal flu has become statistically non-existent, being intentionally misdiagnosed as coronavirus infection. We have witnessed the diabolical deception of civilization by the world's medical industry and the manipulation of the global media to support their plutocratic agenda. The word pharmacy comes from the Greek word Pharmakeia, which translates as the use or administering of drugs; poisoning, sorcery, magical arts; often found in connection with idolatry, and fostered by it; metaph, the deceptions and seductions of idolatry. Big pharma is the arm of the cabal that leads the nations astray and when Mystery Babylon is destroyed, they will fall as part of her corporate family and the world will lament to see her go. "The light of a lamp will never shine in you again. The voice of the bridegroom and bride will never be heard in you again. Your merchants were the world's most important people. By your magic spell all the nations were led astray." Revelation 18:23.

The degree of harm grossly exceeds the benefits. Masks don't work, social distancing doesn't work, lockdowns don't work and testing is monumentally inaccurate. There is nothing that governments have done that have flattened the curve. The virus has a seasonal prevalence just like the flu. There is no significant threat to the vast majority of the population. It is dangerous to the elderly, many of which are in nursing homes where it spreads quickly. However, this does not justify shutting down the economy, incurring mountains of debt in the process which creates numerous other health problems that range from isolation, job losses and other stressors, not to mention the increase in domestic violence and suicides. The cost per human death from COVID 19 is far greater than any benefit to society of the measures taken. The virus may have accidentally escaped from the lab in Wuhan China, but it was quickly exploited as a tool to control populations.

The Vatican is complicit in this façade and uses its power and influence to promote the cabal's narrative while Pope Francis continues to be more interested in world politics than in getting his own house in order and draining the Catholic swamp. By promoting ideologies such as all religions worship the same god and advancing the establishment of a one world religion, the pope is in direct step with the UN and is destined to fulfil prophecy as the false prophet. When was the last time you heard of him preaching the gospel and why does society accept this garbage? The papacy is as much a part of the deep state as the world's financial systems and big pharma. Everywhere we turn we are faced with the same rehearsed recital of civilization's plight. Humanity has proven itself to be malleable and vulnerable to psychological manipulation through the social influence of the cabal.

From China's social credit program to 5G, digital surveillance capabilities have reached a shocking potential for infringement on human rights. Israel has developed Pegasus spyware, a cyber-technology that can infiltrate any cell phone with a "zero click exploit" (meaning you don't have to click on any link in order to activate it), connect it to the hacker's website and take over total control of the phone. For example, it can turn on the camera, microphone, or access any files on the phone. Hackers can listen to your conversations and record interactions right in your home.

Pegasus has been marketed to governments throughout the world as a cyber-security technology used to detect and prevent terrorism and crime. Its sophisticated espionage capabilities make Pegasus a valuable tool for totalitarian regimes and the cost is in the hundreds of millions of dollars. It has been implicated in the tracking and subsequent murder of Jamal Khashoggi, and the surveillance of many journalists working on sensitive projects, investigating wealthy and powerful government personalities.

Under the guise of national security, governments are now capable of setting up complete surveillance states and infringing on human rights with little risk of retribution. In the United Arab Emirates, the company Dark Matter operates under the premise of offensive as well as defensive activity to surveil and compromise the computers of political dissidents both at home and abroad. There are no mathematical limits on the capacity to handle massive digital data by the system. No phone is safe. Any time you turn on your phone they know who you are and where you are anywhere in the world. There is literally nowhere to hide.[113]

All of this data, all of this information they compile on you is their property, not yours. They own the records about you. You don't. Encrypted messages are no longer safe. It doesn't matter whether you are on a free café Wi-Fi network or on your secure Wi-Fi at home. The encryption is compromised on your own phone. Combined with the digital record of the coffee purchase you made at the café, the cell towers you passed on the way to and from the establishment, and the images off of traffic light cameras, governments can construct a pattern of movement and behavior about everything you do. That should scare you.

The deep state has been collaborating globally for centuries in their desire to hoard the wealth of the world to themselves. From the invasions in the name of colonialism to the wars and economic interference between nations of the twentieth century, to drug and human trafficking the cabal's love of money and power has shaped the world we live in. They have orchestrated the global events that have pitted democracy against communism, and the narrative that capitalism is the cause of social inequality, the disparity between rich and poor and between black and white people. In doing so, they have exploited both democratic and communist systems to extort wealth from the populations of the world. The deep state has covertly infiltrated the highest levels of government, monarchies, the global banking system, mainstream media, global corporations and the Vatican. They control our food supply, our medicine and health care systems, global transportation and trade. In a nutshell, they have robbed the people of the world blind.

Their insatiable cupidity has driven them to ruthless and corrupt tactics that attack the very fabric of society. The cabal has championed evolutionary thinking, injected socialist ideology into our education systems, and targeted societal morality by promoting easy divorces, abortions and undermining the traditional family. Anyone with the courage to expose them has been eliminated. JFK and Ronald Reagan both received bullets for their efforts and Trump was steamrolled by their massive corruption. Civilization now finds itself collectively lost when it tries to relate to God and goodness in humanity. The deep state has created a dark state for humanity, where hope seems lost and society suffers from wars, drugs, crime and many must work three jobs to make ends meet. While citizens in developed countries remain preoccupied with entertainment and the pursuit of pleasure, thirty-six percent of the world's population, or 1.89 billion people live in extreme poverty. This didn't happen overnight. It has been systematically and covertly infused into society over time.

We have been provided with the time and space to get our affairs in order. To get the Christian house in order before the final seven years of the Great Tribulation begins. Just as God warned the generation of Noah, he has also warned us. Get right with God before the great and terrible day of the Lord. Jesus said, "Settle matters quickly with your adversary who is taking you to court. Do it while you are still together on the way, or your adversary may hand you over to the judge, and the judge may hand you over to the officer, and you may be thrown into prison." Mathew 5:25. Now is the time to repent and turn from your worldly ways and seek the Lord, but the time is short.

When you read headlines of Bilderberg Group meetings, the WEF's gatherings in Davos, or the UN's Agenda 2030, you must not simply dismiss these events as elite social think tanks but rather acknowledge they are components of a very real and sinister plan to control and hoard the world's wealth at the expense of the greater population. It is an agenda that has been developed in Masonic lodges and followed for centuries and is just now approaching its full potential and culmination. The cabal will one day soon emerge from its secrecy and rule the world in full view of a global society that will prove unable to do anything about its subjugation. In fact, many people will applaud the new world order and gladly capitulate their personal rights and freedoms in the name of safety.

Despite the immensity and avarice of the deep state, it is itself just a small component of much larger forces of universal corruption and darkness. Just when it achieves its goal of global dominance, it will be commandeered by one of its own who will assume a totalitarian one world government. The cabal's power and wealth will be usurped by the antichrist himself. What we are witnessing on earth is an extension of the spiritual battles being fought in the heavenly realms and ultimately part of God's plan for the redemption and judgement of mankind. It is simplistic to label these phenomena as conspiracy theories and prudent to comprehend the gravity of their role in end times prophecy. Wisdom and discernment are found in God's word that explain everything humanity is experiencing and in the end it will be God's truth that will be vindicated.

When we consider the challenges facing mankind that threaten our existence, such as guaranteeing our food supply for our projected population growth over the next 30 years, the shrinking middle class, increasing debt, changing demographics within the population, etc., western culture as we know it is not sustainable. Our population growth is below the rate where we can maintain our population without immigration. As our population ages and more baby boomers retire, the shrinking working class will be saddled with higher taxes to pay for senior's benefits and service an already ballooning debt load. Governments will be forced to run budget deficits to maintain our standard of living and pay for services for a declining workforce, forcing increased taxation of that workforce.

Since the growing immigrant population will out-pace the domestic population growth, there will be a cultural shift away from traditional

North American values to the values of the emerging immigrant ethnicities. It is very conceivable that North America could be dominantly Muslim in the coming decades. Europe is already experiencing this phenomenon and it will continue, and as it does, opposing extremists will clash more frequently on social media and by rioting in the streets. While the Trump administration was proficient at dispensing rhetoric, its impetus to address racism, extremism and gun violence became bogged down in bureaucracy and the result is equal to complacency. In Canada, the existing Trudeau government, in an effort to be all inclusive and tolerant of minorities, confusion abounds as citizens have become frustrated with leadership that is free of focus and has alienated huge segments of the population because if its "wokeness" and in its molly-coddling of special interest groups.

Underlying the challenges mankind is facing is the need for collaboration and acknowledging the problems we face are too big to handle unless all of humanity works together. However, governments are incapable of thinking long term and one political entity's solution automatically becomes the opposing entity's ridicule. Democratic governments' vision only extends up until the next election and they will quickly throw any ideas not palatable with voters under the bus in order to improve their chances of victory in an election. Communist governments all too often become corrupt as individuals in power stockpile wealth or spend disproportionately on their military and leave the common people poor and powerless. The result is a completely impotent and counterproductive world system, incapable of moving forward with holistic, humanitarian policies that address the root causes of our man-made problems. Precipitating from this scrambled conundrum, the UN emerges with its plan for a new world order with implications reaching far deeper into an insidious potential humanity refuses to acknowledge.

Civilization has lost the handle of what is truly important and is grasping at straws as society struggles to strategize as it is caught in a tug of war between the forces of good and evil. The deep state has rendered governments dysfunctional in their handling of world affairs as humanity cannot even agree on societal problems, causes and implications, let alone a course of action to address them. Ultimately, by the time we act, it will in all likelihood be too little too late.

Let's imagine we own a boat that has a small infestation of barnacles on its hull to illustrate this. You discover the area covered by the barnacles doubles every day and will completely cover the hull in 30 days. You are quite busy and decide you will take action when 25% of the hull is covered. How much time will you have to correct the problem before the barnacles completely cover the hull? If you calculate two days, you are correct. The barnacles will cover 25% of the hull on day 28, 50% on day 29 and 100% on day 30. By day 28, any measures you take must be drastic in nature and must not fail. Otherwise we lose the hull and therefore our boat. What day do you think humanity is at with the its current dilemma of corruption and depravity? On January 27, 2021, the Bulletin of Atomic Scientists revealed that it is keeping the doomsday clock at one hundred seconds to midnight for the next year.

While the rich and famous expound upon the virtues of humanitarian causes and the evils of carbon dioxide, their hypocrisy is evident as they travel thousands of miles to convene at gatherings to highlight the imminent climate crisis in private jets and luxury super yachts. Their mansions, collections of fine art, vehicles and personal expenditures are enough to feed and clothe the poor of the world and their closets hide the speculations of conspiracy theorists who suspect (with legitimate cause) covert illegal activities including child trafficking, as was the case with Jeffrey Epstein and a long list of wealthy and powerful elite clientele. The corruption and rot of the principalities and powers that control world affairs, is so great that most would not believe its truth for the incredible grotesqueness of it. "Whoever loves money never has enough; whoever loves wealth is never satisfied with their income." Ecclesiastes 5:10.

When we contemplate the injustices the cabal have inflicted on humanity and their transgressions against the innocent, we must remind ourselves that the world has been Satan's domain for a long, long time. While the spiritual darkness that motivates their corruption and greed, fills their bank accounts and hearts seems formidable, it is nothing compared to the power of the Lord. One day each and every one of them will stand before the judgement seat of God and he will avenge the oppression of their victims. The Prophet Isaiah wrote, "Surely the nations are like a drop in a bucket; they are regarded as dust on the scales; he weighs the islands as though they were fine dust." Isaiah 40:15. He goes on to say, "He brings princes down to naught and reduces the rulers of this world down to nothing. No sooner are they planted, no sooner are they sown, no sooner do they take root in the ground, than he blows on them and they wither, and a whirlwind sweeps them away like chaff." Isaiah 40:23-24.

The things of this world are temporal and while it may seem that life is grossly unfair, we are called to have faith in the Lord. Paul reminds us, "Do not take revenge, my dear friends, but leave room for God's wrath, for it is written: 'It is mine to avenge; I will repay,' says the Lord." Romans 12:19. Perpetrators of injustice may enjoy their riches for a short while, however they will perish having received their comfort in this life. King David wrote, "As a father has compassion on his children, so the Lord has compassion on those who fear him; for he knows how we are formed he remembers that we are dust. As for man, his days are like grass, he flourishes like a flower of the field; the wind blows over it and it is gone, and its place remembers it no more." Psalm 103:13-16. Trust that God will make things right. Isaiah adds, "All people are like grass, and their faithfulness is like the flowers of the field. The grass withers and the flowers fall, because the breath of the Lord blows on them. Surely the people are grass. The grass withers and the flowers fall, but the word of the Lord endures forever." Isaiah 40:6-8.

Jesus said near the end of the world, "Nation will rise against nation, and kingdom against kingdom. There will be great earthquakes, famines and pestilences in various places, and fearful events and great signs from heaven." Luke 21:10-11. He went on predict the fall of Jerusalem and the destruction of the temple which occurred in AD 70 at the hands of the Romans. He added, "Jerusalem will be trampled on by the Gentiles until the times of the Gentiles are fulfilled." Luke 21:24. The Fig tree has long been a symbol for the nation of Israel and Jesus told his disciples a parable, "Look at the fig tree and all the trees. When they sprout leaves, you can see for yourselves and know that summer is near. Even so, when you see these things happening, you know that the kingdom of God is near. Truly I tell you, this generation will not pass away until all these things have happened. Heaven and earth will pass away, but my words will never pass away." Luke 21:

Israel became a nation again in 1948 and Jerusalem's days of being trampled on by the Gentiles ended. The events unfolding in the world today remind us that the hour is late. We are living in the end times before

God will pour his wrath out onto the inhabitants of the world. The middle east today remains a hotbed of diverging nations bent upon conflict with Israel at center stage. Iran continues to supply Hezbollah with weapons by flying them into Damascus and Israel is now bombing the Damascus airport when these weapons arrive. Damascus is still devastated from the Syrian civil war and will be reduced to rubble before this is over in fulfillment of Isaiah 17.

Perhaps the most critical issue to be resolved in Jerusalem as we near the advent of the Great Tribulation is the Temple Mount, which is the most sacred piece of real estate on earth, chosen by God (Psalm 132:13-14) to dwell among his people. The end times temple is a necessity for the fulfillment of Revelation 11:1-2 in order for the antichrist to set up the abomination of desolation (Daniel 11:31, Daniel 12:11, Mathew 24:15-16, Revelation 13:14-15) and will be a physical building and not a spiritual temple. The seven year Israel peace accord will facilitate the building of the third temple and Jerusalem will become the focal point of the last days. "I am going to make Jerusalem a cup that sends all the surrounding people reeling. Judah will be besieged as well as Jerusalem." Zechariah 12:2.

As we witnessed the rockets fly from Gaza into Israel and Israel's retaliation in the spring of 2021, world leaders called for peace. The Palestinian rockets, with little to no navigation capabilities, were fired from launchers imbedded next to hospitals and schools, yet it was Israel who bore the brunt of the criticism for civilian casualties. The UN maintained a twisted, nefarious and purposefully deceptive perception, opposed to Israel, which they promoted and spread across the globe, painting Israel with the negative brush strokes even though the Palestinians initiated the rocket fire.

The press portrayed Hamas as demanding justice for the eviction of Palestinian residents in the Jerusalem neighborhood of Sheikh Jarrah, claiming these were generations deep home owners. In reality, the Jewish plaintiffs' legal chain of title is documented back to 1875 and was illegally confiscated when Jordan invaded Israel in 1948, occupying half of Jerusalem and expelling Jewish inhabitants and seizing their property.

In 1967, when Israel reunited Jerusalem, the Jewish courts respected the new titles, despite the fact they were illegitimately procured through force. As with much of the land that Israel reclaimed after the 1967 conflict, such as the west bank, Israel remains unfairly categorized as the aggressor even though they were backed into a corner by Syria, Egypt and Jordan, desperately outnumbered and overpowered yet triumphant in battle. The UN still does not recognize Israel's right to the west bank as spoils of war. Israel remains in the hot seat on the world stage and is proof that biblical prophecy continues to come true.

The Christian Church was not meant to go astray after the first century, however when emperor Constantine made Christianity the official religion of the Roman empire, the significance of the seventieth week of Daniel's prophecy of the seventy sevens began to take shape. Down through the ages, through the unforced errors of the Catholic church, precipitating the reformation with the likes of Martin Luther, all the way to today's 30,000 Christian denominations, the Christian Church has allowed itself to be persuaded by human reason to wander off God's path.

This all happened so that the prophesies regarding Israel in the last days could be fulfilled in due time and so evil would develop to its fullness and thereby give rise to the man of lawlessness in his appointed time. Jerusalem was trampled on by the Gentiles until the times of the Gentiles were fulfilled and it is now time for the final culmination of God's plan.

Israel is once again at center stage as the world watches and international leaders call for peace. And peace will come in the form of a seven - year covenant that was foretold by Daniel nearly 600 years before Christ (Daniel 9:27).

The wrath of God will soon descend from heaven against all godlessness; onto a lawless generation that suppresses the truth by their wickedness.

The 6th chapter of the book of Revelation gives us a glimpse of Jesus setting in motion this time that will soon be upon us. "I watched as the Lamb opened the first of seven seals. Then I heard one of the four living creatures say in a voice like thunder, 'Come!' I looked, and there before me was a white horse! Its rider held a bow, and he was given a crown, and he rode out as a conqueror bent on conquest.

When the lamb opened the second seal, I heard the second living creature say, 'Come!' Then another horse came out, a fiery red one. Its rider was given power to take peace from the earth and to make people kill each other. To him was given a large sword.

When the Lamb opened the third seal, I heard the third living creature say, 'Come!' I looked, and there before me was a black horse! Its rider was holding a pair of scales in his hands. Then I heard what sounded like a voice among the four living creatures, saying, 'Two pounds of wheat for a day's wages, and six pounds of barley for a day's wages, and do not damage the oil and the wine!

When the Lamb opened the fourth seal, I heard the voice of the fourth living creature say, 'Come!' and there before me was a pale horse! Its rider was named Death, and Hades was following close behind him. They were given power over a fourth of the earth to kill by sword, famine and plague, and by the wild beasts of the earth." Revelation 6:1-8.

Pay special attention to the fact that each horseman was called into action in heaven. This was not precipitated by events on earth. The other point of significance is with reference to the rider of the fourth horse, Death was given the power to take people's bodies and Hades who followed close behind was given the power to take people's souls. There is a spiritual war being fought in the heavenly realms that has immense impact upon the human struggles we are witnessing in our physical world. Whether we acknowledge it or not, our eternal destiny is what is being battled for, so we must take the words of Christ to heart and sincerely contemplate the gravity of what he said. "When these things begin to take place, stand up and lift up your heads, because your redemption is drawing near." Luke 21:28.

The Blessed Hope

Ever since the beginning when Adam and Eve were expelled from Eden, all creation has been groaning under the weight of sin as in the pains of childbirth (Romans 8:22). Jesus said that the signs of his return recorded in Mathew chapter 24 were just the beginning of birth pains (Mathew 24:8). The world we know and the world known before us was not and is not normal to God. When we speak of a new normal, the truth is that it never was. Normal to God was the garden of Eden that was the creation at the beginning. And the most amazing and beautiful thing is that he is going to recreate Eden. He is going to establish a new heavens and a new earth and a new Jerusalem where he will live with us and be our God and we will be his people throughout eternity.

"Therefore, they are before the throne of God and serve him day and night in his temple;

And he who sits on the throne will spread his tent over them. Never again will they hunger;

Never again will they thirst. The sun will not beat down on them, nor any scorching heat.

For the Lamb at the center of the throne will be their shepherd; he will lead them to springs of living water.

And God will wipe away every tear from their eyes." Revelation 7:15.

God has made provision in his perfect plan to reconcile true believers back to himself and his original design for mankind. Through faith in Jesus Christ we are brought back into fellowship with God and become his children and heirs to his kingdom along with Christ. Paul sums it up this way: "As for you, you were dead in your transgressions and sins, in which you used to live when you followed the ways of this world and of the ruler of the kingdom of the air, the spirit who is now at work in those who are disobedient. All of us also lived among them at one time, gratifying the cravings of our flesh and following its desires and thoughts. Like the rest, we were by nature deserving wrath. But because of his great love for us, God who is rich in mercy, made us alive with Christ even when we were dead in transgressions – it is by grace you have been saved. And God raised us up with Christ and seated us with him in the heavenly realms in Christ Jesus, in order that in the coming ages he might show the incomparable riches of his grace, expressed in his kindness to us in Christ Jesus." Ephesians 2:1-7.

What is amazing is that we are seated with him today. This is not a promise of some future suppositional status but rather a reflection of our current position as believers. We are in a structured relationship in the here and now. Therefore, we are no longer children of the world but of heaven.

When we give our hearts to Jesus in response to God's love, we enter an eternal love affair. It becomes our responsibility to be faithful and dedicated to our beloved and submit ourselves to him as we would to a spouse. We are expected to forsake all others and follow him. This is much the same as being betrothed to Jesus and the true Church is depicted as the bride of Christ in scripture. To better understand this relationship, let's examine the components that made up a Jewish marriage proposal in the first century when Jesus made these analogies.

The first step in the process involved the father of the groom paying a dowry or a price for the bride. The father would then take his son to the house of the potential bride and they would enter into an agreement of marriage or betrothal. This would likely include a marriage contract (shetar and/or ketubah) that was signed before two witnesses. The marriage contract included the details of the dowry and the names of the bride and groom as well as their families. Once the contract had been presented to the bride, the groom would pour a cup of wine for the bride and offer it to her. If she accepted the proposal as stated in the contract, she would accept the cup and drink from it.

Unlike an engagement as we understand it in the North American culture today, once a couple were betrothed in Jesus's time, they were considered married, even though they did not yet live together. The woman was often considered "acquired" or "bought with a price" and is a married woman at this stage. If they did not want to follow through with the wedding, they required a divorce. The betrothal was more like phase one of a marriage than an engagement.

The groom would then return to his father's house to prepare a marriage chamber or dwelling for the couple. Hebrew family dwellings usually included several houses and a courtyard where several generations would cohabitate. The important thing to remember here is that the father controlled the timing of everything. In fact, the groom would continue building the marriage chamber until his father said it was ready. At that point he would go and collect his bride. The groom never knew the day or the hour and neither did the bride. She would have kept a lantern filled with oil in the event he came for her after dark.

When Jesus and his disciples ate their last supper together, they celebrated their Passover meal in accordance with their Jewish custom. During the meal Jesus gives thanks and then proceeds to take the bread and break it. Instead of the traditional explanation for the lack of yeast in the bread, he tells those with him, "This is my body given for you; do this in remembrance of me." Luke 22:19. Jesus then takes the cup, and says, "This cup is the new covenant in my blood, which is poured out for you." Luke 22:20.

The disciples then each drank from the cup signifying their agreement to the conditions of the covenant. Following the marriage contract ratification, Jesus then proceeded to pay the price of the dowry. His sacrifice on the cross, infinitely more valuable than an alabaster jar of perfumed oil or the total sum of all the animals sacrificed in the history of civilization, paid for the bride. The apostle Paul wrote, "you were bought at a price. Therefore honor God with your bodies." 1 Corinthians 6:20.

Jesus spoke of his imminent death after they had eaten the last supper and Jesus had washed the disciples' feet. They were troubled by what he was saying so he comforted them with these words: "Do not let your hearts be troubled. You believe in God; believe also in me. My Father's house has many rooms; if that were not so, would I have told you that I am going there to prepare a place for you? And if I go and prepare a place for you, I will come back and take you to be with me that you also may be where

I am." John 14:1-3. His language very closely resembles that of Jewish wedding traditions.

In the 24th chapter of Mathew, Jesus speaks about signs of the end of the age and his return to earth at his second coming in similar language, "No one knows about that day or hour, not even the angels in heaven, nor the Son, but only the Father." Mathew 24:36. In the next chapter, he elaborates using a parable to describe his return, "At that time the kingdom of heaven will be like ten virgins who took their lamps and went out to meet the bridegroom. Five of them were foolish and five were wise. The foolish ones took their lamps but did not take any oil with them. The wise ones, however, took oil in jars along with their lamps. The bridegroom was a long time in coming, and they all became drowsy and fell asleep.

At midnight the cry rang out: 'Here's the bridegroom! Come out to meet him!'

Then all the virgins woke up and trimmed their lamps. The foolish ones said to the wise, 'Give us some of your oil; our lamps are going out.'

'No,' they replied, 'there may not be enough for both us and you. Instead, go to those who sell oil and buy some for yourselves.'

But while they were on their way to buy the oil, the bridegroom arrived. The virgins who were ready went in with him to the wedding banquet. And the door was shut.

Later the others also came. 'Lord, Lord,' they said, 'open the door for us!'

But he replied, Truly I tell you, I do not know you.'

Therefore keep watch, because you do not know the day or the hour." Mathew 25:1-13.

Not only is this parable a lesson in prudence, it has multiple implications for the Christian Church today. As the Bridegroom we are assured that Jesus will return for his bride the Church, though we don't know when that will be. He is in heaven as I write, preparing a place for us who believe. It has been two thousand years since Christ left so we must not be as the foolish virgins and treat the timing with complacency. Peter warns that, "But do not forget this one thing, dear friends: With the Lord a day is like a thousand years and a thousand years are like a day. The Lord is not slow in keeping his promise, as some understand slowness. Instead he is patient with you, not wanting anyone to perish, but everyone to come to repentance." 2 Peter 3:8-9.

While we know that the Church will be raptured at the seventh trumpet we do not know the precise timing of Christ fetching his bride. Many students of theology believe the Church will not be caught up to be with the Lord until Christ returns at the final battle of Armageddon, however this view becomes problematic when the timing of Jesus's second coming is openly provided in scripture as occurring 1260 days after the antichrist assumes control of the world. Additionally, the narrative in Mathew 24 states that, "Then will appear the sign of the Son of Man in heaven. And then all the peoples of the earth will mourn when they see the Son of Man coming on the clouds of heaven, with power and great glory. And he will send his angels with a loud trumpet call, and they will gather his elect from the four winds, from one end of the heavens to the other." Mathew 24:30.

There is no mention of the elect being on earth in this passage which indicates that Paul isn't writing about the return of Jesus to stand on the Mount of Olives when he destroys the antichrist and his allies, "According to the Lord's word, we tell you that we who are still alive, who are left until the coming of the Lord, will certainly not precede those who have fallen asleep. For the Lord himself will come down from heaven, with a loud command, with the voice of the archangel and with the trumpet call of God, and the dead in Christ will rise first. After that, we who are still alive and are left will be caught up in the clouds to meet the Lord in the air. And so we will be with the Lord forever. Therefore encourage one another with these words." 1 Thessalonians 4:15-18. There is intentional ambiguity here for obvious reasons.

There also doesn't seem to be any clear indication of a pre-tribulation rapture in scripture and it is counterintuitive to conclude that God will spare the end times Church from persecution after the last two thousand years during which Christians have been persecuted and martyred continually. Believers are not appointed to wrath however persecution is something entirely different. Jesus said we will be persecuted, "You will be handed over to be persecuted and put to death, and you will be hated by all nations because of me." Mathew 24:9, and, "You will be hated by everyone because of me, but the one who stands firm to the end will be saved." Mathew 10:22.

Proponents of the rapture occurring prior to the tribulation often interpret Paul's second letter to the Thessalonians and his statement concerning the "restrainer" as meaning the true Church is holding the secret power of lawlessness back until he is taken out of the way (2 Thessalonians 2:7). However, the fact that what holds him back is identified as "he" more logically must mean the Holy Spirit. Will true believers be left without the power of the Holy Spirit to endure the tribulation or are they "snatched away" when the restrainer is removed?

Furthermore, the letter to the Church at Philadelphia in the third chapter of Revelation that is directed at those who have kept the word of God and not denied his name states, "Since you have kept my command to endure patiently, I will keep you from the hour of trial that is going to come upon the whole world to test those who live on the earth." Revelation 3:10. How the faithful are kept safe during the hour of trial is debateable. God spared the households that smeared lamb's blood on their door posts for the first Passover in Egypt.

Does the "hour" of trial imply a short period of time during which God's true Church is harbored from the dangers of the Great Tribulation? Will Christians be protected during the coming storm or will they be removed out of the coming storm? The Prophet Isaiah wrote, "Go, my people, enter your rooms and shut the doors behind you; hide yourselves for a little while until his wrath has passed by. See, the Lord is coming out of his dwelling to punish the people of the earth for their sins. The earth will disclose the blood shed upon her; she will conceal her slain no longer." Isaiah 26:20-21.

Adding to the uncertainty, the Greek word apostasia, which Paul uses in 2 Thessalonians 2:3 can be translated as physical departure as well as apostasy or "falling away." This verse could then be understood as, "don't let anyone deceive you in any way, for that day will not come until the departure occurs and the man of lawlessness is revealed, the man doomed to destruction." Even this however, can mean simply departure from the faith.

The Bible's revelations regarding the timing of the rapture are veiled and secretive intentionally so that Satan cannot calculate what will happen when, and thereby force him to maintain a reactive posture. Additionally, believers must rely on their faith to persevere and therefore build strength in their commitment to Christ through adversity as they guard their salvation and focus on the Lord. Each and every one of us will be tested at some point. Jesus said, "For whoever wants to save their life will lose it, but whoever loses their life for me will find it." Mathew 16:25.

When describing the events that would mark the tribulation, Jesus said, "Then you will be handed over to be persecuted and put to death, and you will be hated by all nations because of me. At that time, many will turn away from the faith and will betray and hate each other, and many false prophets will appear and deceive many people. Because of the increase in wickedness, the love of most will grow cold, but the one who stands firm to the end will be saved. And this gospel of the kingdom will be preached in the whole world as a testimony to all nations, and then the end will come." Mathew 24:9-14.

Today one in nine Christians experiences persecution. There are more Christians being persecuted today than at any time in history including at the hands of the Roman Empire. Many of today's martyrs fall at the hands of Islamic jihadists, whose terrorism has become so commonplace that it almost seems normal to hear about it daily. In Africa, entire villages are being wiped out and in the middle east the tragedy is at near genocide levels. In Iran the Christian population has dropped from "1.5 million people before 2003 to less than 120,000." Christians are forced to recite recantations and shot anyway, children are sent into mine fields to set off mines, women are sold as slaves, raped and married off to Islamic fighters. It seems that Christians are the scorn of the earth.

Ever since Jesus was crucified, believers have been despised, imprisoned, tortured and killed because of their faith. The disciples, Paul the apostle, Ignatius of Antioch, Polycarp, Justin Martyr, and a host of others, all lost their lives because they professed Jesus as their Redeemer and the Son of God. They were crucified, sometimes upside down, beheaded, boiled in oil, torn apart by wild animals and burned at the stake. In the tenth chapter of Mathew, Jesus dispels any thoughts of an easy road for those who take up their cross and follow him.

"Do not be afraid of those who kill the body but cannot kill the soul. Rather, be afraid of the One who can destroy both body soul and body in hell. Are not two sparrows sold for a penny? Yet not one of them will fall to the ground outside your Father's care. And even the very hairs of your head are all numbered. So don't be afraid; you are worth more than many sparrows.

Whoever acknowledges me before others, I will also acknowledge before my Father in heaven. But whoever disowns me before others, I will disown before my Father in heaven.

Do not suppose that I have come to bring peace to the earth. I did not come to bring peace, but a sword. For I have come to turn

'a man against his father, a daughter against her mother,
a daughter-in-law against her mother-in-law –
a man's enemies will be the members of his own household.'

Anyone who loves their father or mother more than me is not worthy of me; anyone who loves their son or daughter more than me is not worthy of me. Whoever does not take up their cross and follow me is not worthy of me. Whoever finds their life will lose it, and whoever loses their life for my sake will find it." Mathew 10:28-39.

"Consider it pure joy, my brothers and sisters, whenever you face trials of many kinds, because you know the testing of your faith produces perseverance. Let perseverance finish its work so that you may be mature and complete, not lacking anything." James 1:2-4. In the crucible of our persecution we are refined and defined. I personally have been scorned by members of my own family because of my faith. Perhaps there is judgement because I now speak out against some of the very things I was guilty of before my redemption. Paul wrote, "'My grace is sufficient for you, for my power is made perfect in weakness.' Therefore I will boast all the more gladly about my weaknesses, so that Christ's power may rest on me. That is why, for Christ's sake, I delight in weakness, in insults, in hardships, in persecutions, in difficulties. For when I am weak, then I am strong." 2 Corinthians 12:9-10.

In the same way that Abraham's faith was credited to him as righteousness, Christians today are called to live by faith in Christ and our faith will also be credited to us as righteousness on the day of judgement. Faithful is defined as being loyal and steadfast. I am no longer the person I was before the Holy Spirit came to dwell in me. Jesus paid my debt and gave me a full pardon therefore, I am no longer guilty of sin and I cannot permit it in my life any longer.

Just as a man would expect his betrothed bride to remain faithful and pure in the time leading up to the consummation of the marriage, the Church is also called to remain holy, pure and faithful to Christ. Peter wrote his epistles to stimulate believers to wholesome thinking and Paul said in his letter to the Philippians, "Finally, brothers and sisters, whatever is true, whatever is noble, whatever is right, whatever is pure, whatever is lovely, whatever is admirable – if anything is excellent or praiseworthy – think about such things." Philippians 4:8. Paul also wrote in his second letter to the church at Corinth, "I am jealous for you with a godly jealousy. I promised you to one husband, to Christ, so that I might present you as a pure virgin to him." 2 Corinthians 11:2.

It is our duty, to focus on repentance and goodness and to refrain from sinning against our Redeemer and Bridegroom. Spending time reading the Bible, reading other sources of Christian literature, spending time in prayer and fellowship with other believers, attending church regularly and taking part in bible study and prayer groups, are all important ways to maintain your passion for Christ and ensure you are a worthy bride.

The true Christian Church is eagerly anticipating the return of the Bridegroom, when Christ will come for his bride. Will you be ready? None of us knows the day or the hour of our departure from this earthly life. Whether it is through death or by rapture, it is incumbent to be faithful as a good bride should. Our goal must be to be in attendance at the marriage supper. In the book of Revelation, we are given a glimpse of that banquet in the 19th chapter. "Then I heard what sounded like a great multitude, like the roar of rushing waters and like loud peals of thunder, shouting:

'Hallelujah! For our Lord God Almighty reigns.

Let us rejoice and be glad and give him glory!

For the wedding of the Lamb has come, and his bride has made herself ready.

Fine linen, bright and clean, was given her to wear.'

Then the angel said to me, 'Write this: Blessed are those who are invited to the wedding supper of the Lamb!' And he added, 'These are the true words of God.'" Revelation 19: 6-9.

Through the cup of the new covenant believers are betrothed to Christ and the price for the bride has been paid in full. When Jesus proclaimed with his last breath, "It is finished." (John 19:30), the deal was sealed, the dowry was paid. While the old covenant of sacrificing animals to atone for sin was instituted by God through Moses, it was broken by Israel, so Jesus, who fulfilled it through living a sinless life, instituted a new covenant through himself that is eternal.

All we have to do is accept it. When we celebrate communion with Christ through the breaking of bread and drinking grape juice or wine, we signify our acceptance of the marriage contract and pledge our loyalty to our Bridegroom.

In Mathew 22, Jesus told a parable about a king who was hosting a wedding banquet where the invited guests were either too busy or not interested in attending and even killed the king's servants who delivered the invitations. The disappointed king told his servants, "'The banquet is ready, but those I invited did not deserve to come. So go to the street corners and invite to the banquet anyone you find. So the servants went out into the streets and gathered all the people they could find, the bad as well as the good, and the wedding hall was filled with guests." Mathew 22:8-10.

Israel is represented by those who were initially invited, and their disbelief resulted in the invitation of the Gentile nations who are the people of the streets. Israel killed the King's own Son and subsequently, as believers in Christ, we are invited to take our place at the wedding banquet with Christ. And so, through Jesus, a descendant of Abraham, Jesse and David, the whole world is blessed. Paul wrote that through Christ the Gentiles would glorify God, "As it is written:

'Therefore I will praise you among the Gentiles; I will sing the praises of your name.'

Again, it says, 'Rejoice, you Gentiles, with his people.'

And again, 'Praise the Lord, all you Gentiles; let all the peoples extol him.'

And again, Isaiah says, 'The root of Jesse will spring up, one who will arise to rule over the nations; in him the Gentiles will hope.'" Romans 15:9-12.

The Old Covenant was established between God and Moses on Mt. Sinai in the twenty fourth chapter of Genesis. The Israelites accepted the terms of the covenant by responding with one voice, "Everything the Lord has said we will do." Exodus 24:3. Then Moses went up the mountain to meet with God and receive the stone tablets which God had written the law on. "When Moses went up on the mountain, the cloud covered it, and the glory of the Lord settled on Mt. Sinai. For six days the cloud covered the mountain and on the seventh day the Lord called to Moses from within the cloud. To the Israelites the glory of the Lord looked like a consuming fire on top of the mountain. Then Moses entered the cloud and stayed on the mountain forty days and forty nights." Exodus 24:15-18.

The first truth revealed in this passage of scripture is that God is patient and does not move quickly. He is methodical and everything has purpose. Secondly, the Israelites witnessed firsthand his supernatural glory as they had when they were led out of Egypt. They knew full well they were entering into an agreement with a mighty God. What followed was a short lived loyalty as by the time Moses returned with the stone tablets the Israelites had already committed adultery with an idol and were following their own worldly lusts. How could a people be so superficial and quick to abandon their commitment after all they had been through with God's presence before them and the mighty works performed through Moses?

In the same way, Jesus has been delayed a long time as we wait for his return and many people have been led astray or forgotten his promises. It is only the most committed who have the faith to persist through trials until they finish the race. There is much to learn from the errors of the nation of Israel throughout history that can be applied to the Christian Church today. Even though the bridegroom has been a long time returning the bride must remain faithful and be ready.

Today we are seeing biblical prophecies being fulfilled before our very eyes. The historical record shows that Bible prophecy is always fulfilled literally and what we are witnessing transpire in world events today is aligning exactly with what is predicted for the last days. The world isn't falling apart it is falling into place. Now is the time to have extra oil for your lamp and be prepared.

There is a storm coming and it is incumbent on the Church to remain faithful through the storm. This means we must be ready to defend our faith, stand firm in our faith and be willing to die for our faith. Our loyalty is to Christ above all else, therefore we must forsake all else and prove ourselves worthy as his betrothed bride.

William Shakespeare's Romeo and Juliet is the tale of romance between two young victims of a family feud. They secretly marry with the help of Fryer Laurence who desires to reconcile the two families through the marriage of their children. However, Juliet's father, Capulet, offers her hand in marriage to Count Paris and threatens to disown her when she refuses. In a tragic turn of events, Juliet ingests a potion to induce a forty-two-hour coma the night before the proposed wedding, and mistaken for dead she is placed in the family crypt.

Not knowing of the scheme, because the message did not reach him, Romeo, believing Juliet is dead, drinks poison. When Juliet awakens to find Romeo deceased, she stabs herself with his dagger and joins him in death. In the end, the two families agree to cease their feuding and are ultimately reconciled by the deaths of their offspring. This love story exemplifies the power of pure love that is loyal, honorable and faithful unto death.

Humans are designed to love and love is a compelling factor in the actions we take and the legacy we will be known for. The insurmountable force of love can bring us to the heights of accomplishment or the depths of despair when it is lost. True love is to lay down your life for your lover or your fellow human being. Jesus however, willingly laid down his life for us while we were still his enemies. There is no greater love than this. It is this love that has redeemed humanity because Jesus's love for us put an end to our enmity with God. Our feud is over.

The relationship between a bride and groom is an intimate one. When we accept Christ as our personal savior we recognize his sincere love for us and we reciprocate that love by committing our lives to him. True believers enjoy this intimate relationship with Jesus and forsake the world in favor of our marriage covenant with our Bridegroom. We long for his return to call us to himself, the sound of the trumpet and the promise of a home in heaven for eternity.

"For the grace of God has appeared that offers salvation to all people. It teaches us to say "No" to ungodliness and worldly passions, and to live self-controlled, upright and godly lives in this present age, while we wait for the blessed hope – the appearing of the glory of our great God and savior, Jesus Christ, who gave himself for us to redeem us from all wickedness and to purify for himself a people that are his very own, eager to do what is good." Titus 2:11-14.

We are to live as though Christ will return at any moment. Even the disciples believed the Lord's return was at hand. "Be patient, brothers and sisters, until the Lord's coming. See how the farmer waits for the land to yield its valuable crop, patiently waiting for the autumn and spring rains. You too, be patient, and stand firm, because the Lord's coming is near." James 5:7-8. This doesn't mean the rapture will happen before the Great Tribulation. In reality, scripture tells us we will have to endure tribulation….. but not wrath.

It is critical to be diligent and ready though, because our lives can end at any time. The Bible warns of complacency in how we live with respect to Christ's return. "I know your deeds, that you are neither cold nor hot. I wish you were neither one or the other! So, because you are lukewarm – neither hot nor cold – I am about to spit you out of my mouth. You say, 'I am rich; I have acquired wealth and do not need a thing.' But you do not realize that you are wretched, pitiful, poor, blind and naked. I counsel you to buy from me gold refined in the fire, so you can become rich; and white clothes to wear, so you can cover your shameful nakedness; and salve to put on your eyes, so you can see.

To those whom I love I rebuke and discipline. So be earnest and repent. Here I am! I stand at the door and knock. If anyone hears my voice and opens the door, I will come in and eat with that person and they with me.

To the one who is victorious, I will give the right to sit with me on my throne, just as I was victorious and sat down with my Father on his throne. Whoever has ears, let them hear what the Spirit says to the churches." Revelation 3:15-22.

The return of Christ for his bride is imminent. All of creation anticipates it. The Bridegroom wants his bride. The Father knows the time will soon be upon us when the marriage chamber will be ready. Then the Bridegroom will come for us and we will dwell in the Father's house forever.

FULL ON FOR CHRIST

No one who has had a genuine encounter with Christ and sincerely believes in him can remain unchanged. If you have lost your passion for Jesus or haven't had a bona fide born again experience, then I challenge you to examine your heart and sincerely scrutinize your faith.

Much of my early life was spent questioning my own Christianity, not willing to let go of my affinity for worldly values and pursuits. I thought that I had never been a "bad" person and I intentionally drug my heels to surrender my life fully to Jesus. I had one foot in earthly pursuits and the other in heaven. I was what scripture calls double-minded (James 1:8, 4:4, 1 John 2:15). Jesus said, "No one can serve two masters. Either you will hate the one and love the other or you will be devoted to the one and despise the other. You cannot serve both God and money." Mathew 6:24.

As a result of that rationale, I forged ahead with my dreams without consulting the Lord only to find my plans ended in disaster and amounted to nothing of real significance, not to mention the consequential heartache and pain I suffered. God is omniscient and eternal, knowing the end at the beginning. If we want true happiness in our lives God offers himself as the conduit to success. Perhaps my greatest regret is that I never appreciated God's wisdom and relied on my own instead. Jesus said, "But seek first his kingdom and his righteousness, and all these things will be given to you as well." Mathew 6:33.

God is ready, willing and able to provide and all we have to do is sincerely ask. "Ask and it will be given to you; seek and you will find; knock and the door will be opened to you. For everyone who asks receives; the one who seeks finds; and to the one who knocks, the door will be opened.

Which of you, if your son asks for bread, will give him a stone? Or if he asks for a fish, will give him a snake? If you, then, though you are evil, know how to give good gifts to your children, how much more will your Father in heaven give good gifts to those who ask him!" Mathew 7:7-11.

Ever since I fully surrendered my life to Jesus and chose to walk in total obedience to him, I have received so many good things from the Father. I have changed the way I see life and have found the true fulfillment and happiness I desired before but could never seem to find. The Lord has rewarded my faith with treasure beyond value. "When I called you, you answered me; you greatly emboldened me. Though the Lord is exalted, he looks kindly on the lowly; though lofty, he sees them from afar. Though I walk in the midst of trouble, you preserve my life. You stretch out your hand against the anger of my foes; with your right hand you save me. The Lord will vindicate me; your love, Lord, endures forever – do not abandon the works of your hands." Psalm 138:3, 6-8.

Two days before the Passover, Jesus, who was about to depart for Jerusalem and the culmination of his earthly ministry, shared a meal at the house of Simon the Leper. Not much information is provided about Simon, other than, as his name would imply, he once had leprosy and was now a Pharisee as he is called in Luke's narrative. "While he was in Bethany, reclining at the table in the home of Simon the Leper, a woman came with an alabaster jar of very expensive perfume, made of pure nard. She broke the jar and poured the perfume on his head." Mark 14:3.

It was the custom in those days to welcome someone to your home by greeting them with a kiss, washing their feet and anointing their head with oil. The frequent washing of feet was necessary since the people wore sandals as footwear and went barefoot in the house. "It was also customary to wash the feet before meals and before going to bed." Pouring scented oil on a person's head was both a practical and symbolical custom. It was both therapeutic and cosmetic in that it was capable of masking body odor and penetrating the skin for medicinal purposes. Oil was also used in the making of a covenant, such as the transfer of property or the betrothal of a bride.

Nard or Spikenard is a class of aromatic amber-colored essential oil derived from Nardostachys jatamansi, a flowering plant of the valerian family which grows in the Himalayas of Nepal, China and India. "It was offered on the specialized incense alter when the Tabernacle was located in the First and Second Jerusalem Temples."

Because Nard was an imported item, it was very expensive and in Mark's gospel account, we gain an appreciation that it was of extreme value and not something that would be wasted. So when this woman broke the jar (alabaster jars were usually made in such a way that they had to be broken to be emptied) and proceeded to pour its contents on Jesus, the onlookers reacted. "Some of those present were saying indignantly to one another, 'Why this waste of perfume? It could have been sold for more than a year's wages and the money given to the poor.' And they rebuked her harshly." Mark 14:4-5. If you contemplate a year's wages in today's dollars, you can see why they would think this way.

There is no way of knowing what led this woman to Jesus that day or how she came about possessing such an expensive jar of perfume, but we are told she was a known sinner therefore she must have had a certain reputation. Perhaps she was a corrupt merchant, or a professional thief known to authorities, or maybe a prostitute who had saved her earnings and now sought redemption, we just don't know. Regardless of the how's and the why's, the woman is deeply troubled and comes to Jesus in the spirit of repentance.

Luke's description emphasizes her attention to Jesus' feet rather than his head, "A woman in that town who had lived a sinful life learned that Jesus was eating at the Pharisee's house, so she came there with an alabaster jar of perfume. As she stood behind him at his feet weeping, she began to wet his feet with her tears. She then wiped them with her hair, kissed them and poured perfume on them.

When the Pharisee saw this, he said to himself, 'If this man were a prophet, he would know who is touching him and what kind of woman she is – that she is a sinner.'" Luke 7:37-39.

Christ's response to the woman and her opposition in both accounts not only offers a lesson in humility we can all learn but holds very profound and transcendent intimations. Jesus chastises those who are critical of the immense sacrifice this woman is making. Acknowledging that her heart is breaking as she attends to him, he elevates her as an example for everyone.

To the Pharisee, "Jesus answered him, 'Simon, I have something to tell you.' 'Tell me, teacher,' he said.

'Two people owed money to a certain moneylender. One owed him five hundred denarii, and the other fifty. Neither of them had the money to pay him back, so he forgave the debts of both. Now which of them will love him more?'

Simon replied, 'I suppose the one who had the bigger debt forgiven.'

'You have judged correctly,' Jesus said.

Then he turned toward the woman and said to Simon, 'Do you see this woman? I came into your house. You did not give me any water for my feet, but she wet my feet with her tears and wiped them with her hair. You did not give me a kiss, but this woman, from the time I entered, has not stopped kissing my feet. You did not put oil on my head, but she has poured perfume on my feet. Therefore, I tell you, her many sins have been forgiven – as her great love has shown. But whoever has been forgiven little loves little.'" Luke 7:40-47.

In Mark, Jesus directs his divine dialogue to those who rebuked the woman, "'Leave her alone,' said Jesus. 'Why are you bothering her? She has done a beautiful thing to me. The poor you will always have with you, and you can help them anytime you want. But you will not always have me. She did what she could. She poured perfume on my body beforehand to prepare for my burial. Truly I tell you, wherever the gospel is preached throughout the world, what she has done will also be told, in memory of her.'" Mark 14:6-9.

The sincerity of the woman's repentance is reflected in her humility and reverence, the value of her sacrifice and her selfless actions regardless of how others perceive her. The house of a Pharisee would be a hostile environment for her to enter at any time and this day it was full of guests, nevertheless she braves the embarrassment and reaches out to Jesus seeking forgiveness. This obviously touches the heart of Jesus and he responds by freely giving her a full pardon for her sins.

Repentance touches the heart of the Lord. When we fully surrender to God, from the depth of our soul, earnestly and sincerely reaching out for him, we move him to compassion for us. Just as the woman who suffered from ongoing bleeding pushed her way through the crowd so she could just touch Christ's robe so she could be healed, our passion for Jesus needs to be as unbridled and determined as hers so we can show God our resolve to be his children.

"A large crowd followed and pressed around him. And a woman was there who had been subject to bleeding for twelve years. She had suffered a great deal under the care of many doctors and had spent all she had, yet instead of getting better she grew worse. When she heard about Jesus, she came up behind him in the crowd and touched his cloak, because she thought, 'If I just touch his clothes, I will be healed.' Immediately her bleeding stopped and she felt in her body that she had been freed from her suffering. At once Jesus realized that power had gone out from him. He turned around in the crowd and asked, 'Who touched my clothes?'

'You see the people crowding against you,' his disciples answered, 'and yet you can ask, 'Who touched me?'' But Jesus kept looking around to see who had done it. Then the woman, knowing what happened to her, came and fell at his feet and, trembling with fear, told him the whole truth. He said to her, 'Daughter, your faith has healed you. Go in peace and be freed from your suffering.'" Mark 5:24-34.

In all likelihood Jesus knew who had touched him. He asked for the benefit of the woman herself and the crowd so that he could demonstrate that it was her faith that had elicited the healing of her body and he wanted her to know that she was free. He was illustrating that righteousness comes through faith and redemption is a gift from God, granted freely to those who sincerely seek it.

Much more than just healing her body, Jesus healed her soul. What holds believers back from eagerly and desperately reaching out to Jesus? Are we so fulfilled in our lives from material wealth that we feel we have nothing to gain? Has religion failed us by teaching that through the observance of ritual and ceremony we are justified before God? The Prophet Hosea continually warned the Israelites that their unfaithfulness to God would bring about judgement. He tried to convey the importance of seeking the very heart of God. "For I desire mercy, not sacrifice, and acknowledgement of God rather than burnt offerings." Hosea 6:6.

Our response to God's word has impact in heaven. The Bible tells us the when God wanted Jonah to prophesy to the city of Nineveh, he did everything he could to do the opposite. Nineveh was an ungodly city and Jonah would have been quite content if God destroyed it, yet God prevailed and he reluctantly went to deliver the Lord's warnings.

God was about to punish Nineveh for its sinful ways, and the city was given forty days to repent. They believed Jonah and took God's warning seriously, and from the king down to the peasants, they dressed in sackcloth and ashes and fasted as a sign of their deep sorrow over their sins. Then they urgently called out to God. And they repented of their sinful practices.

"When God saw what they did and how they turned from their evil ways, he relented and did not bring on them the destruction he had threatened." Jonah 3:10. God wasn't moved from anger to compassion by what was said, but rather by what was done. God does not respond to lip service but to the sincerity in our hearts and actions. This is what Jesus meant when he chastised the Pharisees by saying, "These people honor me with their lips, but their hearts are far from me." Mathew 15:8.

God held nothing back when he redeemed us. As much as it must have grieved him to do it, he permitted his one and only son to be crucified at the hands of the Romans as an atonement for our sins. Once and for all, a sacrifice that fully paid for the sins of mankind. Jesus willingly offered himself on our behalf as a sacrifice for sin. Since nothing was held back for us, why do we hold back from God? God knew he needed to lay it all on the table to win the battle. What is holding us back from doing the same?

"For God so loved the world that he gave his one and only Son, that whoever believes in him shall not perish but have everlasting life." John 3:16. God did what he did because of love. He loves us. Do we love him? We may serve him but do we love him? Jesus gave us two commands and said that all of the Law and the Prophets hung on them. Love God with all your heart and all your mind and all of your soul and love each other as you love yourself (Mathew 22:37-40).

When we think of love we often envision the movie version where the hero swims across a sea of broken glass to be with the fair maiden. Are we prepared to do that for Jesus? How many of us would be willing to lay down our lives for Jesus? Are we willing to die for him like he died for us? We are living in a time when it is conceivable that we could be asked one day to take the mark of the beast. What will be our answer, knowing full well that if we refuse we will be killed? What would your response be to a Muslim extremist giving you the ultimatum to denounce Jesus or die?

In the first century after the crucifixion many, many Christians went to their deaths because they refused to deny Christ. The disciples with the exception of John who was exiled to the Island of Patmos, were all killed for their faith in Jesus. Paul, who never shied away from controversy or danger, was beheaded because of his passion for Christ. Throughout the history of the corrupt establishment of the church, a great number of people were burnt at the stake as heretics because of their genuine love for Jesus and the true gospel.

Those were dark days for followers of Jesus Christ. One could not speak openly about the gospel, as one never knew who would overhear, who would sell information to the church or who would run to the Roman authorities. No one knew if centurions would break down the door in the middle of the night and bind them and take them off to prison. Believers lived in constant fear and apprehension over their families, friends and brothers and sisters in Christ. I'm sure you could feel the tension in the air as Christianity spread even while followers of "the way" were constantly sentenced to death in the arena.

In my book *Seeking Truth*, I shared the story of Polycarp. He was an example of living life without inhibition to spread the love of the Lord. The following is an excerpt from *Seeking Truth*:

Polycarp was a disciple of the apostle John. His life and eventual martyrdom are probably the next most recorded testimony after the Acts of the Apostles. Polycarp lived from AD 69 – 155, and his is the oldest authentic account of an early Christian martyr's death. Because he personally knew John and was filled with the Holy Spirit, he was highly revered as a teacher and church leader. He spent his life as a faithful servant of Christ and in his old age, while praying with friends, he had a vision of the pillow under his head in flames. "He said prophetically to those who were with him, 'I will be burnt alive.'" Three days later, he was arrested by the Romans.

When the heavily armed soldiers arrived to arrest him, he spoke with them and offered them food and drink and requested that he be allowed to pray for an hour. The soldiers were amazed at his age and conviction and said, "Why did we go to so much trouble to arrest a man like this?" Filled with the Spirit, Polycarp prayed for two full hours, then he was placed on a donkey and taken into Rome.

"As Polycarp was being taken into the arena, a voice came to him from heaven: 'Be strong, Polycarp and play the man!' No one saw who had spoken but our brothers who were there heard the voice." Before the crowd, the proconsul asked him to deny Christ, to which Polycarp replied, "86 years I have served him, and he has done me no wrong. How can I blaspheme my King and Savior?"

Polycarp was then threatened with wild animals and fire unless he repented, to which he replied, "You threaten me with fire which burns for an hour, and is then extinguished, but you know nothing of the fire of the coming judgement and eternal punishment, reserved for the ungodly. Why are you waiting? Bring on whatever you want."

The wood was prepared, and Polycarp was ready. "But when they went to fix him with nails, he said, 'Leave me as I am, for he that gives me strength to endure the fire, will enable me not to struggle, without the help of your nails.'" So, Polycarp was bound. "He looked up to heaven, and said, 'O Lord God Almighty, the Father of your beloved and blessed son Jesus Christ, by whom we have received the knowledge of you, the God of angels, powers and every creature, and all of the righteous who live before you, I give you thanks that you count me worthy to be numbered among your martyrs, sharing the cup of Christ and the resurrection to eternal life, both of soul and body, through the immortality of the Holy Spirit. May I be received this day as an acceptable sacrifice, as you, the true God, have predestined, revealed to me, and now fulfilled. I praise you for all these things, I bless you and glorify you, along with the everlasting Jesus Christ, your beloved Son. To you, with him, through the Holy Ghost, be the glory both now and forever. Amen.'

The fire was lit, and the flame blazed furiously. We who were privileged to witness it saw a great miracle, and this is why we have been preserved, to tell the story. The fire shaped itself into the form of an arch, like the sail of a ship when filled with the wind, and formed a circle around the body of the martyr. Inside it, he looked not like flesh that is burnt, but like bread that is baked, or gold and silver glowing in a furnace. And we smelt a sweet scent, like frankincense or some such precious spices." [114]

When the Romans saw that his body could not be consumed by the fire, the executioner was ordered to pierce him with a spear. When he did this, a dove flew out and so much blood flowed from the wound that the fire was extinguished. Polycarp's life and death are not only a powerful testimony to the truth and power of God, they are an example that we ought to hold in high esteem. His passion to persevere and the unshakable trust that God is always in control is a precedent we should all aspire to pattern our own lives after.

There are more Christians being persecuted today than at any time in history including at the hands of the Roman Empire. Many of today's martyrs fall at the hands of Islamic jihadists, whose terrorism has become so commonplace that it almost seems normal to hear about it daily. In Africa, entire villages are being wiped out and in the middle east the tragedy is at near genocide levels. In Iran the Christian population has dropped from "1.5 million people before 2003 to less than 120,000."[115] Christians are forced to recite recantations and shot anyway, children are sent into mine fields to set off mines, women are sold as slaves, raped and married off to Islamic fighters.

Jesus said, "Whoever acknowledges me before others, I will also acknowledge before my Father in heaven. But whoever disowns me before others, I will disown before my Father in heaven.

Do not suppose that I have come to bring peace to the earth. I did not come to bring peace, but a sword. For I have come to turn

'a man against his father, a daughter against her mother,
a daughter -in-law against her mother-in-law –
a man's enemies will be the members of his own household.'

Anyone who loves their father or mother more than me is not worthy of me; anyone who loves their son or daughter more than me is not worthy of me. Whoever does not take up their cross and follow me is not worthy of me. Whoever finds their life will lose it, and whoever loses their life for my sake will find it." Mathew 10:32-39.

Today many "Christians" run the risk of losing the race. They are the lukewarm church written of in the third chapter of Revelation. "I know your deeds, that you are neither cold nor hot. I wish you were either one or the other! So, because you are lukewarm – neither hot nor cold – I am about to spit you out of my mouth. You say, 'I am rich; I have acquired wealth and do not need a thing.' But you do not realize that you are wretched, pitiful, poor, blind and naked." Revelation 3:15-17.

Believers who live in abundance and material wealth often have the weakest faiths. When you thirst and desire for nothing there is no unquenchable yearning to be saved. Today people in developed countries have higher standards of living than royalty had in times long past. Even during the COVID 19 lockdowns no one is without food. Very few cry out to God. It often takes a tragedy to touch people's hearts to the point of reaching out and searching for answers to life's existential questions.

It often isn't until we are backed into the corner of drug addiction or alcoholism and at risk of losing our family or our job that we reach for Jesus. Many people don't meet Christ until they find themselves in prison while in the depths of despair. When our hearts break for the same things that break God's heart we surrender to him. "The Lord is close to the broken hearted and saves those who are crushed in spirit." Psalm 34:18.

What is it with human character that is so superficial that we feel we owe nothing to God when times are good? Even the nation of Israel in ancient days existed in an ongoing cycle of prosperity while they followed the Lord, followed by falling away because of that prosperity, and then being punished and suffering under persecution or exile, causing them to repent and turn back to God and be rewarded with prosperity once more. Man was made in the image of God, therefore, our sin and rebellion is not of God. The fallen state of man has produced in us a selfishness and arrogance that can only be attributed to Satan's imprinting upon us.

Adversity produces strength and perseverance. North American churches can be found on easy street. Many Christian churches today are shortchanging their congregations by preaching a candy cane gospel that has no call for heartfelt repentance and obedience to God's word. Rather than being sold out for Christ many church leaders have become bankrupt of the Holy Spirit. Rather than being anointed with the Spirit they are watered down with carnality.

Rather than embracing our role as the "Church" of Jesus Christ, we are trying to worship from a platform of doubt and fear. We are scared of preaching repentance and we are scared of being accused of preaching hate. We cannot afford to be intimidated by a society that revels in the wages of sin. We must not be afraid to offend! Jesus wasn't! He spoke truth and the very same truth that set many free, offended others.

"Then Jesus declared, 'I am the bread of life. Whoever comes to me will never go hungry, and whoever believes in me will never be thirsty. But as I told you, you have seen me and you still don't believe. All those the Father gives me will come to me, and whoever comes to me I will never drive away. For I have come down from heaven not to do my will but to do the will of him who sent me. And this is the will of him who sent me, that I should lose none of all those he has given me, but raise them up at the last day. For my Father's will is that everyone who looks to the Son and believes in him shall have eternal life, and I will raise them up at the last day.

At this the Jews began to grumble about him because he said, 'I am the bread that came down from heaven.' They said, 'Is this not Jesus, the son of Joseph, whose father and mother we know? How can he now say, 'I came down from heaven?'

'Stop grumbling among yourselves,' Jesus answered. No one can come to me unless the Father who sent me draws them, and I will raise them up at the last day. It is written in the Prophets: 'They will all be taught by God.' Everyone who has heard the Father and has learned from him comes to me. No one has seen the Father except the one who is from God; only he has seen the Father. Very truly I tell you, the one who believes has eternal life. I am the bread of life. Your ancestors ate the manna in the wilderness, yet they died. But here is the bread of life that comes down from heaven, which anyone may eat and not die. I am the living bread that came down from heaven. Whoever eats this bread will live forever. This bread is my flesh, which I give for the life of the world.'

Then the Jews began to argue sharply among themselves, 'How can this man give us his flesh to eat?'

Jesus said to them, 'Very truly I tell you, unless you eat the flesh of the Son of Man and drink his blood, you have no life in you. Whoever eats my flesh and drinks my blood has eternal life, and I will raise them up at the last day. For my flesh is real food and my blood is real drink. Whoever eats my flesh and drinks my blood remains in me, and I in them. Just as the living Father sent me and I live because of the Father, so the one who feeds on me will live because of me. This is the bread that came down from heaven. Your ancestors ate manna and died, but whoever feeds on this bread will live forever. He said this while teaching in the synagogue in Capernaum.

On hearing it, many of his disciples said, 'This is a hard teaching. Who can accept it?'

Aware that his disciples were grumbling about this, Jesus said to them, 'Does this offend you? Then what if you see the Son of Man ascend to where he was before! The Spirit gives life; the flesh counts for nothing. The words I have spoken to you – they are full of the Spirit and life. Yet there are some of you who do not believe.' For Jesus had known from the beginning which of them did not believe and who would betray him. He went on to say, 'This is why I told you that no one can come to me unless the Father has enabled them.'

From this time many of his disciples turned back and no longer followed him." John 6:35-66.

There is a day coming and is already here, when we must serve God in true Spirit, not out of some sense of sacrifice - that we are doing God a favor by showing up on Sunday. An impotent Christianity cannot save anyone from the gates of hell. The Christian Church needs to preach the eternal gospel. The Christian Church needs to preach truth. The Christian Church needs to preach repentance of sins. The Christian Church needs to preach Jesus!

As Christians, we must cry out to Jesus, "Son of David, have mercy on me!" Our cries need to touch the heart of God. Our petitions to the Lord must come from a place deep within us in all sincerity. "What is this living water you speak of Jesus?" We must beg to ask Christ the question, "What must I do to be saved?" What is the assurance of our salvation? What do we do in our lives that furthers the kingdom of God? What do we do in our lives that spreads the love of God?

Our hearts were made to be alive and on fire for Jesus. We were designed to yearn for a relationship with the living God. When you truly believe and have the indwelling Holy Spirit awakening your spirit, you are changed from the inside and your heart is set ablaze for the Lord. When your relationship with Jesus is the focal point of your life, it becomes an intentional experience of seeking to know Christ better and to draw nearer to him through prayer and worship each day, sharing your passion for Jesus with others, serving others and meditating on God's word always. Your life will become love in action.

We must be intentional in setting our hearts, minds and souls on Christ. To bask in the love and the joy of being in the presence of the Lord. To feel the Holy Spirit in you welling up like springs of living water that satisfy your thirst for God so that you will never thirst again. Let the fire of Christ burn within you. Fire is consuming, bright and hot, it refines and purifies. Feed the fire with Bible study and fellowship with other believers. Allow yourself to be overwhelmed by passion and love for God, allow the Holy Spirit to wrap you up in joy and peace that transcends all human understanding. Allow yourself to be so full of the Holy Spirit that you cannot contain it.

Jesus Christ is the King of Kings and Lord of Lords, Emanuel who is God with us. He is the way and the truth and the life. The Prince of Peace, Wonderful Counsellor, the Almighty God. Jesus is the Word and the Truth, he is the culmination of all of God's promises, perfect yet humble. "For in him all things were created: things in heaven and on earth, visible and invisible, whether thrones or powers or rulers or authorities; all things have been created through him and for him. He is before all things, and in him all things hold together." Colossians 1:16-17.

When we contemplate what Christ has done for us we ultimately fall short of adequately describing his love for us. When we try to appreciate God, we inevitably fall short. He is beyond our comprehension, he is undefinable yet approachable, he is unsearchable yet knowable, his grace is remarkable, his strength is insurmountable, he is the conqueror of sin, our redeemer and warrior, the Lamb of God, welcoming and inviting. Jesus is the light of the world and he is worthy. Bless his name forevermore.

Live for him! Love for him! Serve Christ Jesus with unbridled passion, as an expression of deep heartfelt gratitude for his sacrifice and atonement on the cross at Calvary. Don't let life pass you by and leave you unsure of your eternal destiny, but rather, finish the game leaving everything on the field, exhausted and satisfied knowing you gave it your all. Then, when you enter heaven, you will hear the Master say, "Well done, good and faithful servant."

When I think of the kind of life that exemplifies what a true Christian ought to pattern themselves after, I think about the passion of Paul. After his encounter with the risen Christ on the road to Damascus, his life was forever changed and the fire of his love for God could not be extinguished. His writings have had a profound effect on me and I dedicated nearly a whole chapter of my book *Seeking Truth* to his legacy. I will share some of that narrative once again here:

Paul was the apostle to the Gentiles, and he is the person I look toward to interpret the gospel for me. His unprecedented understanding of the Jewish perspective and laws and their application through the cross, to non-Jews, like me, make him the undisputed authority on scripture for Christians today. Furthermore, his zealous sharing of the gospel and profound love of Christ exemplify what being a Christian means. Paul had the extraordinary gift of scrutinizing complex concepts and explaining them in simple, easy to understand language that anyone could comprehend.

Paul suffered contempt, beatings, stoning, prison, a shipwreck and was finally beheaded for his faith in Jesus. Yet he never relented in his passion for Christ and immediately went right back to preaching the gospel and reasoning with those who would listen, right up until his death. His zeal and conviction led him to write nearly half of the new testament. Paul's letters have been translated and reproduced more than any other literature in the history of human writing.

Born a Roman citizen, Paul was raised in the Greek culture of Tarsus and educated in Jerusalem, where he studied the Jewish scriptures and religious law under the distinguished rabbi Gamaliel "the Elder" who was a member of the Sanhedrin (Acts 22:3). Paul's father was a Pharisee and Paul's ancestry, was Jewish from the tribe of Benjamin, thus equipping Paul with the ideal toolbox to appeal to the various cultures under Roman rule and to answer the deepest questions with integrity and authority.

While we owe our salvation to Jesus, Paul is responsible for spreading the fire in a way that breathed life into the early church and continues to win hearts and minds for Jesus even today. His passion, compassion, humility, honesty, intelligence and simplicity, combined to make him trustworthy and compelling in his apology of the Christian faith. Paul wrote, "Follow my example, as I follow the example of Christ." 1 Corinthians 11:1.

In the same way that Christ, through his claim to be God, either was who he claimed to be, or he was a complete lunatic, Paul was either the greatest Apostle of Christ or he was a deluded fool. He is honest with this assessment and said, "If only for this life we have hope in Christ, we are of all people most to be pitied." 1 Corinthians 15:19.

He identified personally with Jesus' suffering and as a Jew by blood, his heart ached for his people's unbelief just as Jesus wept over Jerusalem. Furthermore, Paul imitated Christ by making himself vulnerable and sharing in his frailties and personal struggle with sin. He is easy to identify with as we all struggle with temptation and in a similar way to Jesus understanding our humanity because he became human, Paul demonstrates living to please God from a human perspective. Paul considered himself the least of the apostles similar to Christ taking on the very nature of a servant. Paul wrote in Philippians 2:5-8, "In your relationships with one another, have the same mindset as Christ Jesus:

Who, being in very nature God, did not consider equality with God something to be used to his own advantage;

rather, he made himself nothing by taking the very nature of a servant, being made in human likeness.

And being found in appearance as a man, he humbled himself by becoming obedient to death –

even death on a cross!"

Two thousand years later, Paul's writings stand out as applicable and meaningful in an educated and literate western society. His rationality and conceptual reasoning are able to persevere in the face of philosophical challenges from theologians and secular intellectuals alike, yet his language is understandable for those who are less learned. Just as Jesus was able to debate with the religious leaders and teachers of the law in his day and point out their hypocrisy, Paul's letters help to highlight truth in scripture today. Humanity has grossly underestimated the intelligence of God. We cannot even begin to fathom it. In choosing Paul to bring the gospel to the Gentile masses, Christ in his holistic foreknowledge and perspective, established a voice that would transcend the generations and cultures of the world.

Paul preached that what you are inside is what you truly are. It's what is in your heart that is what God is interested in. Your outward appearance and actions are nothing more than hypocrisy if they do not match what you sincerely feel in your heart. You can go through the motions of going to church, giving donations or preaching the gospel but if deep in your heart you lust for money, or sex or have hatred towards someone or something, then you are still under judgement.

Each of us has a conscience provided by God and built into our soul, that guides us and gives a sense of right and wrong. Even those who deny the existence of God are equipped this way. Sin is still sin whether you understand what it is through God's law or if you have never heard of God's laws. Those who suppress the truth by doing what is evil and intentionally betraying their conscience are just as guilty of sin as those who know and practice God's laws and break them. Paul says, "All who sin apart from the law will also perish apart from the law, and all who sin under the law will be judged by the law." Romans 2:12.

Those who welcome the Spirit into their heart and do by nature the things required by the law, ...show that the requirements of the law are written on their hearts, their consciences also bearing witness, and their thoughts sometimes accusing them and at other times even defending them." Romans 2:15.

Repentance requires full submission to the Holy Spirit. Being born again requires full submission to following Christ. Paul demonstrated this by completely changing who he was and what he stood for. Our obedience to God, even though it is imperfect, is made possible through Christ changing our unbelieving and rebellious heart into a heart that longs to please him and delights in serving him. Once we are saved, it is difficult to contain our love and compassion for others and we are highly motivated to share the gospel so that love will spread. We want others to benefit from the saving and transforming power of Christ. We become like Jesus' disciples when he said, "if they keep quiet, the stones will cry out." Luke 19:40.

"Rejoice in the Lord always. I will say it again: rejoice! Let your gentleness be evident to all. The Lord is near. Do not be anxious about anything, but in every situation, by prayer and petition, with thanksgiving, present your requests to God. And the peace of God, which transcends all understanding, will guard your hearts and your minds in Christ Jesus.

Finally, brothers and sisters, whatever is true, whatever is noble, whatever is right, whatever is pure, whatever is lovely, whatever is admirable – if anything is excellent or praiseworthy – think about such things. Whatever you have learned or received or heard from me, or seen in me – put it into practice. And the God of peace be with you.

I rejoiced greatly in the Lord that at last you renewed your concern for me. Indeed, you were concerned, but you had no opportunity to show it. I am not saying this because I am in need, for I have learned to be content whatever the circumstances. I know what it is to be in need, and I know what it is to have plenty. I have learned the secret of being content in any and every situation, whether well fed or hungry, whether living in plenty or in want. I can do all this through him who gives me strength." Philippians 4:4-13.

If only we could all have the faith of Paul. Many have thought that thought. The truth is, you can, and you should. It is so important to fully surrender yourself to the Holy Spirit and give your life to Christ. Jesus never held anything back when he died for us. Paul never held anything back as he was faithful until death. We are called to imitate them by going all in. Jesus said, "Whoever wants to be my disciple must deny themselves and take up their cross and follow me." Mathew 16:24.

Each of us is created with a purpose. When we hear the call of the Lord and heed to it, amazing things happen, and our lives can realize potential we would never attain on our own. Living with purpose and intent can make all the difference in the world, providing energy, hope, happiness and conviction to go the extra mile, put in that extra hour or climb to the next level. What is God calling you to do? Are you willing to step outside of your comfort zone to answer God's call?

The apostle Paul is an example we should all hold vividly in our minds in this time of uncertainty that is coming upon our world. His possessed the kind of spiritual fortitude we will require during our own hour of testing therefore, we would be wise to live with the intent and purpose that Paul displayed. Nearing the end of his ministry and life, he wrote, "I have fought the good fight, I have finished the race, I have kept the faith. Now there is in store for me the crown of righteousness, which the Lord, will award me on that day – and not only to me, but also to all who have longed for his appearing." 2 Timothy 4:7-8.

The time is short! We are living in the age of Elijah. Listen for the sound of approaching hoof beats! Every promise of God will soon be fulfilled. Put on the full armor of God and stand firm in the faith! The hour of testing is almost upon us. Prepare for the battle ahead. Satan will bring that battle to each of us and lay it at our very feet. Be ready!

It is my sincere prayer that you will seek the Lord with all of your heart and all of your mind and all of your soul. That you will pursue Christ, holding nothing back as he held nothing back for you. That as you live your life you will stand faithful knowing that you are a child of the Most-High God, The Almighty. That you be filled with the Holy Spirit and blessed with peace in the knowledge that there is absolutely nothing in heaven or on earth that can pluck you from the Father's hand. I pray that you allow the spark of Christ to ignite in you an eternal flame deep within your soul, that each time a new door opens that the flame is fanned and continues to burn bright and hot. That you will become a city on a hill, giving light to the darkness that surrounds you. May your faith be strong like a lion and as gentle as a lamb. "The Lord bless you and keep you; the Lord make his face shine on you and be gracious to you; the Lord turn his face toward you and give you peace." Numbers 6:24-26. So be it!!!

ENDNOTES

1 https://internationalman.com/articles/the-first-casualty-is-truth/
2 https://www.azquotes.com/quotes/topics/horror-of-war.html
3 https://www.independent.co.uk/news/world/europe/bilderberg-group-conspiracy-theories-secret-societies-new-world-order-alex-jones-a8377171.html
4 https://www.guttmacher.org/fact-sheet/induced-abortion-worldwide
5 https://www.weforum.org/great-reset/
6 https://www.cbc.ca/news/politics/china-totalitarianism-xi-jinping-canada-japan-1.5465067?fbclid=IwAR1omgZbBLdNXHBrtjQgN5F-90Bmpc0Z9lNLCGIygkF8f849U3UCwWjINNY
7 https://populationinstitutecanada.ca/
8 https://extinctionrebellion.ca/
9 https://onlinelibrary.wiley.com/doi/full/10.1111/1758-5899.12721?fbclid=IwAR22YH3Nj_akqhZKOpguduUZTlhAYjHJJwb8VEuCFRgd8XIVj3nCULmw1II
10 https://www.techtimes.com/articles/247711/20200303/dirty-money-who-warns-banknotes-may-pass-coronavirus-looks-towards-cashless-transactions.htm
11 https://medium.com/@topicalthunderseo/implantable-digital-id-vaccination-system-in-development-yikes-ba900cf4017f
12 https://patents.google.com/patent/WO2004092360A2/en
13 https://www.nowtheendbegins.com/big-pharma-microsoft-silicon-valley-id2020-alliance-combine-vaccinations-with-implantable-microchip-digital-id-mark-beast-end-times/
14 http://time.com/collection-post/4589745/fortune-time-global-forum-report/
15 https://www.churchmilitant.com/news/article/catholics-and-non-catholics-hold-globalist-meeting-in-the-vatican?fbclid=IwAR0zRs6_2SDFyOlp3PxJG-OLomJL3QTvMsjaTPbmXPQ9r62Dq77U2i43Q7U

16 https://www.spiked-online.com/2019/12/26/in-2020-we-need-to-fight-the-new-thoughtpolice/?fbclid=IwAR3QjpjzfEurcXv4HOc4GL569sVPiMAOukGeFDvJs5-MD3yi7Is13G2VrI8

17 https://www.spiked-online.com/2019/12/26/in-2020-we-need-to-fight-the-new-thoughtpolice/?fbclid=IwAR3QjpjzfEurcXv4HOc4GL569sVPiMAOukGeFDvJs5-MD3yi7Is13G2VrI8

18 https://www.linkedin.com/pulse/partial-list-over-6000-products-made-from-one-barrel-oil-steve-pryor/

19 https://www.ivey.uwo.ca/cmsmedia/2112500/4462-ghg-emissions-report-v03f.pdf

20 https://en.wikipedia.org/wiki/William_Guy_Carr

21 https://www.globalresearch.ca/the-true-story-of-the-bilderberg-group-and-what-they-may-be-planning-now/13808

22 https://www.globalresearch.ca/the-true-story-of-the-bilderberg-group-and-what-they-may-be-planning-now/13808

23 https://www.globalresearch.ca/the-true-story-of-the-bilderberg-group-and-what-they-may-be-planning-now/13808

24 https://inequality.org/facts/global-inequality/

25 https://www.nytimes.com/2020/07/13/us/politics/george-soros-racial-justice-organizations.html

26 https://niagraindependent.ca/george-soros--casts-a-long-shadow-across-canada-part-4/

27 https://www.goodreads.com/quotes/944478-for-we-are-opposed-around-the-world-by-a-monolithic

28 https://www.theusaexpress.com/index.php/2020/09/17/is-this-john-d-rockerfellers-masonic-creed/

29 https://www.worldbank.org/en/news/press-release/2018/05/24/who-and-world-bank-group-join-forces-to-strengthen-global-health-security

30 https://www.cbc.ca/news/politics/not-isolating-could-threaten-freedoms-hajdu-says-1.5505767?fbclid=IwAR3xXKn6wdS9BGNybWFn9gf4El_hPICal0paSP5pwUxHkw1f703A3c5uH6k

31 https://thetruthaboutcancer.com/coronavirus-panic-pandemic/?fbclid=IwAR06Q9ZJRA8e5F16Yl3yV_qQj-GffUpeJliicsaYxfNYn6GVk69AZzbQeBY

32 https://thetruthaboutcancer.com/coronavirus-panic-pandemic/?fbclid=IwAR06Q9ZJRA8e5F16Yl3yV_qQj-GffUpeJliicsaYxfNYn6GVk69AZzbQeBY

33 https://occamsrazorterrorevents.weebly.com/blog/coronavirus-hoax-jan-2020?fbclid=IwAR04CL8XP2sAuC7327xsO3hmImzH8Um0DCDQHH_0Mj01deaDhklai5rR4Y

34 https://www.youtube.com/watch?v=iH9zqqEHmHM&feature=share&fbclid=IwAR0jhDBcjsbo501J_9Q0fHtt1dwdGMIccQXkYERrkar8357j37QQlr-sOME

35 https://nypost.com/2020/09/11/chinese-virologist-says-she-has-proof-covid-19-was-made-in-wuhan-lab/amp/?fbclid=IwAR32cxpYFHWMufJRZSde3xvVpnaFw8XbwUGDW9tU1M4gDfDXxZE3SSabqbY

36 https://www.toddstarnes.com/values/massie-warns-that-coronavirus-measures-jeopardize-american-freedoms/?utm_source=facebook&utm_medium=social&utm_campaign=social-pug&fbclid=IwAR0u9NclpKsFWVqvZbDJsD_Ubtj05NhVg7CDAW2N98k8O4hYnx_gXtU1-Qk

37 https://www.forbes.com/sites/jasonbrett/2020/03/23/new-coronavirus-stimulus-bill-introduces-digital-dollar-and-digital-dollar-wallets/?fbclid=IwAR3Lhf0pNSzoPfeUf_6KrX2eEFMmcRkrCeNNombgISvqgchu_6ROi7qQGao#7f34c1af4bea

38 https://interestingengineering.com/sweden-how-to-live-in-the-worlds-first-cashless-society

39 https://www.patreon.com/posts/34871937?fbclid=IwAR3kc4pPQrqx0Nz9dSnhqYJAZ3ugoe-9pUP5r-Kgom12GKH1JwBGohYvdOs

40 https://ca.finance.yahoo.com/news/the-richest-got-37-billion-richer-during-covid-19-while-millions-lost-their-jobs-172740845.html

41 https://www.businessinsider.com/billionaires-net-worth-increases-coronavirus-pandemic-2020-7

42 https://www.prophecynewswatch.com/article.cfm?recent_news_id=3933&fbclid=IwAR3wV4YUTyHl8DjCqan4Lkv_yE8zEUnM8FULtL-qYfqLX_1CPtxfh5C0r_I

43 https://en.wikipedia.org/wiki/Bill_Gates_Sr

44 https://www.lifesitenews.com/news/doctors-lay-out-plan-to-punish-people-who-refuse-coronavirus-vaccine-there-is-no-alternative

45 https://www.rfi.fr/en/france/20200624-french-doctor-didier-raoult-championed-hydroxychloroquine-respond-covid-inquiry-france-mps-medicine?fbclid=IwAR21x2h1SF9NA5qzER7iQ0B3ex1OCCJEOrvVfcDjayLvhGVadkrqR516BEM)

46 https://www.facebook.com/lynna.smith.9887/videos/151164299940252

47 https://www.lifesitenews.com/news/twitter-founder-to-send-1b-to-population-control-groups?utm_content=buffer08445&utm_medium=WCEA%2BBuffer&utm_source=facebook&utm_campaign=WCEA&fbclid=IwAR0wzvCy1Ww7CdgZP2tVddcAU2crZhinZv4_cvmO9XJLGnmeHqIEamV5Fc8

48 https://humansarefree.com/2020/10/politician-warns-trudeau-govt-plans-to-build-covid-quarantine-isolation-camps-across-canada.html

49 https://nationalpost.com/news/politics/canadian-government-to-force-incoming-travellers-into-hotels-for-quarantine?fbclid=IwAR3y3241DETFTbil9JbnNnZoCR3NJKgWmi7SqoYdNVqvRURGozOCjzOEBZc

50 https//www150.statcan.gc.ca/n1/pub/71-607-x/71-607-x2020017-eng.htm

51 https://toronto.ctvnews.ca/mobile/ontarians-could-face-restrictions-if-they-refuse-to-get-covid-19-vaccine-health-minister-says-1.5222009?fbclid=IwAR11O-MaRu1egYdRyPQ1tdfYdIC9NIhI-FgGDz6JgQYcOjPNXieL55ziIkzc
52 https://en.as.com/en/2020/11/24/latest_news/1606228590_532670.html?fbclid=IwAR0zC8UB7A1hPs2nnd0lvRW27r6QOaVj34agAhV46E21UM8C08WE3igAnrM
53 https://globalnews.ca/news/7545830/coronavirus-pandemic-big-one-who/?fbclid=IwAR1OXBLVb0zHNlP3pwaU0HFQPWYr8PdC18fsF_IIOqLxbXz6bl2mdczWEPY
54 https://www.guttmacher.org/fact-sheet/induced-abortion-worldwide
55 https://www.cbc.ca/news/politics/grenier-trudeau-ethics-we-1.5645464
56 https://www.cbc.ca/news/politics/trudeau-groping-confident-not-inappropriately-1.4735661
57 https://www.aljazeera.com/opinions/2011/10/27/immunity-and-impunity-in-elite-america/
58 https://www.aljazeera.com/opinions/2011/10/27/immunity-and-impunity-in-elite-america/
59 https://www.foxnews.com/us/st-louis-gun-couple-investigated-clash-protesters
60 https://www.chicagotribune.com/opinion/commentary/ct-perspec-oxfam-sexual-abuse-scandal-0220-20180214-story.html
61 https://www.nytimes.com/2019/08/12/business/jeffrey-epstein-interview.html
62 https://www.rollingstone.com/culture/culture-features/corey-feldman-expose-pedophilia-hollywood-darkest-secrets-825375/
63 https://www.businessinsider.com/elijah-wood-hollywood-pedophile-ring-2016-5
64 https://abcnews.go.com/US/100-sex-trafficking-victims-rescued-us-amid-busts/story?id=64845453
65 https://www.washingtonpost.com/national/missing-children-rescued-in-georgia-sex-trafficking-bust/2020/08/28/eabbc964-e982-11ea-bf44-0d31c85838a5_story.html
66 https://spectrumnews1.com/ky/lexington/news/2020/09/07/us-marshals-rescue-72-children-fromgeorgia-ohio-indiana-september-august
67 https://www.cbc.ca/amp/1.5744766?fbclid=IwAR05Thr_win5Q3gLcW_hn1suzKdP1EB-badNOMh3wxSM6juw5PuEihJjBOE
68 https://www.vanityfair.com/style/2020/10/ghislaine-maxwell-new-legal-hurdles
69 https://www.liveaction.org/news/link-sex-trafficking-abortion-planned-parenthood/?fbclid=IwAR2gZOHo-7pSRfZQo4k7ekKjEv-NOppPWX3vd7t43QegkWStsDHWcPrn354
70 https://www.pewresearch.org/fact-tank/2020/08/31/half-of-u-s-christians-say-casual-sex-between-consenting-adults-is-sometimes-or-always-acceptable

/?fbclid=IwAR3NLA-hcTXcclrqHhGj_p59UUMi1PFYrsxT49rZZ8X51Vlu1_nxLbPCuFU

71 https://www.breitbart.com/politics/2020/09/03/california-legislature-passes-bill-reduce-penalties-oral-anal-sex-willing-children/?fbclid=IwAR16dYQkzw4vObHXFvMv5x7LiccnPwZpshXsU3Z36H-j3Ubu7d4hchpNV50

72 https://www.theguardian.com/news/2019/jan/22/the-new-elites-phoney-crusade-to-save-the-world-without-changing-anything

73 https://www.theblaze.com/wilkow/the-left-is-normalizing-pedophilia?utm_content=buffer5c5b7&utm_medium=referral&utm_source=facebook&utm_campaign=fb-andrewwilkow&fbclid=IwAR1fdQNUPQL2DX4hkasUo7U40aKi7LAKKIpJvJVdNbvE8cIBC1U4CEmzUME

74 https://www.deseret.com/entertainment/2020/10/8/21507515/netflix-cuties-national-center-on-sexual-exploitation

75 https://www.bbc.com/news/world-latin-america-51058029

76 https://newspunch.com/catholic-archbishop-rather-go-jail-than-report-pedophile-priest-who-confesses-his-crimes/?fbclid=IwAR2syxw6NU6ft08RDNOeNA0pyT1BHMtKNNkEVahaQJrT_Nzwb8V8dhIjAt0

77 https://www.goodreads.com/quotes/8804377-i-do-not-believe-that-any-man-can-preach-the?fbclid=IwAR1OS94lRHDzScyxw662bSaZOlq0XGM2eh1kEg69lUIIR-iauQQ0Bhh48cc#:~:text=Lower

78 https://www.biblestudytools.com/commentaries/revelation/related-topics/who-is-the-restrainer.html

79 https://www.biblestudytools.com/dictionary/apostasy-apostate/

80 https://www.timesofisrael.com/liveblog-september-15-2020/

81 https://www.gty.org/library/bibleqnas-library/QA0226/the-man-of-lawlessness

82 https://www.wivb.com/news/the-bibles-antichrist-real-person-or-symbolic/?fbclid=IwAR3MaWYR366p56TGujyYbFwo7TmJQmjcn2KIgBBzzXpkFJhkHrb1tpBABvQ

83 https://www.thekingiscoming.com/blog/2019/2/13/pope-and-imam-sign-one-world-religion-covenant?format=amp&fbclid=IwAR0k72if1q8gyRA_yZOgBmOvISvMeplKLIoW34lttfz2ifoEoV5SC2McZ4g

84 http://themostimportantnews.com/archives/the-pope-and-islams-most-important-imam-just-signed-a-covenant-that-pushes-us-much-closer-to-a-one-world-religion

85 http://themostimportantnews.com/archives/the-pope-and-islams-most-important-imam-just-signed-a-covenant-that-pushes-us-much-closer-to-a-one-world-religion

86 http://catholicnews.sg/index.php?option=com_content&view=article&id=1547:do-christians-and-muslims-worship-the-same-god&catid=119&Itemid=473&lang=en

87 https://www.americamagazine.org/faith/2019/02/04/pope-francis-worlds-religious-leaders-we-build-future-together-or-there-will-be-no

88 https://m.washingtontimes.com/news/2014/jun/9/vatican-makes-history-pope-allows-islamic-prayers-/?fbclid=IwAR0UBRzhoADt67N7O Da5NVDtWFtWqf46Zz9hNerc8- Goc-D zUR2X3-IY

89 https://www.jeremiahproject.com/prophecy/emergence-one-world-religion/

90 https://inspiration.org/christian-articles/the-millennial-reign-of-jesus-christ/

91 https://inspiration.org/christian-articles/the-millennial-reign-of-jesus-christ/

92 https://www.lifeway.com/en/articles/are-you-fighting-a-spiritual-war-priscilla-shirer-armor-of-god

93 https://medium.com/curious/duality-the-dark-side-of-spiritual-awakenings-2104e26a2a8e

94 https://medium.com/curious/duality-the-dark-side-of-spiritual-awakenings-2104e26a2a8e

95 https://www.newdawnmagazine.com/articles/the-spiritual-dimensions-of-the-martial-arts

96 https://www.icr.org/article/creation-quantum-mechanics/

97 https://www.livescience.com/solution-to-worst-prediction-in-physics.html?

98 https://www.youtube.com/watch?v=ei-gfsvt2iM&fbclid=IwAR3BK7G7qcKgTBdkZkSf52e0vbH7bvQao6W9tqdQy30Xs9YV8V5Z9D0E9DU

99 https://pjmedia.com/election/tyler-o-neil/2020/11/30/explosive-michigan-illegally-counted-or-ignored-500k-ballots-lawsuit-claims-n1181826

100 https://www.stopworldcontrol.com/leonardo/?fbclid=IwAR19nCuYZr72acqYXx-ASC FqzZI7hpGZ-qNLCDXJWyEV-GXRj8H-V-niYk

101 https://templeinstitute.org/

102 https://free.messianicbible.com/feature/end-time-prophecy-why-is-the-third-temple-so-important/

103 https://freenorth.news/2020/11/12/evidence-the-great-reset-is-real-heres-why-you-wont-enjoy-it/

104 https://factcheck.afp.com/trudeau-un-speech-sparks-great-reset-conspiracy

105 https://financialpost.com/executive/executive-summary/posthaste-canada-is-leading-the-debt-tsunami-now-sweeping-the-world?fbclid=IwAR3unQU23exNQN NAOFZnSJi2g1ffW5E-TO0YPy9pQwfkhSEHqZnh5Sy06o

106 https://www.weforum.org/agenda/2016/11/8-predictions-for-the-world-in-2030/

107 https://www.qualcomm.com/media/documents/files/ihs-5g-economic-impact-study-2019.pdf

108 https://www.dailywire.com/news/director-of-national-intelligence-china-is-targeting-congress-with-threats?fbclid=IwAR3uGpAHsVINp0qJ0tzg2THz0hljEwcZB2QbiOMcq0xOAKv9H7BhqNHjNrw

109 https://thediplomat.com/2020/04/how-china-is-remaking-the-un-in-its-own-image/

110 https://silview.media/2020/10/04/atomic-bombshell-rothschilds-patented-covid-19-biometric-tests-in-2015-and-2017/?fbclid=IwAR1MavqnBl-X0IJ5zX7EzuwXleJ_1ceeosD-QQcnnu3YBPh3RzVbdX6aag0

111 https://globalnews.ca/news/7545830/coronavirus-pandemic-big-one-who/?fbclid=IwAR2VwKCxRIIhqnHCw--gctOThyFVcKUj-YSkD3Xwq4mHS2Bu2wXcrZTxKOA

112 https://vaxxter.com/

113 https://www.youtube.com/watch?v=lfOgm1IcBd0&fbclid=IwAR3Gj_DHMT5V139m9fd1UKT46wzK5j37lDFP6LA8DKuBoCjerYdwtd1f-8E

114 https://christianhistoryinstitute.org/study/module/polycarp

115 https://www.bIbc.com/news/uk-48146305

Made in United States
Troutdale, OR
08/23/2024

22258162R20170